IDIOT'S
GUIDES.
AS EASY AS IT GETS!

D1278128

Numerology

by Jean Simpson

ALPHA

A member of Penguin Group (USA) Inc.

ALPHA BOOKS

Published by Penguin Group (USA) Inc.

Penguin Group (USA) Inc., 375 Hudson Street, New York, New York 10014, USA • Penguin Group (Canada), 90 Eglinton Avenue East, Suite 700, Toronto, Ontario M4P 2Y3, Canada (a division of Pearson Penguin Canada Inc.) • Penguin Books Ltd., 80 Strand, London WC2R 0RL, England • Penguin Ireland, 25 St. Stephen's Green, Dublin 2, Ireland (a division of Penguin Books Ltd.) • Penguin Group (Australia), 250 Camberwell Road, Camberwell, Victoria 3124, Australia (a division of Pearson Australia Group Pty. Ltd.) • Penguin Books India Pvt. Ltd., 11 Community Centre, Panchsheel Park, New Delhi—110 017, India • Penguin Group (NZ), 67 Apollo Drive, Rosedale, North Shore, Auckland 1311, New Zealand (a division of Pearson New Zealand Ltd.) • Penguin Books (South Africa) (Pty.) Ltd., 24 Sturdee Avenue, Rosebank, Johannesburg 2196, South Africa • Penguin Books Ltd., Registered Offices: 80 Strand, London WC2R 0RL, England

International Standard Book Number: 978-1-61564-425-4
Library of Congress Catalog Card Number: 2013945260

19 18   10 9 8 7

Interpretation of the printing code: The rightmost number of the first series of numbers is the year of the book's printing; the rightmost number of the second series of numbers is the number of the book's printing. For example, a printing code of 13-1 shows that the first printing occurred in 2013.

Printed in the United States of America

Note: This publication contains the opinions and ideas of its author. It is intended to provide helpful and informative material on the subject matter covered. It is sold with the understanding that the author and publisher are not engaged in rendering professional services in the book. If the reader requires personal assistance or advice, a competent professional should be consulted.

The author and publisher specifically disclaim any responsibility for any liability, loss, or risk, personal or otherwise, which is incurred as a consequence, directly or indirectly, of the use and application of any of the contents of this book.

Most Alpha books are available at special quantity discounts for bulk purchases for sales promotions, premiums, fund-raising, or educational use. Special books, or book excerpts, can also be created to fit specific needs. For details, write: Special Markets, Alpha Books, 375 Hudson Street, New York, NY 10014.

Publisher: *Mike Sanders*
Executive Managing Editor: *Billy Fields*
Executive Acquisitions Editor: *Lori Cates Hand*
Development Editor: *Kayla Dugger*
Production Editor: *Jana M. Stefanciosa*

Cover/Book Designers: *William Thomas*
Indexer: *Brad Herriman*
Layout: *Ayanna Lacey*
Proofreader: *Laura Caddell*

Contents

Appendixes

Introduction

In my wildest dreams, I never imagined that a reading from a numerologist would change the course of my life. After my reading, I studied the numbers in my name and birthday and devoured every bit of information I could get my hands on about numerology. Through this study, I discovered my potential. I credit numerology with changing me from a "no" person, to a "maybe" person, and finally to a "yes" person. I went from a shy kindergarten teacher to a confident guest on national television and the author of articles in national magazines and even best-selling books. I've even traveled the world, appeared on television, and was asked to teach at a California university and taught there for 25 years. Without numerology, I might still be teaching kindergarten and probably wouldn't have had the confidence to follow my dreams. It's a great feeling when you discover your true calling in life.

Over the years, I have worked with thousands of people, showing each of them how numerology can guide their lives. Working with these clients over the decades has been as rewarding for me as it has been for them (or so they tell me). There's nothing more gratifying than the feeling I get when someone is at a crossroads in life and doesn't know which path to follow, and I can shed some light and give them direction.

Whether doing my own numbers or someone else's, I've learned the numbers don't lie. Numerology is like a beacon shedding light onto confusion and turmoil. Numbers can point the way and give you direction. Although it doesn't predict specific occurrences, numerology can help you know when to stop and not proceed, when to pause and think things through, or when to go full steam ahead with gusto!

The possibilities are infinite when it comes to how numerology can help you. Perhaps you're looking for insight into yourself, your friends, and your family. Maybe you're hoping to gain a glimpse into what the future holds for you. It's even possible you're hoping to discover whether your romantic partner is your true soul mate, or just looking for your lucky numbers to help you find fortune in the lottery. No matter what brought you to numerology, I hope that you will discover—as I did—that the numbers can change your life.

While we all have control over our ultimate destiny, understanding numerology can give you insight and self-awareness that can help you maximize what the Universe has in store for you. Your name and birth date hold the secrets to your happiness and success. With this book, you hold the key to unlocking the door to your future. I wish you all the best in your journey!

How This Book Is Organized

This book is broken down into five parts:

Part 1, What Is Numerology?, provides an overview about numerology. The chapters in this part explore the history of numerology, including various numerology systems from around the world. This part also explains the basics of Pythagorean numerology (the system covered in this book), the meanings of the letters A to Z, and numerology's various numbers and their meanings.

Part 2, The Secrets in Your Name, features step-by-step instructions for calculating three of your Core (or main) Numbers based on your name—Destiny, Soul, and Personality—and what they mean in combination. You also learn about the parts of the Inclusion Table and Type and Traits Chart, which help you gather information about how the letters in your name affect your life. I even show you how to progress the letters in your name to learn about your true essence.

Part 3, What You Were Born With, explores the meaning behind your birth date. It reveals another of your Core Numbers, your Life Path Number, and your Pinnacles and Challenges. You also learn how to calculate and interpret numbers relating to personal time frames, including years, triads, months, and days.

Part 4, Tying It All Together, discusses some of the lesser-known numbers in numerology that help complete your numerological profile. You learn to determine the numbers that will appear in your more mature years, as well as numbers that may have negative implications. These chapters also show you how to identify important years and periods in your life. I then give you a rundown of the numerology worksheet, which is a great way to collect all of your information in one place.

Part 5, Fun Things to Do and Know, explores keys for choosing important names in your life, such as businesses, home and email addresses, and more. You also learn about choosing the perfect name and birth date for your baby.

Extras

You'll come across helpful notes throughout the book that will provide you with additional information. Watch for the following sidebars:

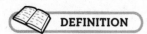 **DEFINITION**

Here, you find definitions of key numerology terms that appear throughout the text.

DID YOU KNOW?

Be sure to check out these interesting facts and insights about specific numbers and numerology in general.

 PYTHAGORAS SAYS

I provide quick tips about key numerological topics in these sidebars.

 IT DOESN'T ADD UP

These warn you about potential pitfalls and calculation errors related to numerology.

Acknowledgments

Heartfelt thanks to Destiny Number 8 Dennis Cohen, the catalyst for the serendipitous beginning of this book, for your decades of friendship and introducing me to your literary agent. Without your collaboration, input, and expertise, this book would not have been possible. I'm endlessly appreciative of your dry humor, off-the-chart intelligence, ability to massage words, and incredible editing expertise!

A gigantic thank you to my eldest Destiny Number 1 daughter Jamie Pagett, a gifted author in her own right, whose understanding of numerology, youthful vision, suggestions, and contributions were invaluable. You've always been able to read my mind and finish my sentences. Thank you from the bottom of my heart for taking time from your family and deadlines to help me meet mine.

And enormous thank yous to my middle Destiny Number 5 daughter, Brooke Finch, and my youngest Destiny Number 4 daughter, Chelsea Caivano, for not dying from embarrassment when I asked every busboy, server, gas-station attendant, postal clerk, and all of their friends for their names and birth dates when I was learning numerology.

And a special thank you to my Destiny Number 4 husband, Saul, for his unconditional love, understanding, and support and for keeping me laughing.

A big hug to each of my grandchildren—Destiny Number 1 Kreider Pagett, Destiny Number 4 Carpenter Pagett, Destiny Number 4 Kendra Caivano, Destiny Number 7 Caelyn Caivano, Destiny Number 6 David Caivano, Destiny Number 7 Regan Finch, and Destiny Number 11/2 Jackson Finch—for understanding when Grammy was busy writing and couldn't attend concerts; plays; open houses; grandparents' days; and baseball, basketball, soccer, volleyball, and lacrosse games. Each of you has a very special place in my heart, and I know you will carry on the family tradition of individuality and excellence.

And to my son-in-laws—Destiny Number 5 Kelly Pagett, Destiny Number 4 Jon Finch, and Destiny Number 6 Kevin Caivano—for loving my daughters and understanding their not-run-of-the-mill mother-in-law.

And thank you to the following:

My literary agent, Carole Jelen of Waterside Productions, Inc., for her calm voice of reason and speed at sealing deals!

Lori Hand, acquisitions editor at Alpha Books, for her interest in this book, wisdom, suggestions, and vision, and Kayla Dugger for her precise editing and thought-provoking queries.

My late but never forgotten numerology teachers, Helena Davis and Earl Miller, for entrusting me with their vast knowledge of numbers. You were both such inspiring, fun-loving mentors, and I miss hearing your uproarious laughter.

Special Thanks to the Technical Reviewer

Idiot's Guides: Numerology was reviewed by an expert who double-checked the accuracy of what you'll learn here, to help us ensure that this book gives you everything you need to know about numerology. Special thanks are extended to Steve Reiss.

Trademarks

All terms mentioned in this book that are known to be or are suspected of being trademarks or service marks have been appropriately capitalized. Alpha Books and Penguin Group (USA) Inc. cannot attest to the accuracy of this information. Use of a term in this book should not be regarded as affecting the validity of any trademark or service mark.

What Is Numerology?

Do you have a favorite number? Do you always choose the same numbers when you buy a lottery ticket? Do you look at the clock at the same time every day? Your preference toward certain numbers goes far beyond simple likes and dislikes. This book shows you how numerology can help you see the science behind your favorite numbers and how using numerology to analyze your birth name and birth date can help you live your life to the fullest.

In Part 1, you learn the history of numerology and its roots in ancient history around the globe. This book focuses on Pythagorean numerology, which was developed from theories set forth by ancient Greek mathematician Pythagoras. The modern adaptation of his theories provides a simple system for analyzing names and birth dates to provide important insight into personality; character; talents; life lessons; and important times for money, health, success, challenges, and more.

In this part, you find out the meaning of letters in numerology and how they correspond to numbers between 1 and 9. I also provide general calculation tips and meanings for the numbers in Pythagorean numerology. I then finish with a brief overview of the number types in numerology, including how they can help you make important life decisions and maximize your talents.

The History of Numerology

Throughout human history and across cultures, people have wanted answers to what the future holds and have looked for assistance when making decisions. Whether these answers are sought through palmistry, astrology, tarot, or consultation with a psychic, seeking foreknowledge is a constant of the human condition.

While many approaches to obtaining guidance are specific to a culture, numerology—in one form or another—has been present in virtually all societies. By definition, *numerology* is a study of the relationship between numbers and events and how this relationship affects your life. Through numerology, you can gain insight into your character and hidden talents, learn about the best time for relationships, find out when your health might be a concern, discern when finances may be at the forefront, or even figure out the right time for a career change.

Some people may consider this link between numbers and events coincidental or even mystical. However, others (including me) have experienced too much consistency in numerology to ascribe it to anything other than reality.

In This Chapter

- The history and various systems of numerology
- Noted numerologists from the twentieth century
- What numerology can do for you

In this chapter, you learn about the history and various systems of numerology, as well as how numerology can help you.

Numerology's Beginnings and the Different Systems of Numerology

Although the word *numerology* didn't appear in the English language until the early twentieth century, the concepts of numerology have been around for millennia.

Prior to the development of number systems, numbers were alphabetic in form. In ancient times, when the Greeks used pebbles to learn arithmetic and geometry, each letter was assigned a numeric value. The letter values in a word were then added to result in a single number, a practice called *isopsephy*. Ancient users of isopsephy believed that words and phrases that shared the same numerical values were divinely connected. Beyond making religious or mystical connections, the practice was also used to predict victors in physical battles—the warrior whose name had greatest numerical value was expected to be stronger. This same technique was later used with the Hebrew alphabet (*gematria*) and the Arabic alphabet (*Abjad numerals*). From the Middle Ages to the Renaissance, a gematria for the Latin alphabet saw wide application.

DID YOU KNOW?

The numerical digits you use today are Arabic numerals, which were derived from Indian numerals around the eighth century C.E.

Arabic numerals made their way into European culture in the twelfth century via the Italian mathematician Fibonacci of Pisa. You may know the name Fibonacci because of the Fibonacci sequence, in which each number in the sequence is the sum of the two numbers that precede it.

Different cultures and belief systems practice different forms of numerology. The following gives you the history of numerology and explores some of the most common forms being used today.

Pythagorean Numerology

Based on the work of the famous sixth-century B.C. Greek mathematician and geometer Pythagoras, Pythagorean numerology is probably the most popular form of numerology, as well as the easiest to learn and use.

These days, numbers are used to quantify and record just about anything, but people don't imbue them with mystical properties outside of "lucky number" superstitions. However, Pythagoras viewed numbers as the greatest achievement of Creation, forming the basis of everyone and everything; this was apparent in his two main teachings, the *Science of Numbers* and the Theory of Magnitude (better known today as arithmetic and music). Every object has a vibration—a higher vibration signals more positive energy, while a lower vibration indicates negative energy. Pythagoras believed numbers are the measure of that energy, with numbers 1 through 9 symbolizing the nine stages of human life.

Since then, the Pythagorean Science of Numbers has continued to evolve and has formed the spiritual basis for many secret societies—such as the Rosicrusians, Masons, Anthroposophists, and the Theosophical Society—as well as provide the foundation for the development of modern numerology in the early twentieth century.

DEFINITION

The **Science of Numbers** is the study of the relationship between letters and numbers. The term *numerology* wasn't coined until 1907 by Dr. Julia Seton.

Pythagorean or "modern" numerology analyzes a person's full birth name and date of birth. The full birth name is said to provide insight into what makes a person tick and in terms of motivation, skills, natural talents, personality, heart's desires, and so much more. The birth date reveals life patterns (such as periods of financial success, health, or love) and elements of timing (such as when to make a career change, enter or leave a relationship, go back to school, or pursue an opportunity).

This book is based on Pythagorean numerology, as I have found it to be the simplest and most accurate system available.

Chaldean Numerology

Originating in Babylonia, Chaldean numerology (sometimes called *mystic numerology*) is an older system than Pythagorean numerology. While some students of numerology consider Chaldean slightly more accurate than Pythagorean, it's less popular because of its fairly high difficulty level of calculation.

Chaldean numerology is based on sounds and vibrations—numbers are assigned to the letter vibrations that they "suit" best rather than in sequential order. The energies represented in the numbers were believed to correspond to planets and other heavenly bodies, in addition to the energies that create life. Those who practice Chaldean numerology believe that the system carries spiritual and mystical messages.

In Pythagorean numerology, the letter-number correspondence follows an easy pattern (with the letters assigned to numbers 1 through 9 based on where they fall in the alphabet; see more about this in Chapter 2); however, as you can see in the following table, the correspondence in

Chaldean isn't systematic, which requires you to memorize the values. Additionally, the Chaldean approach assigns only the values 1 through 8 to letters, reserving 9 as "holy." However, if the sum resolves to a 9, the value is retained. (I warned you that Chaldean is more complicated!)

Chaldean Letter-to-Number Table

1	2	3	4	5	6	7	8
A	B	C	D	E	U	O	F
I	K	G	M	H	V	Z	P
J	R	L	T	N	W		
Q		S		X			
Y							

Another differentiator is that in Chaldean, the name you use for numerology analysis is the one you are most known by, rather than your full birth name. For example, the famous baseball player George Herman "Babe" Ruth would be "Babe Ruth" to the Chaldean school but "George Herman Ruth" to the Pythagoreans.

Kabbalah Numerology

Although it's not a religion, sect, or cult, Kabbalah is a mystical way of approaching life and the universe that explores the relationship between the mysterious Ein Sol (God) and the finite universe. In essence, Kabbalah is an attempt to bridge the physical and metaphysical realms. The discipline provides many tools to help its practitioners attempt to understand the relationship between the finite and infinite—including numerology.

Kabbalah numerology actually doesn't employ numbers at all, but instead uses a person's name as it's expressed in the Hebrew alphabet. Analysis of the name and its constituent sounds tells you how your name affects your actions, thoughts, and feelings.

Chinese Numerology

The Chinese have employed numerology for more than 4,000 years. Chinese numerology varies widely from other forms of the practice in that it assumes that numbers are inherently lucky (good) or unlucky (evil). Luck plays an important role in Eastern culture and is intertwined with the concept of fate; therefore, if someone is lucky, it's believed that it was the person's destiny.

In Chinese numerology, meanings are derived by the sound of the number when said aloud. If a number sounds like a word that is considered unlucky, the number is also considered unlucky. For example, in the Chinese language, the word for "one" sounds like the word for "honor"; the number 1 represents an ability to break down barriers while pursuing higher quests. On the other hand, the word for "four" sounds like the word for "death"; the number 4 indicates great misfortune and is avoided at all costs by people who practice Chinese numerology.

The Chinese also believe in mystical number combinations and relationships. For example, it is believed that the 12 vessels which circulate blood and air throughout the body correspond with the 12 rivers flowing toward the Central Kingdom. Likewise, the 365 parts of the body used in locating acupuncture points is connected with the 365 days in a year.

The simplest method of Chinese numerology is the Lo Shu Square. It is based on the story of the tortoise with nine perfect squares on its shell as seen by Emperor Yu on the banks of the Luo River. The original Lo Shu Square is also known as the "Magic Square" because the numbers in the square add to 15 when added horizontally, vertically, or diagonally. In the following figure, notice that the even numbers are in the corners and the odd numbers form a cross in the center vertical and horizontal rows.

4	9	2
3	5	7
8	1	6

More recently, the Chinese have adopted a modernized version of the original Lo Shu Square to teach Chinese numerology to Westerners that has simpler calculations and doesn't involve *Lunar Years;* it is known as the Hidden Cross (see Chapter 10). In the following figure, notice the difference from the original Lo Shu Square. The squares are numbered 1 through 9, with the rows arranged, top to bottom, 3-6-9, 2-5-8, and 1-4-7.

3	6	9
2	5	8
1	4	7

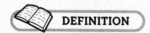

DEFINITION

A **Lunar Year** is 12 lunar months, or a full cycle of the moon through its phases that starts and ends with a new moon. Because a Lunar Year is a little over 354 days, about every 3 years, you get a thirteenth "month" to get back to a full year. This is similar to the concept of leap years.

Interpreting the result requires knowledge of what the squares signify. The bottom row references the practical (for example, coordination, athleticism, and physical labor), the middle row is emotional (for example, feelings and intuition), and the top row is mental (for example, analytical ability). The columns, from left to right, represent thought, will, and action.

To get an idea of how the Chinese interpret squares, look at one of the numerals in the square. For example, a 1 indicates how well a person interacts with others. The number of 1s in your square suggests the following traits:

- **One 1:** You have trouble making your thoughts known to others.

- **Two 1s:** You can make yourself understood by others and can understand what others are communicating.

- **Three 1s:** You can go on and on, but you can also be quiet and moody on occasion.

- **Four 1s:** You tend to be sensitive and caring, but you have trouble verbalizing.

- **More than four 1s:** You may be uncomfortable in large gatherings and have a tendency to overindulge in solitary pursuits, such as overeating.

PYTHAGORAS SAYS

While the modern Western square isn't a true magic square, you might note that the middle row, middle column, and both diagonals each still total 15—the magic number of the magic square.

Abjad Numerals

Predating the eighth-century introduction of Arabic numerals, Abjad numerals assign values to the 28 letters of the Arabic alphabet. In the Abjad system, the first Arabic letter, alif, is assigned the number 1. The second letter, bā', is used to represent 2, and so on. Arabic numerologists use the assigned values to foretell the future and explain the past.

Abjad Letters and Number Values

Value	Letter	Name	Transliteration
1	ا	Alif	'/ā
2	ب	bā'	b
3	ج	Jām	j
4	د	Dāl	d
5	ه	hā'	h
6	و	Wāw	w/ū
7	ز	zayn/zāy	z
8	ح	ḥā'	ḥ
9	ط	ṭā'	ṭ
10	ى	yā'	y/ī
20	ك	Kāf	k
30	ل	Lām	l
40	م	Mīm	m
50	ن	Nūn	n
60	س	Sīn	s
70	ع	'ayn	'
80	ف	fā'	f
90	ص	Ṣād	ṣ
100	ق	Qāf	q
200	ر	rā'	r
300	ش	shīn	sh
400	ت	tā'	t
500	ث	thā'	th
600	خ	Khā	kh
700	ذ	dhāl	dh

continues

Abjad Letters and Number Values   (continued)

Value	Letter	Name	Transliteration
800	ض	ḍād	ḍ
900	ظ	ẓā'	ẓ
1000	غ	Ghayn	gh

Twentieth-Century Numerologists

At the turn of the last century, numerology as we know it today was developed. A series of researchers and writers added their contributions to the field over the past 100 years. Here are some of the most influential of them:

Mrs. L. Dow Balliett became the authority of the modern method of relating names, numbers, and vibrations. She is credited with giving the world a spiritual and pragmatic approach to applying numerical values to people's character. The author of many books, including *The Philosophy of Numbers: Their Tone and Colors,* Mrs. Balliett was a noted teacher of Pythagorean methods. An ardent student of religion and philosophy, her mission in life was to enlighten others and help people view themselves as spiritual beings. She was a trendsetter and ahead of her time, and a frequent presenter in the New Age Thought Movement.

Dr. Julia Seton was a student of Mrs. L. Dow Balliett and is credited with modernizing the Science of Numbers. In fact, in 1907, she coined the term *numerology*. Dr. Seton traveled to South Africa, Australia, and Hawaii to present her theories of the hidden truths in symbols, scrolls, and numbers.

Dr. Juno Jordan was the daughter of Dr. Julia Seton and carried on the family tradition of numerology. A dentist by trade, Dr. Jordan banded together with a group of likeminded, forward-thinking ladies to form the California Institute of Numerical Research. For the next 25 years, they studied every aspect of the numbers and their meanings as related to names. Dr. Jordan wrote the modern "Bibles of Numerology," *Your Number and Destiny,* and (my own personal favorite) *The Romance in Your Name*. In her words, "Numbers do not lie." Amen to that!

Dr. Helena Davis is credited with popularizing numerology from the 1950s through the 1990s. The assistant pastor to the prolific metaphysical speaker and author Dr. Joseph Murphy, Dr. Davis was also a numerologist to the stars and served as William Randolph Hearst's personal consultant. She provided readings in Beverly Hills' most posh hotels and gave weekly lectures on numerology at the Wilshire Ebell Theatre in Los Angeles.

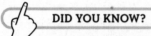

DID YOU KNOW?

Dr. Helena Davis was my numerology mentor. After meeting her at the young age of 22, I was transformed from a shy, insecure caterpillar into a confident butterfly through her readings. Entrusting me with her knowledge of the numbers in the hope that I would carry it on, she worked with me one-on-one for two hours a day for an entire year to teach me everything she knew about numerology. My passion skyrocketed and, after doing numerology readings for thousands of people, I developed my own system, called *Hot Numbers*.

How Numerology Can Help You Now

What can numerology do for you? The possibilities are endless. Here are some common issues in different areas of your life that you can address using numerology:

- **Career:** When is the most auspicious time to focus on your career? Is it the right time to learn new job skills? When should you look for another job? How can you get a new attitude about your current job? What should you name your new business and what telephone number should you choose to increase business?

- **Personal life:** Is your relationship worth repairing, or is it time to move on? When will you meet someone new? What about the people in your life—how can you understand them better? When is the best day to get married? Should you change your name to attract better luck? When should you buy a new car or repair the one you have? What is a good vacation destination?

- **Home:** Should you rent or buy? When's the best time to remodel your home? Is it the right time to buy a new home? Should you choose a home by the address?

- **Health:** Should you pay special attention to my diet now? When should you schedule a physical? Is now a good time to lose or gain a few pounds? When is an ideal time to get pregnant?

Your future is limited only by your beliefs, passion, and imagination. The best is yet to be!

The Least You Need to Know

- Numerology has been around for millennia, taking different forms in different cultures.
- Pythagorean numerology is based on the works of Pythagoras, who believed that numbers can be used to explain everything.

- The twentieth-century writings and research of people such as Mrs. L. Dow Balliet, Dr. Juno Jordan, and Dr. Helena Davis helped shape modern numerology.

- You can use numerology to help you with decision-making and planning and to help you better understand yourself and others.

Getting Started with Numerology

As you've already deduced, numerology is all about numbers. Modern numerology involves converting letters into numbers and performing standard arithmetic operations on those numbers. Don't worry, it's all simple addition and subtraction—no multiplication, division, exponentiation, or logarithms will ever enter the picture.

In this chapter, I walk you through the basics of numerology, starting with the meanings associated with the letters A through Z. You also learn the numeric value of each letter and how to convert letters into numbers. In addition (pun intended), you learn how to add up the numbers and reduce any double-digit numbers to a single digit. I also give you a shortcut that lets you find the single-digit number faster than merely continuing to add and reduce. Not only is the trick simple, it'll save you time as you get deeper into numerology calculations. I also provide a rundown of the general meaning of the numbers for reference. Finally, I close with an overview of the different numbers you can calculate to find out more about yourself.

In This Chapter

- The meanings of each letter of the alphabet
- Letter-to-number correspondence
- Adding numbers
- Reducing numbers to a single digit
- The meanings of numbers and Master Numbers in numerology
- Different types of numbers you'll encounter in numerology

If you're anything like I was when I first learned the basics of numerology, you'll hopefully be intrigued and want to know more. So let's begin your journey along the pathway of enlightenment.

A to Z: The Meaning of Each Letter

As you learned in Chapter 1, before a number system was in place, people used letters to make their calculations. In numerology, each letter has a special meaning. The following are descriptions of the characteristics associated with each letter:

A: This is very powerful as the first letter of a name. A people are their own person—they're sure of themselves and ambitious. Original and creative, they tend to like their own ideas best. Sometimes an indicator of an impulsive individual, A as the first letter also indicates a natural leader who likes action and plenty of it. No grass grows under their feet!

B: B people are prone to sensitivity and must be careful to not take things personally. Wanting to keep the peace, they sometimes acquiesce to others. To be happy, B people need togetherness and companionship. Also drawn to collecting, these people may have treasures displayed or tucked away.

C: This is a lucky letter and indicates strong instincts. C people express themselves clearly and can be enthusiastic and entertaining. They also aren't afraid to wear their heart on their sleeve and tell others how they feel. Mimicking the shape of the letter, which is like a cup turned on its side, C people can spill out their emotions when hurt.

D: D people are solid as a rock and tend to be hard workers. Determined, grounded, and very practical, they don't waste time or money. D people have good systems in place to get things done quickly and efficiently. They can also handle deadlines and pressure, even though they may initially respond negatively to unfamiliar endeavors.

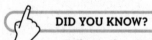 **DID YOU KNOW?**

Differing theories exist on how placement can affect the meaning of a letter. Some numerologists believe the meaning of a letter has greater significance when it's the first letter of your first, middle, or last name, while other numerologists place greater importance on the first vowel in your name. I personally believe that each and every letter is an important part of the whole.

E: This is the letter for activity, restlessness, or uncertainty. E people are powerful and have a strong desire for freedom and fun—the more excitement, the better. These people are versatile and clever, and are able to see many different sides of a situation. Often the life of the party, they have a keen mind and can't be fooled. E also indicates a tendency to be high strung or nervous.

F: Good hosts who are easy to get along with, F people are self-sacrificing and very responsible. Discriminating, particular, and often idealistic, they frequently thrive on helping others, even at their own expense. Because they are warm-hearted and caring, F people have to try not to let other people's problems drag them down.

G: G people are visionaries who have the analytical ability to see the details in the big picture. Often avid readers, they make patient teachers and are intellectually active. Reserved and refined, G people need time alone to charge their batteries.

H: Sometimes emotional yet able to listen to their own inner voice, H people are alert, aware, and watchful. They learn their lessons through experience but aren't easily discouraged from their plan. Even though they enjoy material things, for H people, money can come and go. They also like to spend time outdoors.

I: I people are intense, inquisitive, and able to interpret conditions and events in an intelligent way. Because they feel deeply, I people are compassionate, generous, and loving; however, they sometimes find it difficult to overcome pride and personal feelings. Prone to anxiety, I people need to be balanced.

J: Simply put, J is for justice—fair play and balancing the scales is the name of the game for them. Friendship is their forte, and J people make exceptional friends themselves. Possessing a sense of humor with solid leadership traits, they are sometimes better suited to giving directions than being directed.

K: Psychic, enlightened, and intuitive, K people are often blessed with excellent memories and powers of concentration. Persistent and having strong likes and dislikes, they often go to extremes. Naturally high-strung, sensitive K people need to avoid situations that could trigger their inherent propensity for anxiety. The Master number associated with it, 11 (discussed later in this chapter), is indicative of talent or literary ability.

L: Lively, vital, and powerful, the letter L indicates a heady, honest, and tolerant individual who's generous and kind-hearted. Social and capable of self-sacrifice, L people like their work to be useful and are capable of leadership to that end. They need to watch out for clumsiness or mis-steps when they feel anxious.

M: A dedicated, high-energy worker who likes to see tasks to completion, M people fit well into structured environments. They have their two feet firmly planted on the ground, which makes it difficult to disturb their composure. These faithful homebodies, who need a firm financial base to feel secure, are very loyal and like to help people in their social circle resolve problems.

N: N people are creative and original individuals who are able to think outside the box. They have a strong-willed personality with opinions to match. N people also tend to document their lives in written form, sometimes in journals or diaries. They thrive on change and seem to overcome obstacles with ease. When it comes to their personal life, N people may have their share of romantic entanglements.

O: Self-contained, sensitive, and able to control their emotions, O people need to be careful not to appear self-centered to others. Happiest when there are boundaries, rules, and laws, they have a sense of morality that makes them take the high ground and strive to do the right thing. Because O people feel things deeply, they must try to avoid being possessive or jealous.

P: P people are intellectual with a broad base of knowledge. Though they can often be secretive, others generally have great first impressions of them. Determined but possessed of numerous doubts, they are insistent upon proof of assertions before they're convinced. P people are temperamentally suited for professional and scientific pursuits.

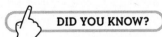 **DID YOU KNOW?**

The first letter of your name—sometimes called the *cornerstone*—provides insight into your overall personality. It also can indicate how you approach life's ups and downs.

Q: Q people are seekers and searchers who ask innumerable questions and have good reasoning skills; however, they can become too deeply wedded to their own ideas. Q people speak their mind eloquently and are money magnets with the ability to be persuasive in business matters. They are often perceived as difficult to read and can be quite mysterious on a personal level.

R: Energetic, exacting, and thorough, R people can be perfectionists to the point that those around them become annoyed by their behavior. They possess strong powers of attraction and are popular with others. Often artistic or musical, R people often have latent talents that need to be developed and expressed.

S: S people are real charmers, with lots of warmth and devotion. Because they possess a kind nature, they are able to work well with others. Often original and artistic, they tend to have an intense life. While S people can be dramatic in their reactions, they are also strong and substantial, able to weather the storm through their frequent up-and-down periods.

T: T people are attentive, thoughtful, conscientious, and sometimes quiet; however, they can be assertive when pushed. Conflicted between a desire for peace around them and having their own way, they are uncertain when standing alone. T people are also charitable, but often consider themselves to be "bearing a cross." They need to keep their feelings in check and not be too sensitive.

U: U people find expression in their fields of interest. They also tend to internalize their feelings and emotions. U people need to tap into their impeccable sense of time and luck to think quickly on their feet and commit wholeheartedly to projects. Pleasing and often entertaining, they are naturally predisposed toward glamour.

V: Often intuitive, V people are tuned in to the universe and get answers from "on high." They have vivid imaginations and therefore need to make sure they are able to separate fact from fiction. V people hate to be controlled. Variety is the hallmark of them, and they tend to have lofty goals. Loving luxury and comfort, travel is a welcome antidote to their restlessness.

W: W people comprise many different experiences and are recognized as willing, spontaneous, outgoing, and versatile. Very charismatic and creative, they surround themselves with interesting people. Because they're mentally active, W people are apt to engage in stimulating conversations. One thing they should be aware of is that travel can upset their home life.

X: Thriving on information extracted from books and other sources, X people tend to have a photographic memory, soaking up information like a sponge soaks up moisture. Mechanical aptitude is often an X trait. X people have a deep love of family and feel a duty to make the world better. Often misunderstood, they can be moody and should be careful to avoid addiction.

Y: Y people love freedom and enjoy pushing the envelope. They tend to be active, but with a carefree, easy-does-it approach. Sometimes faced with forks in the road, Y people need to use their natural gift of intuition while pondering which route to follow in life. They are prone to a curiosity about the supernatural and often have peculiar interests with an intuitive touch. More comfortable when doing solitary pursuits, Y people tend to have artistic or musical interests.

Z: Z is a very strong letter and is common in people who have power over others. While Z people can have a temper, they quickly recover from blow-ups and forgive, forget, and move forward. They are seldom alone in a crowd and make their presence felt to those around them. Because Z people retain knowledge like a walking encyclopedia, they are likely to have a literary bent.

Next, I discuss the numeric value of each letter, which is what you'll be using in your calculations. You don't need to memorize the number that corresponds to every letter, but it's helpful to understand how the numbers are assigned.

How Letters Correspond to Numbers

Following the philosophy of Pythagoras, cycles appear everywhere, including the method by which you assign values to letters. In numerology, each letter of the alphabet is assigned a numeric value from 1 to 9. For letters A through I, you number them based on where they fall in the alphabet—A is 1, B is 2, and so forth. Once you get beyond I, you begin to add the digits together to get a single number.

For example, with J, which is the tenth letter in the alphabet, you add $1 + 0$, which gives you a value of 1. Likewise, because K is the eleventh letter of the alphabet, you add $1 + 1$ to get a value of 2. Can you see the pattern here? This new pattern continues until you get to the letter S; because S is the nineteenth letter of the alphabet, you still have a double digit when you add the separate digits together ($1 + 9 = 10$). In cases like this, you have to add the separate digits again to get the single digit—for S, it's $1 + 0 = 1$. The following table gives you the complete set of values.

Pythagorean Letter-to-Number Table

1	2	3	4	5	6	7	8	9
A	B	C	D	E	F	G	H	I
J	K	L	M	N	O	P	Q	R
S	T	U	V	W	X	Y	Z	

If you compare the Pythagorean table with the Chaldean table (see Chapter 1), you'll be pleased to see that while the Chaldean numbers don't have a simple letter-number correspondence, the Pythagorean numbers are very systematic. Beginning with A is 1, it's as simple as counting to 9 repeatedly to obtain the other values.

Here's another easy way to associate the numbers with their corresponding letters and to remember the letter-number combinations:

- 1s like action and all that jazz (J, A, S).
- 2s are collectors and need a basket (B, K, T).
- 3s are communicators and use clues (C, L, U).
- 4s like rules and structure, like the Department of Motor Vehicles (D, M, V).
- 5s are curious and like things that are new (N, E, W).
- 6s like beauty and may look like a fox (F, O, X).
- 7s are discerning and can spot a gyp (G, P, Y).
- 8s are powerful and have high-quotient zeal (H, Q, Z).
- 9s are universal and interested in international relations (I, R).

 PYTHAGORAS SAYS

Lowercase and uppercase letters have the same values, and spaces and punctuation are ignored. But if you want to think of every character as having a value, you can give them a value of 0, which doesn't contribute to any addition or subtraction operation.

Adding Up the Numbers

Building on what you learned in the previous section, numerology involves calculating with straightforward addition. Like you did when finding the value of each letter, you take the values for each letter and add them up until you get a single digit.

RAUL ALEJANDRO AGUILAR ESCOLAR
9133　13511 5496 1789319　5136219

For example, assume that you want to know the value of the phrase, "We, the people." Here's how you find out:

1. Write down the letters and place the corresponding number values below them (see the "Pythagorean Letter-to-Number Table" if you need a reference).

   WE THE PEOPLE　　　　Now I'm I

   55 285 756735　　　　865 94 9

2. Add up the digits. For the letters in "We, the people," the total should be 58.

   $5 + 5 + 2 + 8 + 5 + 7 + 5 + 6 + 7 + 3 + 5 = 58$

3. Unless the total is a single-digit number, you need to add the digits in the total together until you get a single digit. In this example, you add $5 + 8$, which gives you a value of 13. You then reduce to a single digit by adding 13 as $1 + 3$, giving you 4.

   $5 + 8 = 13$
   $1 + 3 = 4$

If you were a computer program, you would just keep adding, getting a sum, and then adding the digits in the result until you arrived at a single digit. Alternatively, you might arrive at the sum and then just keep subtracting 9 from that sum until you achieve a single-digit result.

However, unlike computer programs, we're human, and we do get bored and tired because we can't perform addition or subtraction at lightning speed. But one thing people can do is perceive patterns, which allows us to make intermediate adjustments. One of the beauties of calculations in this system and the behavior of our decimal (10-based) number system is that intermediate values of 9 can be discarded, as long as there is still something left to total. So you can cross out any 9s or numbers that add up to 9 without changing the result. It's quick, easy, and still accurate.

Try it out. First, add a set of numbers the "traditional way," using the steps you learned in the previous section. For the numbers in this example, the total is 40. You then reduce to a single digit by adding $4 + 0$, which gives you 4.

   9 4 5 8 1 3 6 4

   $9 + 4 + 5 + 8 + 1 + 3 + 6 + 4 = 40$

   $4 + 0 = 4$

Now try adding up the same numbers with the "casting out nines" method:

1. Find any nines and put a slash through them.

   9 4 5 8 1 3 6 4

   The 9 can be crossed out here

2. Look for groups of numbers that add to 9 and put a slash through those groups. Here's how you'd do this for the example set of numbers:

   9 ~~4 5~~ ~~8 1~~ ~~3 6~~ 4

   4 and 5 = 9, so put a line through both the 4 and the 5

   8 and 1 = 9, so put a line through both the 8 and the 1

   3 and 6 = 9, so put a line through both the 3 and the 6

3. Add up the remaining digits that don't have a slash through them. For the example, notice that the only number without a slash through it is the 4. This gives you the single-digit value, which you can see is the same answer you got when adding the traditional way.

Practice by writing down any series of single-digit numbers and first adding them the traditional way and then adding them using the preceding method. You should come up with the same answer no matter which way you do it. Amazing little trick, isn't it?

What Do the Numbers Mean?

Now that you've learned how to add up the numbers, you may wonder how the numbers are applied. In the upcoming chapters of this book, you'll use your name and convert the letters into their numeric values to calculate your most important core numbers—your Destiny, Soul, and Personality Numbers—as well as your Intensification, Karma, Subconscious Response, Point of Security Numbers, and much more. You'll also use your birth date to reveal your Life Path, Personal Year, Personal Month, Personal Day Numbers, and even your Milestone and Highlight years.

But before you get into those more personal and detailed topics, let's take a look at the basic meanings of the numbers you'll be using in numerology.

Numbers 1 through 9

In numerology, each number signifies various traits and characteristics. The following table provides the keywords and basic meanings of numbers 1 through 9. Don't worry about memorizing the meanings; you can always refer to the table. Soon, you'll find that the more you use numerology, the more the numbers and their meanings will become second nature to you.

IT DOESN'T ADD UP

As you progress through the book, you'll learn that while the basic meaning of the numbers remains the same, they have variations depending on the context in which they're used. For example, as a Destiny Number, 1 indicates a leader and innovator; however, when talking about Personal Years, 1 means a fresh start. To help you understand the variations, I've provided plenty of lists for easy reference and usage. Be sure to pay attention to the descriptions of each number as it relates to the topic at hand.

Basic Meanings of Numbers 1 through 9	
1	Masculine influence, beginnings, independence, inventive, original, leadership
2	Feminine influence, cooperation, partnership, tact, diplomacy, harmony, unity
3	Communication, expression, youthfulness, creativity, self-confidence or lack of self-confidence, potential shyness
4	Order, form, restriction, work, patience, values, security, stability, practicality
5	Freedom, changes, variety, travel, activity
6	Love, home, family, responsibility, sense of duty, marriage and/or divorce, nurturing, justice, balance
7	Analysis, wisdom, mystical, spiritual, integrity, solitude, precision, research
8	Organization, money, power, success, business, health, control and authority, mastery
9	Completion, endings, universal, philanthropy

Master Numbers 11 and 22

In numerology, 11 and 22 are considered special; they are known as *Master Numbers*. They are called this because they are believed to be a higher vibration than their reduced number. So Master Number 11 is a higher vibration of 2 (1 + 1 = 2) and Master Number 22 is a higher vibration of 4 (2 + 2 = 4). The following table gives you the meanings of these special numbers:

Master Number Meanings	
Master Number 11/2	Master Number 11 is on a higher plane than the equivalent non-Master or reduced, single-digit number 2.
	Inspirational, uplifting
Master Number 22/4	Master Number 22 is on a higher plane than the equivalent non-Master or reduced, single-digit number 4.
	Inspirational, master builder

Some numerologists believe these Master Numbers are incredibly meaningful and therefore shouldn't be reduced to a single digit. My opinion differs slightly from the norm. When doing calculations, I'm aware of the Master Numbers and make note of them; however, I choose to reduce Master Numbers to single digits—11 to 2 and 22 to 4.

Touring Numerology's Number Types

As befits its name, studying and applying numerology involves many numbers. Some of those numbers derive from your birth name, while others come from your birth date. Together, they give you an understanding of who you are, from what path you'll walk during this lifetime to how others see you.

In this section, I give you an overview of what types of numbers you'll encounter in numerology—including *Core Numbers* and less mainstream numbers—and how they relate to you.

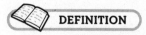

DEFINITION

Your **Core Numbers** are the four main numbers that make up your personal numerology profile. They include your Destiny Number, Soul Number, Personality Number, and Life Path Number.

Notable Numbers Derived from Your Name

If you recall from earlier, while there are 26 letters in the English alphabet, each is assigned a number from 1 to 9 via Pythagorean numerology. Based on this letter-to-number correspondence, your name has many applications in numerology.

Your birth name has a significant impact on who you are as a person. Using numerology, you can discover hidden abilities and talents. You can also gain insight to your innermost desires and how others perceive you.

Using numerology to analyze your birth name helps give you a better understanding of yourself and your abilities, including how you typically act in an emergency and what traits make you most successful.

The following are numerology values you can find using your birth name:

- **Destiny Number:** Sometimes called the Name Number, the Destiny Number is derived from adding the letter values in your birth name. It indicates what talents and aptitudes you were born with, what you are destined to do in your life, and how you can best utilize your talents and interests to be successful (see Chapter 3).

- **Soul Number:** Also called the Heart Number or Birth Force Number, the Soul Number is calculated from the vowels in your name. This number helps you discover the real, inner you, including your values, hopes, wishes, dreams, and innermost desires as well as your thoughts, feelings, and attitudes toward life and love (see Chapter 4).

- **Personality Number:** This number is calculated using the consonants in your name and tells you about the outer you, or what you project to those around you. The Personality Number doesn't always convey the real you—only the impression you make on others (see Chapter 5).

- **Intensification Numbers:** An above-average amount of certain letters and their corresponding values in your name are how you find your Intensification Numbers. They can tell you more about your personality, such as whether you're extravagant or have great self-discipline (see Chapter 7).

- **Karma Numbers:** Any letters you're missing in your full birth name and its corresponding number value indicate your Karma Numbers. These numbers tell you the skills and attributes you may need to cultivate to help you better handle situations in your lifetime (see Chapter 7).

- **Subconscious Response Number:** To get this number, you determine how many Karma Numbers you have and subtract that from 9. This number reveals how you instinctively act in an emergency—in other words, whether you're apt to panic or remain calm (see Chapter 7).

- **Point of Security Number:** This number is derived from adding the amount of letters in your full birth name. The Point of Security Number indicates what you have within you to be successful both personally and professionally, no matter what obstacles come up in your life (see Chapter 7).

- **Hidden Essence and Essence Numbers:** These are calculated by adding the numeric values of the letters in your first, middle, and last names and progressing them on a chart. Your Hidden Essence and Essence Numbers represent conditions and circumstances you may experience at any given age of your life (see Chapter 8).

Notable Numbers Derived from Your Birth Date

All of the numerology values derived from your birth date deal with elements of timing, whether it's a lifetime, a year, a four-month period, a month, or a day. You can use these periods of time to look back, look forward, or even look at where you are currently.

Numbers calculated using your birth date advise you what to do and when to do it based on certain time periods. For example, you may find out that this year is about new beginnings, which can mean looking for a new job, changing your appearance, or moving on to a new relationship. The overarching goals can then be broken down into smaller time frames, such as months or days, so you can work to reach your goal. Think of these calculations as your personal highway, guiding you down life's path.

The following are numerology values you can find using your birth date:

- **Birthday Number:** This number simply comes from the day you were born, reduced to a single digit if necessary. The Birthday Number tells you what traits you have in common with people born on that day, no matter the month (see Chapter 9).

- **Life Path Number:** This number is calculated using the month, day, and four-digit year you were born. Your Life Path Number gives you clues to your opportunities in life and what you may need to learn in order to accomplish your goals (see Chapter 10).

- **Hidden Cross:** Adapted from the Chinese Lo Shu Square, the Hidden Cross is a graphic organizer resembling a tic-tac-toe grid. The digits of your birth month, day, and year are placed in specific squares. Each of the three horizontal rows and three vertical columns give detailed information about how you relate to others and explain your three levels of consciousness (see Chapter 10).

- **Pinnacles and Challenges:** The four Pinnacles and their accompanying Challenges are derived from the month, day, and four-digit year of your birth. Pinnacles give you an overview of positive circumstances and events you may encounter during certain periods of your life, whereas Challenges foretell potential bumps in the road you'll encounter in reaching your Pinnacles (see Chapter 11).

> **PYTHAGORAS SAYS**
>
> Your birth date (month + day + four-digit year) will help you answer questions regarding elements of timing. It will help you know when to go, when to pause, and when to stop.

- **Personal Year Number:** This number is calculated by using your birth month, birth date, and the year in which you last celebrated your birthday. Based on a nine-year cycle, the Personal Year Number indicates the influences for the year you're in, and what you should or can do about it (see Chapter 12).

- **Triad Numbers:** These numbers are calculated using your birth month, day of birth, the four-digit year in which you were born, the four-digit year in which you celebrated your last birthday, your age at your last birthday, and your Life Path Number. The Triad Numbers reveal more detailed information for each of the four-month periods within your Personal Year (see Chapter 13).

- **Personal Month Numbers:** To calculate these numbers, you need only the numeric value of the month in question and your Personal Year Number. Personal Month Numbers help you track how your feelings, attitudes, and circumstances change during the course of a Personal Year (see Chapter 14).

- **Personal Day Number:** You calculate this by using your Personal Year Number and at least one month and day of interest to you. Your Personal Day Number can help you weigh decisions you want to or need to make on any given day (see Chapter 15).

Numerology's Secondary Numbers

There are additional numbers that have lesser import, either because they only impact for a short duration or during a specific part of your life. These numbers can provide insight to your more mature years, help you navigate some less-positive numbers, and detect worldwide trends by year.

The following are secondary numerology values you can use:

- **Maturity Number:** This number is calculated by adding your Life Path Number and your Destiny Number and reducing to a single digit if necessary. This number is meant for your middle-age years and gives hints about how to make the most of your "golden years" (see Chapter 16).

- **Malefic Numbers:** These refer to the numbers 14, 16, and 19. You may see the Malefic Numbers as your calculations for your Core Numbers before you reduce them to a single digit, or they may be around you on addresses, license plates, and so on. Despite the name, these numbers aren't inherently evil—they just point to less positive aspects of your life (see Chapter 16).

- **Universal Year Number:** To calculate this, you simply add the digits of the current year. Known as the "rhythm of the universe," it describes the current year in general terms (see Chapter 16).

Important Year Numbers

The important year numbers are just that—time spans that are interesting in our lifetime. For example, they can refer to the year you graduated from college, made a major physical move, got married, changed careers, had a baby, and so on.

The following are important year numerology values you can find using your birth date:

- **Milestone Years and Overtone Numbers:** Milestone Years are calculated by first taking your four-digit birth year, reducing it to a single digit, and adding it to the full birth year. This gives you the first Milestone Year, which you can then reduce to a single digit and add to that year to get your next one, and so on. These tell you the significant years in your life. The Overtone Numbers are each of the single-digit numbers you get for the years (see Chapter 17).

- **Highlight Year Number:** To calculate this, you add your age now to the age you'll be on your next birthday. This gives you an idea of how you're progressing through life (see Chapter 17).

- **Red-Letter Years:** Sometimes called Forecasting, you find these by taking your first, middle, and last names and adding the numeric value of the current letter to the numeric value of the previous letter. The Red-Letter Years are the ages in your life that are memorable or when something significant occurs (see Chapter 17).

The Least You Need to Know

- Letters of the alphabet are associated with certain traits and characteristics.
- Letters have numerical values in numerology. The letter values in Pythagorean numerology are straightforward and cycle by nines, starting with A having a value of 1.
- When calculating values, continue to add the numbers until you're left with a single-digit result.
- Numbers 1 through 9 each have a special meaning in numerology.
- Numerology can tell you everything from the milestone years in your life to what actions you should take on a certain day.

The Secrets in Your Name

The name you were given at birth holds all kinds of secrets about you as a person, including your innate talents and abilities; your likes and dislikes; your innermost hopes, wishes, and desires; and how others perceive you.

In Part 2, I take you through how to calculate the Destiny, Soul, and Personality Numbers, plus the meanings of them individually and together. I also show you how to dig deeper into meanings in your name by teaching you the significance of the first vowel in your name and how to organize your name with the Inclusion Table and the Type and Traits Chart. This part finishes by showing you how to progress the letters of your name, which you can use to find your Hidden Essence and Essence Numbers.

The Destiny Number

The Destiny Number is one of the most important Core Numbers in numerology. Known by a fair number of numerologists as the Name Number, the Destiny Number is derived from the name you were given at birth. It provides guidelines for describing your character, traits, goals, and impediments and reveals what you need to do to reach your ultimate success.

In this chapter, I take you through what the Destiny Number is, what's required to calculate it, and the meaning of each Destiny Number.

In This Chapter

- The significance of the Destiny Number

- Determining the name you should start with

- How to calculate your Destiny Number

- The meanings of the Destiny Numbers

What Is the Destiny Number?   3

As the name implies, the *Destiny Number* foretells your *purpose* in life—what you must do to fulfill your destiny, not what you are.

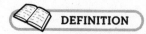

DEFINITION

> The **Destiny Number** is a Core Number that describes your character, talents, and goals, and reveals what you need to do to reach your ultimate success in life. It's derived by adding the numeric values of the letters in the given name you received at birth and then reducing to a single digit.

Knowing your Destiny Number indicates not only how you can, but also should, proceed in your field to be successful and to attain what destiny holds for you. It describes how you react to the stimuli and situations you encounter: Are you to be an active or passive participant? Do you make things happen, or do you take whatever comes? Do you want to play the starring role, or are you happy as an understudy? Additionally, your Destiny Number describes what kind of people you work well with and how you relate to others.

Your Destiny Number isn't always easy to implement, because sometimes what you think you want to do isn't what your Destiny Number says you must do. The Destiny Number truly embodies the union of your inner self and the persona you project to the rest of the world. (In Chapters 4 and 5, you'll learn about the separate inner and outer self with the Soul and Personality Numbers.)

What Name Should You Use?

To get the most accurate interpretation of your Destiny Number, you need to use your name *exactly* as it appears on your birth certificate, birth registration, or whatever document officially records the name you received at birth, even if you've never used or been known by that name.

That also means even if your name is misspelled, it says "Baby Boy" or "Baby Girl" where your name should be, or your mother's maiden name is included with a hyphen after your father's name, you still use it! The following are some other special situations that might arise:

- **Lost or misplaced birth certificate:** What should you do if your birth certificate has been lost or misplaced? What if you were born at home and the midwife neglected to report your birth? Not to worry! Birth certificates can be ordered from the Office of Vital Statistics or Registrar in the county or state where you were born in the United States, and similar resources exist in other developed nations. So go online and search for the appropriate government office. If all else fails, use the name that was listed on your school records as a child.

- **Taking an additional name later:** Per the customs of some countries and religions, you may have been given an additional name when you were baptized or the equivalent. Or perhaps Aunt Tilly promised to leave you her entire estate if you took her name. As much as you might want Tilly's treasure trove by assuming her moniker, revert to the full name on your birth certificate when you calculate your Destiny Number.

- **Adoption:** Many times adoption records are sealed and adoptees have difficulty obtaining their original birth certificate. If this is the case for you, search online for agencies that specialize in researching adoption records. Ideally, it's best to use the name you were given at birth, even if it was only used temporarily until your adoption. If all else fails, use the name your adoptive parents gave you.

 DID YOU KNOW?

> When adoptees are able to see their original birth certificate and do their Destiny Number based on that, many frequently discover that their original Destiny Number is the same as for the name they were given by their adoptive parents.

- **Born in a foreign country:** Perhaps your parents were living in Japan at the time of your birth—lo and behold, when you look at your birth certificate, you see Kanji characters instead of the name your parents intended. Or maybe your mother was on a trip to the Middle East when you were born and there are Arabic or Hebrew symbols on your birth certificate. If you confront this issue, use the name your parents intended and the full name you used as a child.

- **Junior, II, or III:** Do you have a generational suffix, such as "Jr." or a Roman numeral, as part of your name? If so, numerology experts agree that using your full name *without* the added letters or Roman numerals provides the most accurate interpretation of your Destiny Number. This is because it's considered an add-on rather than a true part of your name.

- **Name changed due to marriage or legally:** I believe that the exact name on your birth certificate, even if there was a misspelling, is the name you carry with you for life on a numerological level. Even if you changed your name for professional reasons (due to marriage or simply because you don't like your given name), or you have a nickname and no one has ever heard your given name, you should only use your complete birth certificate name when calculating your Destiny Number and other various Core Numbers. Let's face it: a changed name is not what you were born with and is therefore not the name your destiny in life is determined by.

Calculating Your Destiny Number

To calculate your Destiny Number, the only information you need is the full, exact name on your birth certificate (or the name you used as a child if you are one of the exceptions I talked about in the previous section). Use the following steps to walk you through the process.

1. Print the letters of your name, leaving a bit of space between each letter. It's easiest to leave some space between your first, middle, and last names because the numbers will be easier to add in smaller groups. Also, leave plenty of space underneath for your calculations.

2. Below each letter, write the number that corresponds to that letter (you can refer to the "Pythagorean Letter-to-Number Table" in Chapter 2 if you get stuck). As I mentioned earlier, generational references such as Junior or II are ignored, so numbers for that shouldn't be included.

3. Add the numbers in your first name and reduce the answer to a single digit.

4. Add the numbers in your middle name and reduce the answer to a single digit.

5. Add the numbers in your last name and reduce the answer to a single digit.

6. Finally, to get your Destiny Number, add the numerical value of your first, middle, and last names and reduce the answer to a single digit.

IT DOESN'T ADD UP

Always check to make sure you put the correct numbers under each letter (this is even more important until the letter-number correspondences become second nature to you). If you're arithmetically challenged or just want to be certain of your addition, consider using a calculator.

Here's an example to help you see the calculation process in action. Considering the person I used for this calculation is arguably the most well-known individual on Earth at this time, that his birth certificate was (and possibly remains, for some) an issue of some controversy, and his name has one of the exceptions listed earlier (the Roman numeral II), I thought this would be a fun one to work through.

For Barack Obama, I first wrote down his full name with spaces in between the first, middle, and last names.

B A R A C K   H U S S E I N   O B A M A   II

I then wrote the corresponding numbers for each letter of his name. As I mentioned earlier, generational references such as Junior or II are ignored, so I didn't include any numbers for it here.

B A R A C K   H U S S E I N   O B A M A II
2 1 9 1 3 2   8 3 1 1 5 9 5   6 2 1 4 1

For his first name, I added the numbers and reduced to a single digit. As you can see, Barack has a value of 9.

B	A	R	A	C	K
2	1	9	1	3	2

2 + 1 + 9 + 1 + 3 + 2 = 18

1 + 8 = 9

I next added the numbers in his middle name and reduced to a single digit. The numerical value of Hussein is 5.

H	U	S	S	E	I	N
8	3	1	1	5	9	5

8 + 3 + 1 + 1 + 5 + 9 + 5 = 32

3 + 2 = 5

I then added the numbers in his last name and reduced to a single digit. I got a value of 5 for Obama.

O	B	A	M	A
6	2	1	4	1

6 + 2 + 1 + 4 + 1 = 14

1 + 4 = 5

Finally, I added the first, middle, and last name values and reduced to a single digit.

BARACK	HUSSEIN	OBAMA
9	5	5

9 + 5 + 5 = 19

1 + 9 = 10

1+ 0 = 1

The Forty-Fourth President of the United States has a Destiny Number of 1.

In the steps, I showed you how to add your first, middle, and last names separately to make the process easier as you're learning it. But if you add the numbers for your first, middle, and last names all together and reduce to a single digit, you'll see that you get the same answer. Using Barack Obama's name again:

B A R A C K + H U S S E I N + O B A M A

2 1 9 1 3 2 + 8 3 1 1 5 1 5 + 6 2 1 4 1

$2 + 1 + 9 + 1 + 3 + 2 + 8 + 3 + 1 + 1 + 5 + 1 + 5 + 6 + 2 + 1 + 4 + 1 = 64$

$(6 + 4) = 10$

$(1 + 0) = 1$

DID YOU KNOW?

A lot of 1 values (A, J, S) indicates a pioneering spirit, a leader, and someone with new ideas and a take-charge attitude. Multiple 5 values are characteristic of an active person who enjoys being busy. Check out the forty-fourth president's numbers and see how well this fits.

And you don't have to just do this for your own name. It's fun to go back in your memory bank and find the Destiny Number for important people in your life or from your past—your favorite teacher, your parents, your grandparents, or even your family pet. When you perform the calculations and check the interpretations of numerology's for the Destiny Number and other numbers that you'll learn about in the rest of this book, you can gain a lot of insight into the people you care about. Going back and doing the numbers of the people you know best is a great way to prove to yourself that numerology's interpretations are accurate.

Destiny Number Meanings

Now that you've calculated your Destiny Number, it's time to check out the meaning. As you read about your Destiny Number, you'll undoubtedly experience some "aha!" moments. Hopefully, reading about your various traits and characteristics will give you greater understanding as to why you do the things you do, and why you do them in a certain way. Have fun as you read about your Destiny Number, or even the Destiny Numbers of those close to you.

Destiny Number 1

With a Destiny Number of 1, you are an independent person who wants to be the leader of the pack. Determined and self-sufficient, you're able to stand on your own two feet. You're also competitive and like to be front and foremost. With a no-nonsense approach to living, you aren't afraid to roll up your sleeves and do what needs to be done to succeed. You're ambitious, strong-willed, and determined, with an ability to set your sights on a goal and then single-mindedly work to accomplish the desired result. An innovative pioneer, you're inventive and seem to be able to do old things in a new way. One of your passions is to originate new ideas and develop new projects.

Whether working on your own or directing others, you're determined to do things your own way and don't always care what others think. Original in your thinking processes, you tend to like your own ideas best. As a 1, you also have your own systems for doing things and don't like to be told what to do or how to do it. Not one to waste time, you can accomplish tasks in an efficient manner.

Decisive and instinctive, you can make up your mind quickly; you have definite likes and dislikes and instinctively know what you want and don't want. This can sometimes mean you're hasty in making remarks. You love freedom and suffer when others try to put restraints or limitations on you.

Not afraid to dress in a trend-setting manner, you like the latest styles that are unusual and stand out from the pack. You're unafraid of being unique and actually enjoy being the center of attention.

Remember that other people have opinions, too! Be careful of your natural tendency to dominate—others may see you as domineering or aggressive. Learn to be a team player and develop the skill of listening and working with others.

 DID YOU KNOW?

Destiny Numbers don't just apply to humans! My favorite pet was our beloved Basset Hound Sam. The Destiny Number of 3 achieved by calculating his name of Sam Simpson didn't suit his personality. However, the name given to him by the breeder was Santana Mandeville's Samson; when I used his given name, bingo! The Destiny Number of 1 fit him to a T. Independent, original, and persistent, he knew what he wanted and pulled out all the stops to make his wants known. At dinnertime, he would park himself in the middle of the kitchen, bark once, and stare at the clock until he was fed.

Destiny Number 2

Cultured and refined, you're an insightful, intuitive, and sensitive soul who picks up on the feelings and thoughts of others—in other words, you can easily "read the room." As a 2, tact and diplomacy come naturally to you. You would never do or say anything that would intentionally hurt someone else.

Destiny Number 2 also indicates you prefer to be the force behind the scenes rather than the person leading the parade. Able to do two or more things at once, you're a natural multitasker who can successfully juggle multiple projects. Teamwork is your forte; you enjoy working in tandem with kindred spirits and naturally defer to their opinions. You're also able to influence others and encourage them to be the best they can be.

A good listener, you instinctively put others at ease and have the ability to get others to open up and tell you their deepest secrets. Lost strangers also feel comfortable coming up to you to ask for directions.

As a 2, partnership and togetherness mean everything to you. Enjoying companionship and harmonious relationships, you're a firm believer that it "takes two to tango." The quintessential friend, you're very helpful to those you care about. You don't quarrel easily, but if you're pushed too far, you'll fight for peace.

A perpetual student, you're a collector of things, ideas, and information. Because you're resourceful and good at research, you excel at gathering and compiling facts and data. You may be considered a "walking search engine" who others call when they need to find the weird and the wonderful.

Although you're naturally a giving person, you resent it when others try to take advantage of you. If someone takes you for granted, you have no problem slamming down the drawbridge to your heart.

Don't be fussy or take things personally. Avoid being overly sensitive and pouting when your feelings are hurt. Be more decisive—don't say "yes" if you mean "no." And remember that fear is false evidence that appears real.

Destiny Number 3

As someone with a Destiny Number of 3, you have a way with words. Possessing the gift of gab, you can sell someone their own car or "sell ice to Eskimos" with your power of persuasion. With your unique imagination and innate creativity, you have the ability to write or speak in a fascinating manner. Trying to manage many projects simultaneously, your life is often a juggling exhibition.

"Laugh and the world laughs with you" was written with a Destiny Number 3 in mind. When you feel comfortable in a situation, you can be quite charming, entertaining, and humorous. The perfect party package, you can lighten up the dullest event.

Self-expression, enthusiasm, happiness, and friendship are your ruling passions with Destiny Number 3. Depending on your mood, you can vary between gregarious and shy. When you focus on the positive, you're optimistic and see the glass as half full. Eternally youthful, you can be joyful and childlike, sometimes to the point of being a bit egocentric or petulant—for instance, you may like to play practical jokes on others but don't necessarily enjoy it when the favor is returned. You also have keen powers of observation and an uncanny ability to imitate how others walk and talk. You like gadgets and toys and are apt to be the first on the block to have the latest product or invention.

While this could be true of any Destiny Number, a 3 in particular enjoys attention from others. Concerned with appearance, you have a knack for choosing accessories that add some sparkle to your outfits. Fortunately, the older you get, the happier you'll be and the more self-confidence you'll have. However, don't let all the compliments about "discovering the Fountain of Youth" go to your head.

Keep your commitments—don't take on more than you can deliver. Focus and avoid being scattered or irresponsible. Work on becoming more self-confident. Also, realize that money doesn't grow on trees.

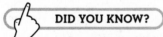 **DID YOU KNOW?**

> If your Destiny Number is 3, you're quite complex and can either be overly self-confident or very shy. As you mature, you'll develop more self-confidence and become happier in life.

Destiny Number 4

When you have a 4 for your Destiny Number, you're considered structured and reliable. Responsibility, reliability, and patience are your mantras—you're tenacious and don't give up easily. Conscientious and hard-working, you stick with tasks until they are completed.

As a 4, you're a detail-oriented and highly organized person who's able to transform practical ideas into reality. A lover of routine and order, you're happiest and work best when you have a schedule and a plan to follow. With your highly logical and organized mind, you're able to focus and concentrate on a project from beginning to end. Because of your strong dislike of change, being interrupted is one of your least favorite things (and that's putting it mildly!). You also have a memory like an elephant and remember trivia and minute details.

Accurate and precise, you're punctual and make good use of your time. In your desire to save time and money, you have or look for a system to do everything and enjoy making lists. You can be quite frugal but need to remember not to be stingy.

Steadfast, honest, and sincere, you are a loyal and sentimental friend. Solid as the Rock of Gibraltar, you're down to Earth and a good citizen, with a strong love of your country and your fellow man. However, you have no patience with undisciplined, lazy people.

Avoid being stubborn and learn that change is an inevitable part of life. Discover that it's fun to be frivolous once in a while. Although you have your own system for accomplishing tasks at work, your methods may not be right for everyone. It's best if you allow others to complete tasks using the system they prefer.

 IT DOESN'T ADD UP

These numbers are indicators of tendencies and don't rigidly define your actions. You have free will to make your own decisions, but the numbers can help guide you in making the choices that you consider right for you.

Destiny Number 5

Like a five-pointed star pointing in several directions at one time, as a Destiny Number 5, you can successfully multitask—you're able to watch TV, listen to the radio, talk on the phone, and cook dinner all at the same time. Eternally restless and seemingly in perpetual motion, you need to keep busy to avoid depression. Also, because you dislike monotony, you need to vary how and when you complete your "to-do" list.

Quite versatile and a Jack of all trades, you're not only multitalented but also multifaceted. As a 5, you're curious and always asking questions; in fact, your favorite word is "why." However, even though you're good at making inquiries, you dislike being questioned yourself. A quick thinker, you often change your mind and are willing to take chances.

A Destiny Number of 5 also indicates you use all five senses simultaneously and are quite sensual. Always flexible, you have some gypsy in your soul and enjoy travel. Because you're impulsive and spontaneous, you're willing to drop things on the spur of the moment to have fun. Clever and outgoing, you're a party waiting to happen and can liven up the dullest room.

Focus and stick to one thing at a time, and make sure to finish what you start. Slow down and take time to smell the roses. Discover that it's fun to have a quiet evening at home once in a while!

Destiny Number 6

A Destiny Number of 6 reveals a nurturer. Love, home, and family are the keys to your happiness. With your affectionate and loving nature and your desire for harmony, quarrels and arguments are not your cup of tea. Highly reliable and responsible, you're happy sharing with and taking care of others. You're also a gracious and sociable host who delights in entertaining.

As a 6, you're a service-oriented person who often volunteers to work on civic projects and isn't afraid of taking on more than your fair share of responsibility. And with your honesty, integrity, and sense of values, you're considered a solid citizen.

With a Destiny Number of 6, you personify the mantra, "Let there be peace on Earth and let it begin with me." You have a congenial and even-tempered personality, and you desire for everyone to get along. A sympathetic listener and giver of sound advice, others often seek your counsel.

Always enjoying the best of everything, you desire comfort and quality with a capital Q. You're interested in art, music, and beauty and have a keen eye for color and design. Because of your tastes, you may find you can make money through any product or service that caters to women or enhances comfort and beauty.

Before giving your great advice, make certain that the person really wants to hear what you have to say. And remember, even with your champagne tastes, it can still be fun to shop for bargains.

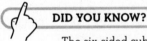

DID YOU KNOW?

The six-sided cube is the most easily recognized solid in geometry—steady and balanced. The Destiny Number 6 person provides a solid base around which others congregate.

Destiny Number 7 ▶

A Destiny Number of 7 indicates you have a highly developed analytical mind, which allows you to precisely examine objects and situations and see patterns and trends. Mildly skeptical, you generally require proof. You also need tranquility and time alone to recharge your batteries; in those times, you enjoy reading to help you relax.

Although you aren't overly demonstrative, as a 7, you feel things deeply. A lover of nature in all forms, you have respect for all creatures great and small. Having a pet brings you pleasure.

Conservative, dignified, and well-groomed, you tend to be a perfectionist. You're a person of refined tastes and culture who appreciates the finer things in life. An observer of others with an ability for imitation, you have the talent to act. Because of your extensive vocabulary, you're able to express your thoughts, particularly in written form. You also know how to ask keen questions and think on your feet.

Even though you may appear aloof and not easy to get close to, as a 7, you're a very loyal friend. You dislike gossip and the people who spread it, and because of your highly developed sense of integrity, you're extremely ethical and honest in your dealings.

As a believer in karma, you strive to do the right thing—even when no one is watching. An intuitive old soul with an interest in metaphysics, you're also a seeker of truth.

Be more sociable—make the first move, greet others warmly, and learn the art of small talk. Remember that stimulants (and depressants) affect you differently than they do most people because you're often naturally pensive and melancholy.

Destiny Number 8

If you have a Destiny Number of 8, you often tend to have goals more than dreams. A very powerful person, you're driven by money, power, and success. You're a born leader who likes to be the boss or in charge of things. With innate managerial skills and individual methods for doing things, you first need to know what's expected of you and then prefer to be left alone to do your job.

An ambitious promoter who's able to get others on the bandwagon, you can always be counted on to complete the project. You're a resilient, take-charge person who seems to handle whatever comes your way. Because you're capable and have your own way of doing things, you chafe at being micromanaged; you don't like to be questioned or prodded for updates on the status of a project. As an 8, you feel that such interrogation just consumes valuable time and that your history of performance should speak for itself.

While you're levelheaded in emergencies, you may be emotional after the crisis has passed. You function well under pressure, but after the lid is off, all that steam dissipates. Because you are interested in fitness and health, you monitor your health, diet, and exercise routines carefully. Unless you have an H, Q, or Z in your given name, as a Destiny Number 8, you may get emotional and have a tendency to gain or lose weight when you are under stress.

Try to keep emotions on an even keel by avoiding highs, lows, and sometimes in-betweens. Learning to balance your life—eight hours for work, eight hours for play, and eight hours for rest is essential for you. With your nose always to the grindstone, you may not take enough time for romance.

Be tactful and allow others to express their own viewpoints. Work hard to avoid projecting the attitude, "If I want your opinion, I'll give it to you!"

PYTHAGORAS SAYS

Destiny Number 8s have the capacity to be fair, balanced, and keep their lives on an even keel. If you're a Destiny Number 8, make sure others stop, look, and listen to you.

Destiny Number 9

You're a humanitarian who appreciates art, music, and beauty and has an innate desire to express your own literary, artistic, or musical talents. As a 9, you also have the ability to influence others and can shed your light on those who are less evolved. An understanding soul, you want peace on Earth and have difficulty understanding why people can't get along.

A geography buff, the world is your oyster. You're a good traveler who's tolerant of others and has a genuine concern for mankind; you want to see the world and mingle with people of various cultures.

A Destiny Number of 9 indicates you have visionary tendencies. You see the big picture and think of things on a grand scale that have universal appeal. Adaptable and able to fit in easily with diverse groups of people, you often try to be all things to all people.

With a friendly and outgoing personality, you're kind-hearted and generous—sometimes to a fault. You also possess a strong desire to make life easier for others. Always willing to give of yourself, you sometimes want appreciation for your thoughtful (and random) acts of kindness.

Be forgiving of others who aren't as thoughtful and generous as you are. Avoid trying to be an "A" person (all things to all people at all times).

Master Destiny Number 11

The Master Destiny Number 11 is a higher vibration of the Destiny Number 2. A very idealistic leader who's diplomatic and well-liked, you're able to inspire others. Highly intuitive and inspirational, you can also be high-strung.

As an 11, you may be interested in metaphysics. A natural storyteller, you tend to exaggerate and are able to elaborate on the truth.

Avoid being petty. Save yourself the trouble—some people want to stay in the valley and not be on the mountaintop with you.

Master Destiny Number 22

The Master Destiny Number 22 is a higher vibration of the Destiny Number 4. You know what you're talking about and can charm the birds out of the trees with your influence. Respected by others, you're the authority on many things.

Avoid being stubborn. Finish what you start. Be aware that some people have to learn things on their own and don't want to hear what you have to say.

The Least You Need to Know

- Your Destiny Number comes from the name on your birth certificate or the equivalent.
- Knowing your Destiny Number indicates how you can and should proceed in your field to be successful and to attain what your destiny holds for you.
- Each part of your name (in other words, your first, middle, and last names) contributes to and impacts on the whole you.

The Soul Number

In the previous chapter, you learned that the first vowel of your name has special meaning. This chapter takes it a step further, showing you how in Pythagorean numerology, all the vowels in your name have great meaning. The collection of vowels, when added and reduced, reveals your Soul Number. Tucked away and sometimes hidden, your Soul Number reveals the inner you.

In this chapter, I tell you about the Soul Number: what it is, how to calculate its value, and what your Soul Number indicates about you.

In This Chapter

- Learning what the Soul Number is
- How to calculate your Soul Number
- Interpreting the Soul Numbers

What Is the Soul Number?   4

Your *Soul Number* is hidden inside your name and reveals your innermost thoughts, hopes, wishes, dreams, and desires. It also tells you about the inner you, what you value most, what you long for, what you daydream about, what you want to express in this lifetime, and what feeds your soul. It's your inner spirit—the *you* that few, if any, in the world ever see. Your Soul Number also indicates talents you might possess, whether they're developed, exhibited, or still dormant. What's revealed by your Soul Number might amaze your friends, loved ones, and even your closest confidants.

 **DEFINITION**

> Sometimes called the Heart Number, the **Soul Number** is a Core Number that represents the inner you, including your values, hopes, wishes, dreams, and innermost desires as well as your thoughts, feelings, and attitudes toward life and love. It is the reduced sum of the numeric values of the vowels in your birth name.

Knowing and understanding your Soul Number can point to aspects of yourself that you may not even realize are there. Or, if you do know your hidden qualities and are a private person, these may be things that you may dread others finding out about you, either from embarrassment or fear of ridicule.

For example, if you're a male with a Soul Number 6, you may not want it known that you have very tender feelings toward children, animals, and older people. Likewise, an executive with a Soul Number 2 would prefer to keep her easily hurt feelings under wraps with coworkers.

Knowing and understanding your Soul Number can bring you greater happiness and deeper personal insight. It can help you with family and personal relationships, as well as with decisions in your career. Your Soul Number also explains why you do certain things the way you do.

And knowing the Soul Number of loved ones gives you more insight and understanding of their inner nature, regardless of how they appear on the outside. At work, knowing the Soul Number of your boss and coworkers helps you know what motivates them and how to connect with them in a manner they can relate to. If you have or know children, knowing their Soul Number is the key to helping them achieve their heart's desire.

Calculating Your Soul Number

The vowels in your name, along with their numeric values, combine to disclose your Soul Number. When calculating, remember that Y or W aren't used as vowels—only A, E, I, O, and U. In the following steps, I walk you through how to calculate your Soul Number.

RAUL ALEJANDRO AGUILAR

Vowels	A U		A	E	A			O	A	U I	A	
Name	1 3		1	5	1			6	1	3 9	1	

Use this worksheet to fill in information for steps 1 through 3.

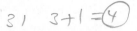

31   3+1 = ④

Write your Soul Number in this heart, as indicated in step 4.

1. Print each letter of your full name, exactly as it appears on your birth certificate. It's important to leave some space above your name, because that's where the numeric values of the vowels are written.

2. On the top line, place the numeric value of every vowel (A, E, I, O, and U). Remember: A is 1, E is 5, I is 9, O is 6, and U is 3.

3. Now add up all of the numeric values of the vowels and reduce to a single digit. You can either add the numbers horizontally all the way across the entire name or, if it's easier for you, add the first, middle, and last names separately and then add the sums together—whichever way it's done, you get the same result. That number is your Soul Number.

4. Write your Soul Number, also known as your heart's desires, in the heart.

Here's how this process is applied to the name of former president Dwight David Eisenhower. I've provided the two ways Eisenhower's name can be added, so you can judge which way is right for you.

I first entered Eisenhower's name in the chart.

Vowels																					
Name	D	W	I	G	H	T		D	A	V	I	D		E	I	S	E	N	H	O	W	E	R

I then inserted the values of the vowels at the top of the chart.

Vowels		9						1		9				5	9		5			6		5	
Name	D	W	I	G	H	T		D	A	V	I	D		E	I	S	E	N	H	O	W	E	R

Finally, I added and reduced until I got a single-digit value. The first chart shows Eisenhower's entire name being added at once, while the second chart shows the first, middle, and last names being added separately before their sums are added together.

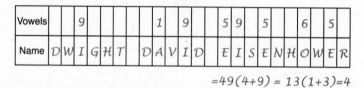

=49(4+9) = 13(1+3)=4

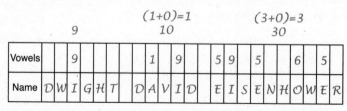

$$9 \qquad \begin{matrix}(1+0)=1 \\ 10\end{matrix} \qquad \begin{matrix}(3+0)=3 \\ 30\end{matrix}$$

=13(1+3)=4

Whatever way you add it, Eisenhower had a Soul Number of 4.

When calculating your Soul Number, you also have the option of "casting out" or ignoring the nines. Here's how the calculation for Eisenhower's Soul Number looks when doing so.

Vowels		9̸						1		9̸				5	9̸		5			6		5	9̸
Name	D	W	I	G	H	T		D	A	V	I	D		E	I	S	E	N	H	O	W	E	R

1+5+5+6+5=22(2+2)=4

If you recall from Chapter 2, you also have the option to get rid of groups of numbers that add to 9. Whatever you decide to do, you should still get the same answer.

 PYTHAGORAS SAYS

Even if you have two or more middle names or a hyphenated name on your birth certificate, use them all. Hint: If you have several names, be sure to start on a large piece of paper or turn the paper to landscape (horizontal rather than vertical).

Soul Number Meanings

Now that you know how to calculate the Soul Number, you can delve deeper into the meaning. The following provides information about each Soul Number and how they reveal your heart's desires and innermost feelings.

Soul Number 1

A Soul Number of 1 indicates that in both your personal and professional lives, you have a strong need to manage situations. Ambitious and determined, leading and directing are your forte. Regardless of the circumstances, you want to be in charge and the leader of the pack. Goal-oriented, you thrive in a fast-paced environment and act quickly to accomplish your objectives. Because you like your own way best, you probably dislike taking orders from anyone and work best alone rather than in tandem with others.

As a 1, you prefer to be respected for your keen mind rather than your appearance. Original and creative, you need to find outlets for your artistic talents. You also have the ability to find new solutions to old problems. An idea person, you have high-flying plans and the talent to concep-tualize large projects yet like to leave the details to others—creating original ideas is fun and exciting for you, but mundane details seem boring.

Liking others around you to be as independent as you are, you tend to avoid those who are needy and possess the ability to say "no." You're also content to spend time alone, enjoying your own company.

Because you're a born leader, you may resent being placed in a subordinate position. Also, due to your ability to work at lightning speed, you may get impatient when others dawdle. Work on developing friendships and the ability to work with others, and be careful not to dominate situations and people. Also, avoid being boastful, egotistical, or too critical when people disagree with you.

Soul Number 2

If your Soul Number is 2, you desire harmony above anything else and are able to get along and cooperate with all different types of people. Sympathetic to your core, you have a gentle heart and pleasant way about you. You also have excellent manners and social skills due to your courtesy and politeness. An eternal optimist, you see the best in everyone.

A team player and an inspiration to others, you prefer to work à deux rather than solo and excel at arbitrating, negotiating, or teaching. But in your desire to weigh all the options, you may take a while to make up your mind. Because you're good at details and aren't afraid to ask for help when you need it, you usually pick up the pieces when others drop the ball. As a Soul Number 2, you also have the ability to embellish the truth and get others on the bandwagon with you.

As a 2, you're an avid collector of both objects and friends. A lover of beauty and culture, you appreciate the finer things in life. Although you desire economic security, wealth is your primary goal; however, your ability to share helps you get along well with others.

You find it difficult to make choices and are sometimes indecisive. Influenced by others' opinions, you require careful handling and lots of tender loving care. Because you fear criticism from others and desire to please them, you're easily persuaded and can be gullible. If this happens and makes you feel taken advantage of, you tend to shut down. Rather than trying to get peace at any price, you may have to force yourself to be assertive in business dealings.

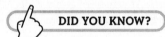

DID YOU KNOW?

Some numerologists call the Soul Number the *Urge Number* because it represents your deepest and innermost feelings and subconscious urges.

Soul Number 3

Romance never dies for a Soul Number 3. You have a natural artistry and an innate desire for self-expression. With your joie de vivre, you're popular and well-liked. A natural flirt, your youthful good looks and appearance are important to you. You enjoy receiving compliments and are comfortable basking in the attention they bring.

As a 3, the happiness of others is essential to you. Optimistic when you feel secure, you can be quite entertaining and can use your gift of gab to liven up a party or dull event.

As a bon vivant, you enjoy living the good life and all of the trappings that go with it. Flexible and resilient, you can roll with the punches and take life as it comes.

Because you're not always focused on the task at hand, you tend to scatter your forces and spin your wheels. Also, you may be too optimistic and see the world through rose-colored glasses.

Avoid tooting your own horn. People around you aren't sure who they are going to get—the fun, social butterfly or the shy introvert.

Soul Number 4

If you're a Soul Number 4, you crave a practical and disciplined life and are tethered to your calendar. With your highly developed work ethic, you roll up your sleeves and get to work without hesitation. You also tend to have a mind and memory like a steel trap, making you the King or Queen of trivia. (Try to get on *Jeopardy!*)

Time is money to you, and you hate to waste either. When it comes to time, you dislike surprises or being interrupted. As for money, when you make a purchase, you expect to receive value and quality for money spent.

You love tradition and take a practical approach to matters of the heart. Extremely conscientious and reliable, you're precise, exacting, and able to tackle the smallest of details. With your keen eye for design, you often straighten crooked pictures as you walk by.

Because you need routine, you may feel disconnected when faced with change. You must also be wary of being stubborn, narrow-minded, or rigid in your thinking. You don't mean to be bossy—you simply think that your ideas are best. However, your critical nature makes others wish you were more flexible. Therefore, try to avoid being too miserly or stingy. Also, take the time to look at the big picture rather than focusing only on minute details.

 IT DOESN'T ADD UP

If you're a Soul Number 4, you probably have a strong desire to provide for your loved ones, which can lead you to be a workaholic. Temper your organizational skills with some flexibility to bring balance to your work and family lives.

Soul Number 5

As a 5, you thrive on routine and crave an organized life. A person of many talents and diverse interests, you can multitask with the best. Because you're blessed with an ingenious mind, you're an unconventional thinker who grasps difficult or abstract concepts quickly and easily. And with your natural curiosity, you like to ask questions.

A whirling dervish, you're happy when you're in the center of the action and love to shock people. You're able to spin a story like no other and can tell a fib with a straight face. However, honesty and loyalty are your middle names. Quick to forgive, you're able to let go and move on.

As a Soul Number 5, your passion is variety—trying new restaurants, taking a new route to work, or meeting new friends. You enjoy change and are content to change course midstream. Adventurous, you would have hopped on the first wagon heading west. Because of this, you're apt to have your travel agent's phone number on speed dial. Overall, you hate the feeling of being trapped and require freedom at all costs.

You're apt to be overly restless or impatient at times. Because you tend to jump from activity to activity, you rarely finish what you start. You also may think the grass is always greener somewhere else when doing boring, routine work. In the personal realm, commitment is difficult for you, and others may perceive you as unreliable because you change your mind at the drop of a hat.

Soul Number 6

If you're a Soul Number 6, your motto is "the best or nothing." The quintessential romantic, love, home, and family are essential for your happiness. As a 6, you treasure family values and traditions. Generous and loving, you are a magnet for children and animals and often rescue stray animals and people.

As a 6, you're recognized by others for your good common sense. The epitome of a peacemaker, you're a natural counselor who strives for harmonious relationships. Because you're always responsible, you willingly assume more than your fair share of the workload.

Although wealth is not very important to you, security and financial stability are crucial. A fair deal for all is essential to your happiness. Big on commitments, you write them in pen, not pencil, and your handshake and word are golden.

With a Soul Number of 6, you play for keeps and would never be heard singing the lyric, "do you want to make love or do you just want to fool around." Idealistic and trusting, you see the best in people; however, you aren't afraid to speak your mind if you feel someone has been unjust or unfair.

You tend to put the needs of others before your own. In your desire to help others, be careful not to smother them. Also, know that some people may take advantage of your caring and generous nature. In an argument, your emotions can get the best of you.

 IT DOESN'T ADD UP

Because loving others brings the Soul Number 6 great happiness, you may become too involved in the lives of your loved ones. Remember that children fail to develop critical independence and decision-making skills when their parents are too overprotective. Give them room and let them know you'll be there if and when they fall.

Soul Number 7

Your mantra is "silence is golden." Pensive and reflective, as a 7, you enjoy your own company best and crave tranquility away from the maddening crowd. Just like a good poker player, you're able to keep your emotions in check and your thoughts to yourself.

As a Soul Number 7, you often feel misunderstood by others, though your ability to imitate others is uncanny. Always intuitive, you have no use for phony people and can spot them a mile away—no one can fool you for very long (if at all). You avoid petty gossip and appreciate meaningful conversations. Because you're so selective, you have a small but valued circle of friends.

A seeker of the truth, you have great wisdom. Because you're analytical and insightful, you know what questions to ask. You also don't speak until you're sure of the facts because you hate to be wrong.

Because you repress your emotions, others may have a hard time getting to know you. Avoid being an introvert and isolated from others.

Soul Number 8

A Soul Number of 8 indicates that power and position in life are essential to your happiness. Full of ambition, you strive to make your mark in the world. And because you equate money with power, financial independence and security are important to you.

Taking charge is your natural instinct as an 8. Self-contained, you work hard and feel as though you have the right to succeed. Checking accomplishments off your bucket list is fun for you. You also have a resilience and tenacity that makes you not give up easily. A good judge of human character, you prefer to direct and supervise, leaving the actual tasks to others.

As a Soul Number 8, you make your presence known wherever you go. Strong and authoritative, you need an organized mate who is as independent as you are. However, you're often too busy for romance. You mainly need to feel important and be respected by others.

It's important for you to balance your emotions. Because others may see you as overly domineering or stubborn, try being open to the ideas of others. Also, avoid being extravagant and boastful in an effort to demonstrate your financial prowess to others. Keep a careful eye on your health in times of trouble, as you gain or lose weight easily when you're upset or stressed.

Soul Number 9

As a Soul Number 9, you have the power to influence others. Friendly, easy to get along with, and well liked, you have universal admiration and appeal. A Soul Number of 9 also indicates that you're a self-sacrificing philanthropist who enjoys helping mankind.

Possessing a flair for artistic pursuits, art, music, and beauty are important to you. You also have a keen sense of perfection and aesthetics. A tolerant and understanding teacher, you're sought out by those who want to emulate you.

As a 9, you're idealistic about love and feel emotions deeply even though you may not always express them. You also embrace and personify the phrase "brotherly love." Having experienced your own disappointments, you're highly empathetic toward others. But even with your altruistic nature, you're able to quit giving when you feel taken for granted—when you express love and appreciation for others, you need to have the favor returned.

You tend to get resentful if others don't show enough appreciation for your kind deeds and may express your feelings too strongly at times. A dreamer, you can be overly impressionable. You may also often feel disappointed by the lack of perfection in yourself and others.

Master Soul Number 11

Master Soul Number 11 is a higher vibration of Soul Number 2. Thus, in addition to the challenges and characteristics of a 2, you're sensitive and intuitive, sometimes to the point of being psychic. An old soul and wise beyond your years, you get hunches and do best when you listen to your inner voice. You also want to be the star of the show and refuse to play the role of understudy. Remember that others are on their own path during their journey through life and need to follow their own intuition.

Master Soul Number 22

Master Soul Number 22 is a higher vibration of Soul Number 4. Thus, in addition to the challenges and characteristics of a 4, you have a strong desire and the talent to build a better world than the way you found it. Using your leadership abilities, you're able to change the world one person at a time. You also need practicality in all you do and thrive on a sense of security. In terms of challenges, others often need to learn life's lessons for themselves—let them.

The Least You Need to Know

- Your Soul Number reveals the inner you: your hopes, wishes, and heart's desires.
- Your Soul Number can indicate desires and talents that are developed, exhibited, or still dormant.
- The Soul Number is calculated using only the vowels in a name.

The Personality Number

Think of your name and all of the letters in it as a box that holds a birthday present. The box as a whole is your Destiny Number (see Chapter 3). The inside of the box represents the inner you, or your Soul Number (see Chapter 4). The wrapping on the outside of the box is your Personality Number, or the outer persona you may or may not be aware you're projecting.

In this chapter, I tell you about the Personality Number, show you how to calculate it, and give you a rundown of the perceptions associated with each number.

In This Chapter

- Learning what the Personality Number is
- How to calculate your Personality Number
- Interpreting the Personality Number values

What Is the Personality Number?

The *Personality Number* reveals the "outer you" and discloses how others perceive you, which can be different from how you see yourself. For example, you may know people who are fun-loving when in small groups or among friends but are introverted when in a crowd; conversely, there are people who let their hair down in public but are more reserved when amongst those whose opinions matter to them.

When it comes to your own outer self, maybe you have a pleasant and outgoing façade to mask your insecurity and reclusive nature. Although the old saying goes, "you can't judge a book by its cover," people get their first impressions from the cover you project. Understanding your Personality Number can give you some clues as to how others see you. And, if you want to, you can use this information to make adjustments in how you present yourself in order to be seen as you want to be seen.

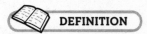 **DEFINITION**

The **Personality Number** is a Core Number that represents the outer you, or the traits perceived by others. It is obtained by adding and reducing the numeric value of the consonants in your birth name.

Remember that the impressions that people have of you can have significant impact on your life, both personally and professionally. So being able to make good first impressions can go a long way toward happiness and prosperity. Your Personality Number can show you where to start.

Calculating Your Personality Number

The numeric values of the consonants in your name, when added and reduced, disclose your Personality Number. In the following steps, I show you how to calculate this important number.

Name	PAUL ALEJANDRO AGUIAR
Consonants	9 3 3 1 5 4 9 7 3 9

Use this chart to enter the information for steps 1 through 3.

Write your Personality Number on the package, as indicated in step 4.

1. On the top row of the chart, write your name as it appears on your birth certificate.

2. On the bottom row, place the numeric values of the consonants below each occurrence.

3. Add the numbers and reduce to a single digit. The single-digit sum is your Personality Number.

4. Write your Personality Number on the package.

To show you how this process is done, here's an example using former president Dwight David Eisenhower. First, I wrote his full name in the chart.

RAUL ALEJANDRO AGUILAR ESCOBAR = 49

Name	D	W	I	G	H	T		D	A	V	I	D		E	I	S	E	N	H	O	W	E	R
Consonants	9			3		3	1			4 9						7		8	9			1 3 2 9		

I then wrote the numeric values corresponding to the consonants below them.

Name	D	W	I	G	H	T		D	A	V	I	D		E	I	S	E	N	H	O	W	E	R
Consonants	4	5		7	8	2		4		4		4				1		5	8		5		9

Finally, I added the numeric values of the consonants and reduced to a single digit.

$$4 + 5 + 7 + 8 + 2 + 4 + 4 + 4 + 1 + 5 + 8 + 5 + 9 = 66$$

$$6 + 6 = 12$$

$$1 + 2 = 3$$

As you can see, Eisenhower had a Personality Number of 3.

PYTHAGORAS SAYS

Note that during the reduction process for Eisenhower's Personality Number, I could have just ignored the nines and 9 combinations (4 and 5; 7 and 2; 4, 4, and 1; and the 9). This would have left me with a sum of 30, which also reduces to 3.

Now I'm going to show you a shortcut to calculating your Personality Number that's not only easy but will save you time. The Destiny Number is the single-digit value you get from adding and reducing the letters in your name. Because the Soul Number comes from adding the vowels while the Personality Number comes from adding the consonants, the Soul Number and Personality Number add together to the same digit as the Destiny Number. In a nutshell, that means if you know your Destiny Number and your Soul Number, you can skip the step of adding up the numeric value of the consonants. Why? Ask yourself a simple question: What number, when added to your Soul Number, results in the same number as your Destiny Number? Without having to add up your consonants, the missing number is your Personality Number. So to get your Personality Number, you can use the following formula:

Soul Number + Personality Number = Destiny Number

But what if you only know one of the values for the formula? Let's see what this shortcut looks like using the Soul Number and the Destiny Number from examples in previous chapters.

In Chapter 4, I calculated Eisenhower's Soul Number, which was 4. The following is his chart filled out with his name and numbers for the vowels, along with the calculation I did to get the Soul Number.

Vowels			9					1	9		5	9		5			6		5	
Name	D	W	I	G	H	T	D	A	V	I	D	E	I	S	E	N	H	O	W	E	R

$$=49(4+9) = 13(1+3)=4$$

To get his Destiny Number to help figure out his Personality Number, I wrote his full name on another chart and put the numeric values below every letter. I then added and reduced the numbers, which gave me 7 for his Destiny Number.

Name	D	W	I	G	H	T	D	A	V	I	D	E	I	S	E	N	H	O	W	E	R
Values	4	5	9	7	8	2	4	1	4	9	4	5	9	1	5	5	8	6	5	5	9

$$115 (1+1+5)=7$$

Next, I plugged Eisenhower's Soul Number and Destiny Number into the formula. I then figured out what number, when added to Soul Number 4, gave me a Destiny Number of 7. This told me Eisenhower's Personality Number was 3.

If you recall from Chapter 3, I calculated Obama's Destiny Number, which is 1. In this case, I didn't know his Soul Number, so I needed to add and reduce the numeric value of the vowels to find it. This gave me a Soul Number of 9 for him. In the following chart, you can see the information for both his Destiny Number and his Soul Number.

27(2+7)=9

Vowels		1	1			3		5	9		6	1		1
Name	B	A	R	A	C	K	H	U	S	S	E	I	N	O	B	A	M	A
Values	2	1	9	1	3	2	8	3	1	1	5	9	5	6	2	1	4	1

64 (6+4)=10(1+0)=1

To find out Obama's Personality Number, I had to figure out what number, when added to his Soul Number (9), results in his Destiny Number (1). It's actually 1, as 9 + 1 = 10, which reduces to 1 + 0, or 1.

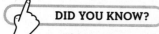

Let's check to make sure 1 is really his Personality Number. You'll notice that only the numeric values of the consonants are written below his name, so the Personality Number is easier to figure.

$$27(2+7)=9$$

Name	B	A	R	A	C	K		H	U	S	S	E	I	N		O	B	A	M	A
Consonants	2				3	2		8		1	1			5			2		4	

$$28 \ (2+8)=10(1+0)=1$$

It all adds up! This proves that President Obama's Personality Number is 1.

If you'd like to learn more about the combinations of Destiny, Soul, and Personality Numbers, check out Chapter 6.

Personality Number Meanings

Now, let's discover what characteristics are common to the different Personality Numbers. The following takes you through a number of traits, characteristics, and impressions for each Personality Number.

Personality Number 1

If your Personality Number is 1, you appear to be self-sufficient and the center of attention; you're seen as comfortable standing out from the crowd. People see you as strong-willed, determined, and in control. They think you're self-reliant and have your act together.

As a Personality Number 1, you come off as courageous, with a no-holds-barred attitude. That courage spills over into fashion, as you're perceived as being fashion-forward with a unique sense of style that may include bright colors. You appear content with your individuality and are independent to the point where it may seem as if you don't care what others think about you.

Personality Number 2

If your Personality Number is 2, you appear to be friendly, pleasant, and at ease talking with others. People think you're tactful, diplomatic, and able to use the perfect words to make others feel comfortable and understood.

You're perceived as cooperative and easy to get along with, often deferring to the opinions of others. They find you charming and are often apt to see you with a companion. Sometimes you seem shy or quiet, but you'll happily participate when asked.

Perhaps people find you plain looking at first glance, but you're neat, clean, and careful with details. Your clothes are always pressed, and nary a hair is out of place. They see you as wearing comfortable, soft, flowing clothes in a gentle color palette.

Personality Number 3

If your Personality Number is 3, you appear to be the life of the party. You're seen as good with words, expressive, and animated, sometimes to the point of hogging the spotlight. People also perceive you as a natural entertainer who tells jokes and may talk a lot.

You're seen by others as a practical joker or prankster with a wonderful sense of humor and the gift of gab. People say you're a flamboyant speaker who's most comfortable talking about yourself and an exaggerator who livens up stories with many details about yourself.

You're seen as someone who wears artistic, creative clothing, often with glitzy accessories. People think you're an eternal optimist.

 DID YOU KNOW?

Beauty surrounds the Personality Number 3. Whether you're a man or a woman, you're strikingly attractive, look younger than your years, and appreciate fine clothing and jewelry.

Personality Number 4

If your Personality Number is 4, you appear to be a planner who impresses others with your keen organizational skills. You're concerned with following rules and policies and driven by deadlines and budget constraints. You're also perceived as reliable and hardworking.

People think you're always punctual and respectful of others' schedules. Loyal and honest, you're dedicated to displaying proper behavior and good manners.

Very level-headed and astute, you're concerned about finances and generally quite thrifty. And when it comes to your daily attire, you're seen dressed in very tailored, neat, and sturdy clothes.

Personality Number 5

If your Personality Number is 5, you appear to be energetic and restless, with "ants in your pants." You're seen as exciting and fun-loving with a zest for life. You're outgoing and willing to jump in and do what others are doing. You're also always aware of the latest scoop or big news.

People also think you're touchy-feely, with a habit of putting your left hand on top of their right when shaking hands. You're curious and able to make anyone comfortable by asking thoughtful questions.

At work, you're seen as a multitasker who can text or read emails during a conversation or meeting. However, you're often seen as running late and frequently rushed.

People see you as wearing fashion-forward clothes or sportswear that's loose or nonconstricting. You also tend to be dressed in clothes that work for day or night in the event of a last-minute change of plans.

Personality Number 6

If your Personality Number is 6, you appear to be easy to talk to and are always ready with a warm and gentle greeting. People feel you're readily adaptable to any group's dynamic, as you seem comfortable in social situations and have impeccable manners.

High fashion and brand names mean little to you. When you're with another person, you look beyond physical appearance and get to know them for their personality and inner beauty. When it comes to your own style, you're viewed as wearing comfortable, flowing clothes made of soft fabrics in pleasant colors.

You treat others fairly, and people find your words and actions nonjudgmental. You're seen as very dependable and concerned with the welfare of others, with a willingness to pitch in where needed. You're also sympathetic, a good listener, and a giver of valuable advice. Nurturing and helpful, you're perceived as always helping those less fortunate.

 DID YOU KNOW?

The Personality Number 6 has a strong sense of justice. If you're a 6, others see you as a peacemaker. Because you also radiate warmth and compassion, you're also a trusted confidante to many.

Personality Number 7

If your Personality Number is 7, you appear to be impeccably groomed with a refined appearance. Aloof and dignified, you tend to be dressed in quality fabric in a neutral color palette.

Others feel you're private and reluctant to discuss personal matters. They see you as intense, self-absorbed, and deep in thought. You're also considered mysterious and slow to warm up to others.

Although you're able to look straight through someone and know what he or she is thinking, people see you as trustworthy and unwilling to betray a confidence, with great integrity.

You're perceived as intelligent, with keen observational skills. You're also considered analytical to the point where you may appear negative or skeptical.

Personality Number 8

If your Personality Number is 8, you appear to be positive, outgoing, and self-assured. People find you confident, powerful, and influential. They also find you authoritative and concerned with the first impression you make. You're capable and in control, though courteous and concerned, and you always have impeccable manners.

People think you're wealthy, even if you're not. You're seen as dignified, looking the part of a CEO even when you're wearing jeans. You're thought of as impeccably dressed in fine fabrics and tailored clothes.

Personality Number 9

If your Personality Number is 9, you appear to be magnetic, warm, and welcoming to everyone you meet. People find you approachable and a natural conversationalist who's comfortable in any environment. You're also seen as a very generous person who's often happy to pick up the check.

People think you're younger than you actually are because you may have a good complexion. You're also either the picture of good posture or a slouch. You're usually dressed in comfortable clothes and may have a flair for the dramatic through ethnic or unusual accessories.

A frequent volunteer, you're admired by others. People think of you as friendly with people from all walks of life, cultures, and countries. Tolerant of others, caring, and kind, you're seen as devoted to justice for all.

Master Personality Number 11

Master Personality Number 11 is a higher vibration of Personality Number 2. If you encounter a number 11 when reducing the sum of the numeric values of your consonants, you are a Master Personality Number 11. If you have a Master Personality Number of 11, you appear to be more spiritual than most—at the very least, you're inspirational. You're considered highly intelligent and a visionary. People also think of you as intuitive or even psychic.

Master Personality Number 22

Master Personality Number 22 is a higher vibration of Personality Number 4. If you encounter a number 22 when you're reducing the numeric values of your consonants, you're a Master Personality Number 22. In addition to the persona perceptions of a 4, as a 22, you also appear competent, focused, and unwavering. People see you as a problem-solver who plans for success and follows through. When it comes to dress and appearance, you tend to be conservative.

 PYTHAGORAS SAYS

> Master Personality Number 22s have their act together and are ready to take it on the road. Able to handle any situation, you're destined for greatness and could rule the world.

The Least You Need to Know

- Your Personality Number is the "outer you" and indicates how others perceive you.
- By modifying your actions, you're able to control how others perceive you.
- Your Personality Number is calculated using only the consonants in your name.
- Because your Soul Number and Personality number equal your Destiny Number when added together, you can use your Destiny Number and Soul Number to more quickly find your Personality Number.

Destiny, Soul, and Personality Number Combinations

As you learned in Chapter 3, your Destiny Number is determined by the combination of the inner and outer you. Because of this, your Soul and Personality Numbers (see Chapters 4 and 5) add and reduce to your Destiny Number. This means, for example, that if your Soul Number is 4 and your Personality Number is 6, your Destiny Number is 1.

Each Destiny Number has nine possible combinations when combined with the various Soul and Personality Numbers. Thus, there are 81 possible Destiny, Soul, and Personality Number combinations. Interpreting these 81 combinations takes care and experience. It's necessary to blend the three separate parts into a cohesive whole and weigh the strength of each influence—sometimes the Destiny Number is dominant, sometimes the Soul Number takes the lead, and occasionally the Personality Number shines the brightest.

In this chapter, I discuss the combinations of Destiny, Soul, and Personality Numbers and the information behind them.

In This Chapter

- How your Destiny, Soul, and Personality Numbers are linked
- Potential combinations of the numbers
- The meaning behind the Destiny, Soul, and Personality Number combinations

Table of Potential Combinations

While you should learn how to calculate each of the numbers to fully understand the process, the following is a handy table of the different combinations of Destiny, Soul, and Personality Numbers.

Destiny Number 1	Soul Number 1	Personality Number 9
Destiny Number 1	Soul Number 2	Personality Number 8
Destiny Number 1	Soul Number 3	Personality Number 7
Destiny Number 1	Soul Number 4	Personality Number 6
Destiny Number 1	Soul Number 5	Personality Number 5
Destiny Number 1	Soul Number 6	Personality Number 4
Destiny Number 1	Soul Number 7	Personality Number 3
Destiny Number 1	Soul Number 8	Personality Number 2
Destiny Number 1	Soul Number 9	Personality Number 1
Destiny Number 2	Soul Number 1	Personality Number 1
Destiny Number 2	Soul Number 2	Personality Number 9
Destiny Number 2	Soul Number 3	Personality Number 8
Destiny Number 2	Soul Number 4	Personality Number 7
Destiny Number 2	Soul Number 5	Personality Number 6
Destiny Number 2	Soul Number 6	Personality Number 5
Destiny Number 2	Soul Number 7	Personality Number 4
Destiny Number 2	Soul Number 8	Personality Number 3
Destiny Number 2	Soul Number 9	Personality Number 2
Destiny Number 3	Soul Number 1	Personality Number 2
Destiny Number 3	Soul Number 2	Personality Number 1
Destiny Number 3	Soul Number 3	Personality Number 9
Destiny Number 3	Soul Number 4	Personality Number 8
Destiny Number 3	Soul Number 5	Personality Number 7
Destiny Number 3	Soul Number 6	Personality Number 6
Destiny Number 3	Soul Number 7	Personality Number 5
Destiny Number 3	Soul Number 8	Personality Number 4
Destiny Number 3	Soul Number 9	Personality Number 3

Destiny Number 4	Soul Number 1	Personality Number 3
Destiny Number 4	Soul Number 2	Personality Number 2
Destiny Number 4	Soul Number 3	Personality Number 1
Destiny Number 4	Soul Number 4	Personality Number 9
Destiny Number 4	Soul Number 5	Personality Number 8
Destiny Number 4	Soul Number 6	Personality Number 7
Destiny Number 4	Soul Number 7	Personality Number 6
Destiny Number 4	Soul Number 8	Personality Number 5
Destiny Number 4	Soul Number 9	Personality Number 4
Destiny Number 5	Soul Number 1	Personality Number 4
Destiny Number 5	Soul Number 2	Personality Number 3
Destiny Number 5	Soul Number 3	Personality Number 2
Destiny Number 5	Soul Number 4	Personality Number 1
Destiny Number 5	Soul Number 5	Personality Number 9
Destiny Number 5	Soul Number 6	Personality Number 8
Destiny Number 5	Soul Number 7	Personality Number 7
Destiny Number 5	Soul Number 8	Personality Number 6
Destiny Number 5	Soul Number 9	Personality Number 5
Destiny Number 6	Soul Number 1	Personality Number 5
Destiny Number 6	Soul Number 2	Personality Number 4
Destiny Number 6	Soul Number 3	Personality Number 3
Destiny Number 6	Soul Number 4	Personality Number 2
Destiny Number 6	Soul Number 5	Personality Number 1
Destiny Number 6	Soul Number 6	Personality Number 9
Destiny Number 6	Soul Number 7	Personality Number 8
Destiny Number 6	Soul Number 8	Personality Number 7
Destiny Number 6	Soul Number 9	Personality Number 6

continues

continued

Destiny Number 7	Soul Number 1	Personality Number 6
Destiny Number 7	Soul Number 2	Personality Number 5
Destiny Number 7	Soul Number 3	Personality Number 4
Destiny Number 7	Soul Number 4	Personality Number 3
Destiny Number 7	Soul Number 5	Personality Number 2
Destiny Number 7	Soul Number 6	Personality Number 1
Destiny Number 7	Soul Number 7	Personality Number 9
Destiny Number 7	Soul Number 8	Personality Number 8
Destiny Number 7	Soul Number 9	Personality Number 7
Destiny Number 8	Soul Number 1	Personality Number 7
Destiny Number 8	Soul Number 2	Personality Number 6
Destiny Number 8	Soul Number 3	Personality Number 5
Destiny Number 8	Soul Number 4	Personality Number 4
Destiny Number 8	Soul Number 5	Personality Number 3
Destiny Number 8	Soul Number 6	Personality Number 2
Destiny Number 8	Soul Number 7	Personality Number 1
Destiny Number 8	Soul Number 8	Personality Number 9
Destiny Number 8	Soul Number 9	Personality Number 8
Destiny Number 9	Soul Number 1	Personality Number 8
Destiny Number 9	Soul Number 2	Personality Number 7
Destiny Number 9	Soul Number 3	Personality Number 6
Destiny Number 9	Soul Number 4	Personality Number 5
Destiny Number 9	Soul Number 5	Personality Number 4
Destiny Number 9	Soul Number 6	Personality Number 3
Destiny Number 9	Soul Number 7	Personality Number 2
Destiny Number 9	Soul Number 8	Personality Number 1
Destiny Number 9	Soul Number 9	Personality Number 9

PYTHAGORAS SAYS

Each time you increase the Destiny Number and start with Soul Number 1, the Personality Number starts descending, beginning with one less than the Destiny Number. Like almost everything else in numerology, the pattern is cyclic.

Let's now take a look at the meanings behind each combination, in order by Destiny Number.

Destiny Number 1, Soul Number 1, Personality Number 9

You're a leader, not a follower. A natural politician, you have a strong inspirational effect on others and can motivate large groups with your persuasive and glad-handing demeanor.

People are impressed by your range of influence and the scope of your ideas. You think big and strive for success. Because you inspire trust in others, they readily sign on to your program and help promote your ideas. An expert planner, you often stage events or organize campaigns that benefit others; however, it's always a win-win arrangement, as they also burnish your reputation and further your career.

Just as you thrive on competition and challenge in your career, you enjoy the chase in your personal relationships. The compliments of an attentive mate can make you very demonstrative. You're also an impulsive lover, and your restless nature means you're easily bored in matters of the heart when your mate doesn't share your take-charge approach.

Destiny Number 1, Soul Number 2, Personality Number 8

Your self-sufficient persona tells others you have the world by the tail. However, beneath that confident exterior is a romantic soul who seeks to love and be loved.

Although aggressive and independent in a work environment, you're an excellent listener and want to cooperate with others, even if you don't always do so. You project an aura of prosperity that impresses others.

You have the tendency to let pride get in the way of the personal relationships you crave. Seek out a mate who recognizes the sensitive soul hidden beneath your protective shell and can provide the reassurance you need.

Although you often take things personally, you have the fortitude to overcome your feelings. When you direct your sensitivity toward others, you can read between the lines and give yourself a decided edge in both personal and professional dealings.

Destiny Number 1, Soul Number 3, Personality Number 7

You live a fast-paced life, ignoring people and activities that don't interest you. With an insatiable appetite for variety, you require a spectrum of creative outlets. Unless you can find like spirits to surround you, you're content keeping your own company. You possess an independent, nonconformist streak and hate being dominated by others.

Others may see you as aloof and difficult to approach, but this contrasts with the appeal of your youthful appearance and great vitality. An admirer who flatters you and can keep up with your pace will discover your friendly and fun-loving side.

A keen observer, you enjoy entertaining others with your impressions and impersonations. You're in constant pursuit of self-expression and enjoy time alone to refine your act.

Destiny Number 1, Soul Number 4, Personality Number 6

You work and play hard, demanding a lot of yourself and those around you. Your strength and independence means you prefer to do things your own way. Others often describe you as stubborn and set in your ways, but you've earned a reputation for being fair and keeping your word.

You're practical and self-sufficient. Although you find ways to do good deeds, you do so in a way that ensures your contribution is noticed and recognized. Strong drive and determination mean you always see projects from concept to completion.

Dedicated to quality, you instill confidence in others through your ability to coordinate a smooth, economical process. You seek the best deal on the best product, are compelled to surround yourself with comfort and beauty, and thrive on providing luxury to your loved ones.

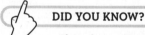 **DID YOU KNOW?**

If you have a Destiny Number of 1, it's likely that your Destiny Number will be dominant over your Soul and Personality Numbers. This is because Destiny Number 1s generally indicate powerful people.

Destiny Number 1, Soul Number 5, Personality Number 5

You embody the admonition of "expect the unexpected." Energized by a fast-paced schedule, you do things on your own time and resist the restriction of a 9-to-5 job. You're also full of creative ideas and need the freedom to implement them.

Unconventional and original, you aren't usually affected by the opinions of others. However, you easily incorporate new ideas and concepts into your planning. Even though you tend to like your ideas best, you're able to modify your point of view when the situation calls for it. Fortunately, you've learned when to stand firm and when it's wisest to bend to the wishes of others around you.

You court risk and yearn for adventure. In the country's early days, you would have been one of the pioneers who headed West. Independent, you crave being in the middle of the action in any space. When you want to, you can be very flexible, but you have a short attention span when things get dull and often drop what you're doing to go where the action is.

Destiny Number 1, Soul Number 6, Personality Number 4

Your goal in life is to help others and participate in loving and harmonious relationships. Even while striving for fairness and avoiding confrontation, you feel the need to express your opinions and crave the last word.

Responsibility is a serious matter for you, and you exhibit honor when protecting others' welfare. Even though you approach matters in a strong and determined manner, those on the receiving end of your advice need to understand that you're a solid individual whose word can be trusted.

Your quick and creative mind helps you present a logical appearance. When resolving problems, you seek the prudent and conservative course of solution. Avoiding hasty decision-making, you analyze all sides of a prospective endeavor first. You always finish what you start and only undertake projects that show potential.

With an excellent eye for balance and design, your home and surroundings are comfortable and attractive. This is a good thing, as home is where you prefer to be. Also an expert bargain shopper, you're especially pleased when quality can be found at a reasonable price.

Destiny Number 1, Soul Number 7, Personality Number 3

The first impression you make doesn't reflect your inner self. At your core, you're strong willed and determined, but you present yourself as an easygoing and sociable companion. And although you're sociable and entertaining in group settings and appear to enjoy everyone's company and attention, you're actually somewhat reserved and very selective in who you let get close. Basically, you aren't always as confident and self-assured as you make others believe.

Your innovative ideas can elicit significant improvements in your career. Lively discussions invigorate you, and you enjoy expressing your opinion when analyzing a subject or situation. You can be withdrawn and introspective when trying to unravel difficult situations. If people get too inquisitive or intrude on your personal space, you back off and drop them from your circle. However, you can turn on the charm to elicit the information you seek.

Destiny Number 1, Soul Number 8, Personality Number 2

Your considerate and laid-back appearance conceals a person of independent mind and who loves to get his or her own way. While others see a sensitive and cooperative demeanor, you actually have a strong will and fierce determination.

While you solicit and consider the opinions of those around you, you're the ultimate decision-maker. You may listen to the input of others, but overall you're reluctant to change your mind once it's made up. With a strong code of ethics, you make up your own rules and often have innovative ideas and approaches.

Your organizational and leadership skills let you develop and execute custom plans, resulting in successful and profitable endeavors. Diplomatic when giving direction, you readily inspire others to follow your lead.

You're patient, even when dealing with those who can't keep up. Although you thrive on challenge and love competition, you're willing to forego some success to have others join in your achievements.

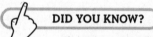

DID YOU KNOW?

The Destiny Number 1, Soul Number 8, and Personality Number 2 weighs all factors at hand before coming to a decision. However, you often lack the flexibility or willingness to make mid-course corrections based on new information.

Destiny Number 1, Soul Number 9, Personality Number 1

This combination indicates a person of great energy with original ideas and a penchant for leadership. Despite great determination and a tendency toward independence, you still find it within yourself to be generous toward those around you. You take great pleasure in helping others and do a lot to make your corner of the world a better place.

You initially impress others with the enthusiasm and energy you devote to attaining your goals, but people become even more impressed when they realize your ambition isn't purely personal. You use your ability to come up with concepts that grow any business or project in which you're involved. Big plans and your personal imprint are part of everything you do.

Although you're at home wherever you go and fit in easily anywhere, you stand out in a crowd. You enjoy receiving the praises of others and take great pride in your achievements and capabilities. Therefore, taking orders or direction from others is something you dislike.

Destiny Number 2, Soul Number 1, Personality Number 1

Agreeable and accommodating up to a point, you listen to other people's opinions but ultimately follow your own judgment and convictions.

You're observant enough to recognize when resentment is festering and instinctively know when to clear the air tactfully. People respect your ability to simultaneously stand up for yourself while cooperating in joint ventures. They find you inspirational and persuasive and are glad to follow your lead.

Depending upon your mood, you're either willing to work alone or partner with someone efficient. However, you can be patient with someone who's making an honest effort. When on a creative tear, you work better alone but will take the time to let others recognize your contributions.

You make a serious attempt to consider all aspects of a situation in order to achieve a mutually satisfactory result, even though you know what you want (and appear to get it).

Destiny Number 2, Soul Number 2, Personality Number 9

You inspire many and therefore have a lot of devotees. Because you're an authority in your field, others tend to seek your expertise, and you're happiest when sharing your knowledge and insights. Others also find you readily available when a thoughtful touch is needed.

Although you have a wide circle of acquaintances and are gracious to all, a caring and intimate relationship is essential to your happiness.

You're a patient and understanding audience who exercises great diplomacy in going that extra mile to help others. A highly regarded student of human nature, people buy into your vision of how things ought to be.

You're not wild about change and will often go back and forth or rely on the opinion or advice of someone you trust before coming to a decision. Sensitive to the feelings of others, you also like to avoid being the bearer of ill tidings.

Destiny Number 2, Soul Number 3, Personality Number 8

You're an effervescent person who has a knack for storytelling and strives to be the life of the party. Although you may occasionally be shy, you never give that impression. You can be very funny when you're comfortable with good friends and just let loose.

Using your charm and gift for gab, you have the know-how to get almost anything you want from others, whether it's the last piece of pizza or the signature on a big contract.

By paying careful attention to your diet and health, you possess tremendous energy for both your social and business lives. You also project a prosperous image by maintaining a youthful and polished appearance that draws others to you.

Your outward appearance of organization and control can conceal a disorganized inner you. You'd rather be with a companion having fun than sitting alone in your office organizing your files and straightening your desk.

 IT DOESN'T ADD UP

The Destiny Number 2, Soul Number 3, and Personality Number 8 tends to rely more on your personality than your talents. If something is really important, try to push your skills rather than your charisma. Remember that personality can get you elected, but a failure to perform is what everyone will remember once you've left your post.

Destiny Number 2, Soul Number 4, Personality Number 7

Although you like to help others and listen to all viewpoints, you find it difficult to walk in another's shoes. You prefer small groups where conversation is one-on-one and are very cautious in forming friendships.

Although generally amicable, you avoid small talk, making it difficult for many to see beyond your shyness and reserved exterior. The special person in your life knows that although there's frost on the surface, there's fire in the furnace.

You often react emotionally and find it hard to express your feelings without revealing more of yourself than you wish to share. Keeping things bottled up, you're sometimes resentful about not speaking your mind in order to avoid hurting someone's feelings.

You feel duty-bound to finish what you start and have a compulsion to be and appear put-together. People respect you for your ordered life, even if they perceive you as somewhat nitpicky. And while you're usually prudent and economical, you're generous with yourself and those close to you on occasion.

Destiny Number 2, Soul Number 5, Personality Number 6

Your kind, loving personality attracts a wide circle of friends. People think of you as someone they can count on in hard times due to your warmth and hospitality. Those who know you well admire your curiosity and sense of adventure, suspecting a hint of wanderlust under the surface.

Your stability and responsibility are evident, though many appreciate that you also have an adaptable and easygoing nature. You're often called upon to resolve disputes and settle controversy due to your deserved reputation for tact and diplomacy, as well as your ability to listen to all sides of an issue.

You absorb information like a sponge and are happiest when involved in simultaneous projects. You often come up with new ideas for your next project while still chasing your current pursuits.

Freedom is essential to your personal happiness, but your sense of right and wrong precludes you from pursuing it if it would mean shirking your responsibilities.

Destiny Number 2, Soul Number 6, Personality Number 5

Although a homebody at heart, you appear outgoing and adventurous to others. Broad interests and a busy schedule make you also appear exciting and full of curiosity.

You're a loyal friend with few prejudices who derives great pleasure from being of service to others. Happy to offer advice, know that some may choose to ignore your input.

Your enthusiasm and promotional talents make it easy to get others to jump on your bandwagon. Because you tend to make value judgments, you love to root for the underdog. You have a strong sense of justice, especially considering your desire to please everyone. You also frequently adjust your opinions to avoid hurt feelings and confrontation.

Your romantic nature calls for an honorable and understanding mate. Because harmony is so essential to your happiness, you work hard to promote and maintain a loving relationship.

Destiny Number 2, Soul Number 7, Personality Number 4

People are unaware of how much thought and effort you put into analyzing a situation and choosing your words—they only see your ability to do or say the right thing at the right time. You avoid speaking out of turn, and your sense of propriety prevents you from telling some lively stories. Guarding your feelings carefully, you choose when to participate and when to stay silent.

Sensitive by nature, you sometimes require solitude to sort out your feelings. In an attempt to keep everyone happy, you find it difficult to say "no."

You project a conservative and orderly image in both your appearance and surroundings. Susceptible to petty annoyances, you prefer all aspects of your life to be neat and orderly.

Your honor and integrity inspire your friends, who count on your considered and practical advice. You also employ keen powers of observation and intuition in pursuit of the truth. Although you don't always call people on their misrepresentations, you're aware of them and don't let anyone pull the wool over your eyes.

 IT DOESN'T ADD UP

If you're a Destiny Number 2, Soul Number 7, and Personality Number 4, your bywords are "watch, listen, and learn." However, this can lead you to be less than trusting of others. Try to understand that little white lies may be used to avoid hurting your feelings rather than to conceal something sinister.

Destiny Number 2, Soul Number 8, Personality Number 3

While you appear patient, sociable, and charming, people are unaware of the iron will at your core. You express yourself well, both in spoken and written word. Using your sense of humor to make a good story even better, you bask in the attention of a receptive audience.

Your organization and efficiency let you get your work done with energy to spare, regardless of the number of tasks you undertake. You also find it impossible to sit back and do nothing when you witness something being done poorly or incorrectly. Jumping right in to do the job right, you always perform up to your own high standards.

You're a good listener, fascinated by the complexities of human nature and interaction. You do what it takes to make people feel special, but you also like to get your own way. While most of the time you are content to humor people, sometimes your emotions get the best of you when you don't get your way.

Destiny Number 2, Soul Number 9, Personality Number 2

You're an idealist and humanitarian who sacrifices for those you love and those in need. In return, you receive the understanding and affection essential to your psyche.

Always a soft touch for a hard-luck story, you're perpetually sentimental and hate to turn anyone down. You're also able to forgive and forget any disappointments in the name of love.

A natural student, you possess the extensive knowledge and patience that make you an excellent teacher. You're typically mild-mannered and tolerant, carefully deliberating before offering a solution in an attempt to make everyone happy.

Normally quiet, you can display a surprising ire when provoked sufficiently or hurt. Deep emotions guide you through your relationships and manifest in an appreciation of art and music.

Destiny Number 3, Soul Number 1, Personality Number 2

Your ability to wrap people around your little finger helps you lead a charmed existence. You're friendly, personable, and socially graceful, leading others to seek your company. Also, your diplomatic skills result in people giving you what you want.

A busy schedule combined with a youthful exuberance make you almost legendary among those who know you. You make it all work because you crave outlets for your energy and creativity. Because of your facility with words, you can talk your way into and out of almost anything. You conceal your impatience and get others to accomplish much for you in pursuit of your many goals.

Your priority list is topped by a need to be recognized as popular and unique. Because a youthful appearance is essential in your life, you want to remain young and gather praise while others collect the wrinkles. In matters of the heart, you need a communicative and fun-loving partner who can join you in outdoor activities while still being sympathetic to your need for independence.

Destiny Number 3, Soul Number 2, Personality Number 1

Your facility with words and ability to put others at ease make you especially persuasive. Your confidence inspires others to see you as a master multitasker. Sensitive to others' feelings, you avoid controversy in an attempt to keep everybody happy. When asked to join your campaign, people gladly enlist because they see you as someone who will lead them to victory.

You will have to make many choices in your lifetime regarding friends, careers, and romantic partners. Although you project a strong and decisive front, each choice will be the result of somber deliberation. You often find it difficult to choose which of the many ideas that run through your mind to pursue.

Your individualized manner of dress projects your fondness for luxury and beauty. Combined with youthful enthusiasm, your carefree and optimistic outlook attracts people of all ages, particularly children. People generally give you what you want with a smile as you charm and entertain them with great humor.

 IT DOESN'T ADD UP

If you are a Destiny Number 3, Soul Number 2, and Personality Number 1, your ongoing deliberations can lead to indecisiveness. Tackle issues head-on rather than vacillating ad infinitum if you want more of your ideas to see fruition.

Destiny Number 3, Soul Number 3, Personality Number 9

Always in contact with one or more people, you're a master networker. You're never at a loss for words, but you desire to be seen as well as heard.

Your imagination and charisma help you spread the word about any cause you choose to promote. Flirtatious and intoxicated by applause and appreciation, you can be quite entertaining.

You're optimistic, generous, and truly care about your fellow man. Because you love to attract attention with your appearance, you may spend extravagantly, particularly when it comes to your wardrobe.

Overly constrained by a 9-to-5 existence, you come into your own when given the freedom to set your own schedule. There's also a bit of the gypsy in your soul, as you love to travel and roam.

Destiny Number 3, Soul Number 4, Personality Number 8

Your belief in hard work has obviously paid off, as people tend to see you as successful. You appear to others to be in charge and surrounded by the fruits of your labor. You have a well-earned reputation for keeping your word and fulfilling your responsibilities. Others admire you for your logic and ability to express yourself when finding solutions to problems.

You strive to get the most for your dollar and always enjoy a good bargain. Creativity and the ability to analyze how things work help you design and build systems that do the job well.

You've built your life on a solid foundation, and you seek tangible results from all that you do. Looking young, being in good health, establishing financial security, forming long-lasting relationships, and maintaining family traditions top your priority list.

Always convinced that you know the answer, you choose your words carefully and employ your charm to influence others. Although unwilling to show others your feelings, you can be quite blunt when angered.

Destiny Number 3, Soul Number 5, Personality Number 7

Variety is central to your life and needs, and an optimistic outlook compels you to experiment with new ideas. You're always on the go and prefer to travel in the fast lane. In relationships, you don't just ask for freedom, you take it by the horns.

You're a natural promoter, quickly sizing up situations and people and employing your verbal skills to sell your ideas to others. Your enthusiasm is contagious, and you demonstrate genuine interest with perceptive questions that flatter your audience. Always curious about what makes others tick, you're reticent to reveal what drives you.

You might spread yourself too thin with multiple concurrent projects, even though others might think of you as a perfectionist and expect more than you might deliver. Some people might also see you as evasive and wonder about the inner you. Not seeing your secretive, analytical side, others are unable to recognize your inner shyness or sense that you might be lacking in self-confidence.

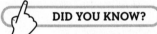 **DID YOU KNOW?**

If you're a Destiny Number 3, Soul Number 5, and Personality Number 7, politics— whether corporate or governmental—is a possible venue for you.

Destiny Number 3, Soul Number 6, Personality Number 6

You have tremendous charisma and attract a legion of admirers. Although you love being the center of attention, you derive more pleasure from helping others and are generous with advice and support.

Your family depends on you to lead the way, and your personal choices are the consequence of focusing on their welfare. Home is your haven, and you always have an open-door policy.

With a strong desire for harmony, you do everything within your power to keep those around you happy and content. You attempt to right all wrongs in your quest for justice. Convinced of your own correctness, you expect others to agree with you.

Always generous, you seek quality for yourself and others. If the best is out of reach, you bide your time until you can afford it.

Destiny Number 3, Soul Number 7, Personality Number 5

Outwardly friendly and full of sociability, you're actually somewhat shy and don't warm up to strangers as quickly as others think you do. Just when they think that they've gotten to know you, people are often surprised by the deeper facets of your personality.

You combine glibness with an analytical mind, often engaging in long monologues covering a range of subjects. You're versatile but greatly enjoy having talented mentors in a variety of areas.

Your written skills are excellent, as is your ability to critique; you quickly differentiate between ordinary and extraordinary effort and results. Your perfectionism drives you to try new approaches and tactics to improve performance.

Attractive to the opposite sex, you really seek and need that special someone who can bolster you when you feel misunderstood.

Destiny Number 3, Soul Number 8, Personality Number 4

You're organized, even when you have myriad new ideas. An expert delegator, you expect and demand that the people you choose are up to the task.

Multifaceted and farsighted, you're very creative. Your enthusiasm occasionally lets you be distracted, but your organizational skills generally see you through.

You're eloquent, which is a decided advantage when convincing others to share your vision and opinion. A natural communicator and motivator, you easily win friends and influence people. Others sign on because they know and trust your record of accomplishment.

Your major goals are financial success and the respect of your peers. You walk a high wire confidently from vision to reality.

Destiny Number 3, Soul Number 9, Personality Number 3

You can charm anyone while using your gift of gab to entertain others and promote your ideas and pet projects. Before an audience, you can make even dull material interesting.

You have a large circle of friends and acquaintances and are often hosting affairs where you're praised for your sense of humor. The way you preen when complimented only enhances the show.

You're generous and extravagant, spending money freely. Not wanting to disappoint your fans, you purchase the best of everything and shower your friends with gifts.

Even though you want to get your own way, your heart of gold leads you to indulge your loved ones. And when lacking outside activities, you have a tendency to be overprotective of those close to you.

When you get out and meet interesting new people, you consider it a day very well spent, with your optimism spreading cheer wherever you go.

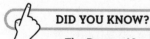 **DID YOU KNOW?**

The Destiny Number 3, Soul Number 9, and Personality Number 3 is a social butterfly, flitting and fluttering about. Always attracting a large audience, you make even the most mundane story exciting.

Destiny Number 4, Soul Number 1, Personality Number 3

You're determined and possess great patience. You keep your goals in mind and are willing to do whatever it takes to achieve them. Recognizing that the devil is in the details, you tackle routine tasks with the same energy and focus you place on larger ideals of leadership and creativity.

To maintain your reputation, you make sure that any job with your name attached to it is done to the highest standards. You hate being rushed or pressured and seek the opportunity to see your plans through to fruition. You specialize in projects that are both original and practical.

You work best and are happiest when part of a team that shares your vision and high standards. People enjoy working with you because of your outgoing and pleasant persona. Others would be wise to do their homework before contradicting you or trying to prove you wrong.

Destiny Number 4, Soul Number 2, Personality Number 2

Your common sense is allied with a good mind that absorbs facts like a sponge. You impress others as a reliable, cooperative, and hard worker who notices all details and inspire them when you share what you know and what you've learned. Your ability to assemble seemingly disparate items into something working and useful is another facet of you that amazes people.

Extremely loyal, you go out of your way to please others. Your winning personality and kindness make others feel comfortable around you, even when you seem set in your ways. When surrounded by those about whom you care, you exercise patience and compromise as necessary.

You internalize hurt feelings rather than risk uncomfortable situations and confrontations. Caring about what other people think, you make an effort to listen to them.

It's fortunate that you're good at finding bargains, because you can be generous to a fault. You also desire meaningful relationships and freely give of yourself when pursuing them.

Destiny Number 4, Soul Number 3, Personality Number 1

A strong public persona and an aura of practicality make people see you as a strong leader. They value your ability to explain complicated subjects and concepts in comprehensible terms.

You have an eye for design and a highly developed imagination, both of which enhance your versatility. Strong determination drives you to get your own way.

A master planner, you have the ability to balance hard work with spontaneity. You often spend more time than necessary during the planning stages of a project to make certain that everyone understands where you're coming from. However, your desire for tangible results can be counterbalanced by a tendency to procrastinate.

You epitomize the saying that "many a truth is said in jest," as you are reluctant to reveal your true feelings. When not fully confident, you can be defensive. Though occasionally unsure of yourself, you tend to mask that uncertainty and come across as in control.

Destiny Number 4, Soul Number 4, Personality Number 9

Unless someone can demonstrate a superior method or technique, you stick with what works—you avoid experimentation when a working model exists. You will, however, tweak what's there for improved performance, reliability, or cost-effectiveness.

You demand excellence of yourself and others, making every effort to finish what you start. People also know that you're reliable when it comes to meeting schedules and staying within budget. You're methodical and keep constant track of your progress.

Your nature is to be punctual and frugal, but your musical and artistic talents give you a less practical outlet. Your emotions run deep, but you aren't always able to express them.

You demonstrate generosity within the constraints of your frugal nature. For example, you only contribute to charities where you know your donations will be put to effective use. You also derive great pleasure from giving and receiving appreciation.

 DID YOU KNOW?

With a Destiny Number 4, Soul Number 4, and Personality Number 9, you possess a unique mix of practicality and artistic expression that makes you a Renaissance Man (or Woman). You have to work to control your ebullience in order to meet those schedules and stay within budget, but the results justify that effort.

Destiny Number 4, Soul Number 5, Personality Number 8

You have the energy to manage large projects to completion and work alongside your subordinates to ensure success. If it takes getting your hands dirty to achieve the desired result, you'll look for the soap later.

Very self-disciplined, you're painstaking and meticulous in your work. After hours, you're dedicated to enjoying the company of a wide assortment of friends, all of whom you keep in regular contact with.

You dress well and take care of yourself, contributing to making a good impression. Your friends know that a down-to-Earth soul is sheltered within that impressive wardrobe. Even when suffering from inner turmoil, you present a solid front.

An outer balance combined with a complex inner self make you a puzzle to many. Even when given a logical reason to change your mind, you tend to be quite stubborn. And your conservative and practical façade conceals a free spirit with a case of wanderlust. This multidimensionality can be a surprise to others.

Destiny Number 4, Soul Number 6, Personality Number 7

A generous heart beats within your reserved shell. You're discriminating and cautious, but some take that for aloofness. Once people understand your true nature, they value your patience and ability to avoid jumping to conclusions.

You have a tendency to take on more than your share of the load when you're in service to others. Trying to be helpful, you offer advice, even when it will be ignored. Although you mean well, some people take your suggestions as criticism.

You diligently avoid confrontation and hate to argue. Sometimes, especially when you don't fully agree, you find it difficult to adapt to others.

Your tendency to analyze helps you find superior quality at good prices. Dishonesty or insincerity put you off, and superficiality and inferior products offend your senses. This analytical bent also helps you sort out facts and come to fair and just conclusions.

Destiny Number 4, Soul Number 7, Personality Number 6

A strong sense of responsibility and a logical mind are at your core. You take a practical approach, proceeding cautiously and paying attention to detail. You also ask pertinent questions and take the time to seek the answers, chafing when pressured or rushed to come to a decision. Although you enjoy luxury, you strive more for quality.

When in a discussion, you tend to listen and avoid speaking off the cuff. You also don't like to make decisions or pronouncements until you're sure of the facts and your conclusions. Once committed, though, you keep your word.

You hate being questioned about yourself, but you want to know the who, what, when, and why of any situation you encounter. People don't always realize just how long it takes for you to make close friends; they only see the result of your steadfastness toward those friends.

Destiny Number 4, Soul Number 8, Personality Number 5

Once you make up your mind to do something, you're single-minded in your pursuit of the goal. You seek power and prosperity and work hard to attain both. Your frugality helps you budget and track every penny.

You strive to stay mentally and physically balanced in spite of a busy, almost frantic, social life. You seem so carefree and fun-loving that people are often surprised to see you're happiest when in control and doing things your way. You appear to be game to try anything new, so it's sometimes surprising to others just how steadfast a friend you can be. Anyone who knows you well, though, recognizes your stable center.

People appreciate and acknowledge how you approach even routine tasks with energy, often turning chaos into order. Your flexibility lets them forgive your perfectionist tendencies.

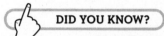 **DID YOU KNOW?**

> As a Destiny Number 4, Soul Number 8, and Personality Number 5, you want everything to be perfect. However, you realize that perfection is a goal never achieved. Your best characteristic is recognizing when "good enough" is good enough.

Destiny Number 4, Soul Number 9, Personality Number 4

People see you as dependable and trustworthy, with strong organizational skills. You're a stickler for playing by the rules, which is something people recognize about you. You also have talents in art or music and the corresponding sense of design or rhythm.

Deeply concerned about others' welfare, you have strong humanitarian instincts. You temper your natural heart of gold with logic and practicality.

You're set in your ways and have a history of prudence, but you also have an urge to do something grandiose and extravagant. Your generous urges are balanced by a need for financial security and thrifty habits. You feel great satisfaction when your good deeds are recognized and appreciated.

You're patient and sympathetic when confronted by the problems of others. Sentimental and romantic, you share your true feelings with only a select few.

Destiny Number 5, Soul Number 1, Personality Number 4

Your traditional persona conceals the fact that you're really a nonconformist who hates to be pinned down. People see you as reliable, solid, and a pillar of strength—they would be surprised that you wish to eschew the traditional and try new approaches.

Happiest in a leadership position, you can provide direction to individuals and groups. One benefit of being in charge is that you can often make your own hours and set a schedule that provides time to relieve stress and pressure.

You work to appear patient, even when you feel the urge to finish other people's sentences. You're adaptable and react quickly, which lets you accomplish more in less time than most people.

Your outward appearance of a wide range of friends conceals a core that needs a lot of "me time." Seeking like souls, you gravitate toward people who cater to your need for freedom and independence.

Destiny Number 5, Soul Number 2, Personality Number 3

You enjoy being in the spotlight, surrounded by an appreciative audience. Engaging and entertaining, you're possessed with a natural talent for self-expression. Your audience is impressed by the way you present yourself, a product, or an idea. When moved to express your insights, you can be inspirational.

You love to love and be loved, leading you to seek companionship and group activities. An interdependent relationship with a supportive mate who is as fun-loving and flexible as you are is the perfect kind of union for you.

Involved in myriad activities, you give the impression that you can accomplish anything you set out to do. However, your sociability and confidence conceals an inner sensitivity. You have a personal Jiminy Cricket on your shoulder—your conscience keeps your adventurous side from writing checks that your outer enthusiasm and energy can't help you cash.

Destiny Number 5, Soul Number 3, Personality Number 2

You have a talent for expressing original ideas through spoken and written words. A quick and agile mind compels you to share your ideas and conclusions with an audience. But you often get ahead of the audience, making your next point while they're still struggling with the previous one.

You welcome change and the accompanying challenges in your battle against boredom. Just as you occasionally leave a sentence unfinished, you sometimes leave a project incomplete.

Others call upon you frequently to referee disputes or settle arguments, as even difficult personalities seem to respond to your friendly manner. You can also be attractively flirtatious to others.

It's not that you can't make up your mind; it's just that new information has you frequently changing your opinion. You're an optimist and find that a change of direction just makes life more interesting. You tend to live in the present, rarely looking back or worrying what the future might hold.

IT DOESN'T ADD UP

Others may see the Destiny Number 5, Soul Number 3, and Personality Number 2 as unpredictable. While you find that impulsiveness makes life interesting, those around you might not hold the same view. Work on knowing when new data is not consequential—if it isn't, then hold the course.

Destiny Number 5, Soul Number 4, Personality Number 1

Others see you as a leader—one who is determined and capable of coping with any situation. Being congenial and gently persuasive, you make a great advocate or salesperson.

You have an active imagination, and new ideas flow from you like water from a spring. You also have a practical side and methodically impose order on your creative ventures.

You leave no stone unturned when researching your projects. You carefully analyze data, separating fact from fluff and continuing only with what's useful.

Your sense of responsibility prevents your personal preferences from interfering with deadlines or fulfilling a commitment. And your practicality and desire for security usually wins out over any impulsive actions.

You have a rare ability to keep your eye on the prize and still deal with the unexpected, both good and bad, that life throws your way.

Destiny Number 5, Soul Number 5, Personality Number 9

You're especially adept at dealing with the public and have the energy to exercise your many talents in that pursuit. Your friendly and gracious nature gains you the trust of diverse people.

Compassion for the problems of others is a big part of your persona. A fascination about what makes people tick combined with a talent for character analysis drive you concerning other people's activities.

People see you as someone who has seen it all, is well-traveled, and is constantly on the go—they envy your exciting life. Schedules nettle your free spirit; the thought of punching a time clock sends you running for the hills. You would rather be busy than bored, and your occasional impatience can impel you to start something new before you've dotted the Is and crossed the Ts of your latest venture.

Destiny Number 5, Soul Number 6, Personality Number 8

You appear to others as a winner, unflappable and stable. Regardless of how busy you are, you always seem to land on your feet.

You possess the extra drive to take on a large new project while still completing your current endeavor or planning the next. Your sense of duty drives you to meet all your commitments.

Home and domestic responsibilities win out over your restless side that's curious about what's around the bend. You frequently rearrange furniture or redecorate in order to discharge your creative urges and your restless side.

You have many friends, and your commitment to them is as important to you as your desire for freedom. Your air of authority draws people to you, and they respect the fairness you demonstrate in your dealings with others. Friends and neighbors often rely upon you to resolve disputes with no hurt feelings.

Destiny Number 5, Soul Number 7, Personality Number 7

You possess an eagle eye for discovering flaws and a sixth sense in uncovering inconsistencies. Combined with a knack for finding clues and solutions in apparently unlikely places, you come up with answers and solutions. Perceptive questioning and a relentless search for clues help you arrive at accurate conclusions.

You're more comfortable posing questions than you are answering them. Mistaking your amicable exterior as an open invitation, some people make the error of invading your privacy. Your adverse reaction to this kind of attention from others makes you appear enigmatic. You sometimes feel misunderstood and have trouble understanding why others may not think as you do.

You have a quick mind and require a lot of mental stimulation to be happy. Knowledgeable people willing to share that knowledge are your favorite companions. Someone who's flexible and willing to grant you alone time is the ideal partner.

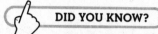 **DID YOU KNOW?**

The Destiny Number 5, Soul Number 7, and Personality Number 7 needs to understand—especially when dealing with others who share your numbers—that it's okay to answer questions and not just ask them. In fact, your own answers can lead you to consider new lines of inquiry.

Destiny Number 5, Soul Number 8, Personality Number 6

You have a good head for business; in fact, one of your ideas is going to prove lucrative in the future. Your people skills are the basis for your success. Able to organize skillfully, you can assemble top-notch people into an effective team.

Your flexibility inspires others. Although you can multitask and adapt to change, you really require stability and organization to be at your best.

You aren't one who likes to be questioned about personal matters yet you're curious and have a knack for getting others to reveal juicy details about themselves.

You lead an active life, with an emphasis on fitness and health. You strive hard to maintain your good reputation as well as your appearance and know you're on the right track when you receive praise from others.

Destiny Number 5, Soul Number 9, Personality Number 5

Happiest when you're busy, a quick pace and mental stimulation are basic requirements for you. Boredom has you frantically searching for new challenges.

A teacher at heart, you excel in both formal and informal settings. You vary your approach to keep your students interested and involved. This same approach helps you sell others on new ideas.

Sympathetic to those less fortunate, you enjoy helping others. A considerable amount of your time and attention is devoted to charitable activities. Although you would do it anyway, receiving appreciation and recognition makes it all the more worthwhile to you.

Restless energy and a desire for a change of scenery puts travel high on your list of personal pleasures. Between the major trips, you look forward to three-day weekends—an excuse for revelry.

A romantic at heart, you are in love with the thought of love. However, a possessive person is anathema to you.

Destiny Number 6, Soul Number 1, Personality Number 5

You have the desire and ability to lead and seek out groups where you can exercise those traits. At heart you're a pioneer, even if you're currently following a conservative path.

A natural problem solver, you're goal-oriented and idealistic. You like having your peers look to you for advice and leadership. Although you listen to their input in an attempt to keep everyone involved and happy, you usually end up doing things your own way.

You accomplish a lot and have the reputation of an energetic doer who's always in the middle of the action. You keep up with the latest news and trends, which leads people to look to you for new ideas.

Many people find you attractive, so it takes a novel approach to get your attention. You desire independence in a prospective mate and abhor possessiveness.

Destiny Number 6, Soul Number 2, Personality Number 4

Your courtesy and adaptability draw others to you. Polite and well-mannered, you're a good and attentive listener. Others value your meticulous attention to detail and ability to synthesize information.

A square dealer, you strive to make wrongs right. People respect you for always keeping your word and consistently delivering on your promises.

In your desire to be well-liked, you may go overboard and allow people to take advantage of you. You have a deep need to love and be loved, and having someone with whom to share your life makes living worthwhile. Generally frugal, you make exceptions for loved ones and purchase items of high quality.

Destiny Number 6, Soul Number 3, Personality Number 3

You exude charm and have a gift for gab, making you Mr. or Ms. Personality. You're never at a loss for words and can engage anyone in conversation—even if they're initially reticent, you fill the silence with a monologue until they are engaged.

You can be uncomfortable when part of a group that isn't getting along. But your excellent peace-making skills help convert the discord to harmony.

Your joie de vivre is contagious, and your good cheer and optimism attract a loyal following. People around you count on you to be responsible and keep your promises. Because you have a tendency to overcommit, this occasionally makes you nervous.

You're a clotheshorse whose wardrobe expenditures contribute to the economy. Always in search of a creative outlet, you see your wardrobe as a way to project your individuality.

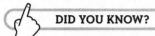 **DID YOU KNOW?**

If given the choice, as a Destiny Number 6, Soul Number 3, and Personality Number 3, you should consider diplomacy over politics—it better matches your personality and skill set.

Destiny Number 6, Soul Number 4, Personality Number 2

Home and family are the center of your existence. Your home is your sanctuary, a revered place where you can live according to your principles. You do what it takes to maintain peaceful relationships both inside and outside the home.

Your warmth and spirit are magnetic, drawing others to you. You have a talent for putting people at ease and go the extra mile to fill their emotional needs, providing counsel according to your principles and beliefs. Although laced with common sense and practicality to your way of thinking, your advice might not be appropriate for those counseled. Whether or not they take your advice, they respect your good intentions.

You're dependable in personal interactions and reliable on the job. You work hard to build a solid foundation in order to fulfill your ambitions. Your honesty makes you shun any business practices that might damage your reputation or credibility.

Destiny Number 6, Soul Number 5, Personality Number 1

You're amiable and outgoing, genuinely enjoying the company of others. When in the mood, you attract friends with your protective and nurturing nature. You like to give good advice but have a tendency to overdo it. Nonetheless, people value your objectivity and the effect you have on them. You help people see and understand their situation through the application of logic rather than emotion.

Your determination and sense of responsibility make you a touchstone for reliability and just decisions. Personal ethics keep you from being party to unscrupulous practices—you have no future in politics.

Despite a strong desire for independence, you're loving and devoted to your family and friends. You enjoy a lot of mental stimulation and keep a large and diverse group of friends and acquaintances with whom to interact. Comfort and even luxury are on your wish list, making you willing to wait until you can afford the best.

Destiny Number 6, Soul Number 6, Personality Number 9

You draw upon your ability to work in concert with others to achieve the harmony you seek in your relationships. You give of yourself and sacrifice to make those around you happy, which brings contentment to you.

Gracious and sociable, you have the ability to reach out to all kinds of people. Your amiable and helpful approach nets you a wide circle of friends and contacts. Willing to give someone the shirt off your back, all you need is a simple thank you in return.

Curb your tendency to inundate others with your advice—you have a propensity to wear out your soapbox. While most people realize that you're trying to help, your way is not the only way to do things and may not be the right way for everyone else.

Destiny Number 6, Soul Number 7, Personality Number 8

You strive for a balance between two personal priorities—the time you spend helping others and the time you spend pursuing your own interests. You're a social animal but are slow to befriend those who come on strong. You need to get to know someone well before you divulge personal information.

Able to handle whatever life throws at you, you project an image of strength. With finely tuned analytic skills, you know how to find workable solutions to any problem. When you see someone who can benefit from your help, you gladly pitch in. While you project emotional stability, it may mask private insecurity.

You're always ready to proffer well-considered advice, but you don't seek it from others. This could make you an excellent therapist, as you're willing to help people by getting them to talk about themselves and their issues without sharing your own inner thoughts. When pressed, you might lose your cool rather than reveal anything of yourself.

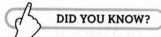 **DID YOU KNOW?**

Although a Destiny Number 6, Soul Number 7, and Personality Number 8 like you might consider being a therapist, other possible lines for you might be as an interviewer, journalist, or even a detective.

Destiny Number 6, Soul Number 8, Personality Number 7

You're complex and often difficult for others to understand. You vacillate between being lovable and keeping a distance from others. Appearing self-contained to others, it's important for you to always project an image of self-control.

You're organized and accept challenges in pursuit of your ambitions. You covet a big title, an impressive office, a substantial salary, and the opportunity to manage large groups. Always fair, with good judgment when delegating responsibility, you seek harmony in your presence and offer only the most unbiased opinions.

The image of tastefulness, you buy only the best, even if it limits the extent of your wardrobe—this is an area where quality trumps quantity for you.

Community affairs benefit from your excess energy. But know that you may meet resistance when you attempt to organize your loved ones like one of the committees you chair—back off at the first sign of opposition.

Destiny Number 6, Soul Number 9, Personality Number 6

Helping others is your mission in life—you have a penchant for helping to solve people's problems. Having survived your own personal disappointments helps you provide compassionate advice. Attempting to help loved ones can involve you in larger causes; in fact, the political arena isn't outside of your sphere.

A romantic at heart, you make relationships a priority. You're gracious and get along well with everyone, preferring to give in rather than fight. You also constantly adapt and subordinate yourself to the needs and wishes of others, particularly your family. This makes them feel they can depend upon you.

Your love of travel competes with your love of home. When you do travel, the short trips you take are typically in service to others.

Destiny Number 7, Soul Number 1, Personality Number 6

Well-groomed, tastefully attired, and impeccably mannered, you present a class act. Friends regard you as dependable and available for helpful consultation. Although warm and affectionate, you never gush, preferring to carefully consider what you're about to say before speaking.

You avoid pushy and clingy people, and your radar detects phonies a mile away. Not one to get too close to others too quickly, people must be trustworthy and willing to do their share before you let them into your inner circle.

Preferring to be in control, you choose to follow your instincts and do as you wish. Be cautioned that your self-sufficiency can make you impatient with people who don't understand your approach. Although others often perceive you as a loner, you actually crave praise and recognition more than most.

Destiny Number 7, Soul Number 2, Personality Number 5

You appear impulsive, frenetically pursuing multiple projects. However, there is a method to your frenzied pace—you're masking a shy and introverted inner you.

Casual acquaintances see you as someone who doesn't need people around, but your close friends know otherwise. Your confidantes also know that you take pride in your tact and diplomacy.

You prefer solitude when gathering information and analyzing problems. Lacking absolute proof, you can waver when trying to make a decision.

Although talented and capable in a variety of areas, you tend to specialize your interest. You have the ability to teach, and others come to you for your sage advice.

Destiny Number 7, Soul Number 3, Personality Number 4

You work hard at your specialty and, when asked, give sound advice. Don't take on too much, though—you may overcommit in an effort to gain the praise and recognition you crave.

You're an optimist at heart, with big dreams and great expectations. Foremost among your talents is a facility with words. Given an audience and the opportunity, you're very entertaining. Be glad that you like to think before you speak, because when you don't, you have a tendency to talk too much.

Although you're shy at times, you can also be sociable and charming. Your friends understand that you need alone time because you don't like exhibiting your inner feelings. A strong sense of loyalty makes you capable of sacrifice for others. Proud of your honesty, you expect a lot of yourself and those around you.

 IT DOESN'T ADD UP

You're at your best as a Destiny Number 7, Soul Number 3, and Personality Number 4 when given a chance to think before you speak. Therefore, you should stay away from situations where you have to ad lib. Scripted comedy is more your forte than improv.

Destiny Number 7, Soul Number 4, Personality Number 3

You have a deep sense of responsibility, exemplified by your care in financial matters and your desire to have others rely upon you. Sentimental when it comes to romance, a dependable and practical partner finds you a patient and loyal match.

Your goal is perfection, and you seek it methodically through your pragmatic approach to life. When confronted by new products or ideas, your motto is "try before you buy."

Your tastes are traditional and refined. At ease socially, you exhibit a clever sense of humor. However, you're careful about what you say and reticent to reveal too much about yourself.

You sometimes think that your approach to life is unique. When feeling introspective, give yourself ample time alone to figure things out. Communing with nature or working with your hands aids you in those times.

Destiny Number 7, Soul Number 5, Personality Number 2

You present an amicable and pleasant persona. People around you value your perceptive questions and the attention you pay to the answers. Your curiosity can lead you to take some risks, such as trying new venues or following a friend's impulses in pursuit of new experiences.

Concentrating on a situation and choosing your words with care can give others the mistaken impression that you're aloof. When confronted by a flawed argument or dishonest claim, you avoid direct confrontation, filing the information away for future reference. However, you're only patient to a point; you're apt to push tolerance aside when you think the other party isn't behaving appropriately.

Unconventional personalities and curious minds intrigue you. While you like to learn what makes others tick, you're unwilling to reveal your innermost dreams and desires.

Destiny Number 7, Soul Number 6, Personality Number 1

You're a self-sufficient and determined leader with an air of authority. Because of the aura of mystery about you, the first impression people have is that you're aloof—a consequence of your quiet and reserved nature. You play everything close to the vest, revealing only what is absolutely necessary in any given situation. In your mind, silence is golden.

Contrary to the perceptions of others, you have a strong desire to help others and live harmoniously. Never one to boast or brag, your love of family is evident by the perfectly framed photos facing you on your desk.

You set high standards of achievement for yourself, striving to be the best at whatever you do. To you, quality is economy—you insist on having the finest and won't accept second best. You want to be loved and respected, but most of all, you want to be understood.

Destiny Number 7, Soul Number 7, Personality Number 9

You're poised and in control—the picture of refinement. Your behavior and appearance are always in good taste. Accepting only the best, you're very particular about your possessions.

You seek knowledge and are intrigued by mystery. Dealing with the mental challenges you set for yourself requires time alone, often in the tranquility of nature.

People respect your astute mind and keen powers of observation. Because you need to see proof before embracing a concept, you take nothing on faith. You have the ability to reach the masses when spreading your knowledge.

While your real desire is to be alone with chosen friends, you have a gracious quality and exhibit acting ability when dealing with the public. Able to spot a phony a mile away, intellectual challenge beats out superficiality and false flattery every time.

You demand a lot of yourself and others in pursuit of perfection. Although you insist on honesty and don't lie, you conceal things in order to preserve your privacy. Others rightly trust you with their secrets, and you're equally careful with your own, revealing them only when you find someone equally trustworthy.

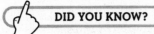

> **DID YOU KNOW?**
>
> As a Destiny Number 7, Soul Number 7, and Personality Number 9, you have a talent for observation. When combined with your natural skepticism and ability to convince an audience, you could do well as an investigative journalist.

Destiny Number 7, Soul Number 8, Personality Number 8

To maintain a tasteful appearance, you buy only the best and are finicky about your possessions. Equally selective in your choice of friends, you can be somewhat snobbish, seeking only people of your social station or higher.

You can be secretive when asked direct questions, lest you reveal something personal. Problems are puzzles to be solved, and in your search for truth and answers, you don't take "no" for an answer.

Very ambitious, you aspire to a position of great influence. You're a workaholic who demands high standards for yourself and those around you. With a clear view of the big picture, you use your organizational skills to set up and efficiently manage a system. You're also a proficient manager who delegates well and wisely. Your planning skills could be your ticket to achieving your goals.

Destiny Number 7, Soul Number 9, Personality Number 7

You're a perfectionist and very picky about everything in your life, from your possessions to the people around you. Only people you can trust can penetrate your inner circle. Although you appear aloof to others, those closest to you know that appearances can be deceiving.

Although basically honest, you can be less than forthcoming to avoid offending someone or being misunderstood. You're especially reticent unless you know someone well, and even then, you speak out only when you're absolutely sure of your position. One of your greatest fears is being wrong and looking like a fool.

Not one to fall for a quick-talking salesman, you study the pros and cons of products before you buy. You're a natural researcher and scrutinize everything to discern patterns and meanings in your search for truth. Always curious as to why and how and fascinated by the details of complex issues, you listen carefully to pick up clues.

Destiny Number 8, Soul Number 1, Personality Number 7

You're energetic, always on the go, and climbing the ladder toward success. The prospect of an important position inspires you to work hard. Driven by a quest for money and the power it brings, you want only the best in life.

Others find you pleasant and easy to get along with but difficult to get to know. You don't need a lot of people in your life, and solitude doesn't faze you.

There's no real demarcation between your personal and professional life—you never pass on an opportunity to make new contacts or to follow a lead. You know the company to keep and where to be seen in order to advance socially and professionally.

You like being considered a trendsetter but don't really seek or need the approval of others. Physical fitness and a good appearance are important to you, so you schedule time to exercise regularly. You like athletic competition and enjoy the contacts that come from participation in sports.

You're better at giving orders than taking them and can't tolerate anyone breathing down your neck. Though you prefer your own way of doing things, you're an effective delegator. The slow or lazy can make you impatient, but you listen to the input of others. You also make decisions quickly, but they often reflect the input received from those around you.

Destiny Number 8, Soul Number 2, Personality Number 6

Happiest when in love, you seek a devoted mate to pamper. And because you give love freely, you desire reciprocation and can have your feelings hurt when your partner wants a little space.

You're patient and go out of your way to be helpful and cooperative at work and with friends. You gladly help others and give due credit when the favor is returned. Placing a strong value on harmony, you live by your personal credo of "peace at any price."

You're willing to meet challenges and accept responsibility to further your ambitions. While happy to carry more than your share of the load, you effectively unite factions within groups. Your attention to detail and skill at handling others makes you an effective manager.

You ride an emotional rollercoaster, which can impact your health and your weight. You find decision-making difficult when emotions are involved. Because you consider people's feelings and can see both sides, you can become indecisive. When pressured, you may let your heart rather than your head control you.

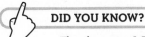 **DID YOU KNOW?**

The character J. Pierrepont Finch in Shepherd Means' 1952 bestseller *How to Succeed in Business without Really Trying* (later a musical on Broadway and on screen), could have been written with the Destiny Number 8, Soul Number 2, and Personality Number 6 in mind.

Destiny Number 8, Soul Number 3, Personality Number 5

Essentially an optimist, you avoid worries that your busy schedule might cause by keeping things light. Most people can't maintain your pace, but when you have the freedom to set your own hours and make the rules, your organizational skills see you through.

Your love of the spotlight and verbal skills make you an excellent entertainer. Socially adept, you have a talent for making important contacts and can use your charm to convince others to give you what you want. By paying attention to your physical and mental health, you maintain the energy necessary to pursue your many projects. Every passing year brings you closer to your goal of position and power and increases your confidence level.

Destiny Number 8, Soul Number 4, Personality Number 4

Leading a disciplined life, you make the most of every hour and day. An ambitious approach helps you accomplish a great deal, and your keen business judgment and logic make you an effective organizer. Once you've set up the system and delegated responsibility, you expect performance. You don't like to make changes and, so long as everyone follows your instructions precisely, you don't feel the need.

You take commitments seriously and expect the same from others. Naturally frugal and never extravagant, you still require quality for your dollar. Financial security is a higher priority to you than outward signs of success.

You're devoted to your loved ones and desire deep, meaningful relationships. If your mate falls short, you let your disappointment be known. However, if the situation calls for it, you can bottle up your feelings.

Destiny Number 8, Soul Number 5, Personality Number 3

You thrive on variety and are happiest when involved in multiple, simultaneous ventures. A hectic schedule doesn't impair your organization. Making your own schedule and creating your own rules go hand-in-glove with your flexible approach.

Your curious and versatile mind generates original—and often unconventional—ideas. You grasp concepts and size up situations quickly, coming to almost instantaneous decisions. Quick to exploit an opening, you rely on charm and an ability to articulate to involve others in business ventures. When the stakes are high, with money to be made, you welcome business challenges and competition. You also never pass up the chance to make a new contact or take advantage of an opportunity.

Your humor and energy make you attractive to others. However, you hate to be tied down and don't deal well with obstacles in your path to personal freedom.

Destiny Number 8, Soul Number 6, Personality Number 2

Strong-willed but with a surprisingly soft heart, you're an effective leader. Although you like being in charge, you want those around you to get along and be happy. You listen to the ideas of others and care about their feelings; therefore, community projects often benefit from your involvement. You're particularly effective at organizing fundraisers.

You're adept at putting others at ease and are frequently in demand as a mediator. If you had your way, peace and fairness would be the order of the day. Although you're blessed with common sense, you need to avoid letting your feelings get in the way when making decisions.

Because your family is important to you, creating a pleasant home environment is critical. With high expectations of yourself and others, you also expect your family to reflect well upon you. Although you're responsible and want people to depend upon you, you'll pitch in if you see people unable to hold up their end. When you feel that someone has taken advantage of you, you're still able to communicate your disappointment in a nice way.

 IT DOESN'T ADD UP

Either the expression "You're known by the company you keep" or "If you lie down with dogs, you get up with fleas" could apply to the Destiny Number 8, Soul Number 6, and Personality Number 2. Be careful of the company you keep if you want them to reflect well on you.

Destiny Number 8, Soul Number 7, Personality Number 1

You're seen as an independent leader with the courage to act on your own ideas. People recognize you as efficient and capable, able to analyze what's needed in any situation and to efficiently manage people to accomplish the task at hand. You work best alone without anyone breathing down your neck—taking orders is not your strong suit.

You're career-oriented, but your skills are evident in any setting. You take pleasure in attacking and solving challenging problems. You arrive at sound conclusions through careful thought, keen powers of observation, and good intuition. Able to turn a profit in almost any venture you undertake, your emotional balance and determination can put a prosperous future within reach.

Essentially private, you reveal your inner feelings only to those you really trust. You respect other people's privacy, and in turn they trust you not to reveal their secrets.

Destiny Number 8, Soul Number 8, Personality Number 9

You take pride in knowing all the right people, and you use these contacts to accomplish worthwhile community projects. People appreciate your ability to see the big picture and communicate it effectively. You're nobody's fool and don't let anyone take advantage of you.

You like to be in control and accomplish a lot when you're able to do things your way. You tend to delegate the details but spend long hours making sure everything is done and works together. You have your own timetable and system for completing projects and chafe when asked for an update on your progress.

A workaholic by nature, the one area of your life that's lacking is time for yourself to enjoy the fruits of your labor. The result of taking your responsibilities seriously is a shortage of time for recreation.

Destiny Number 8, Soul Number 9, Personality Number 8

You have an air of authority—you not only appear to be in charge, you also readily give the orders to back up that impression. Organized and efficient, you work well with large groups of people. A necessary but enjoyable aspect of your work, travel fills your need for freedom.

You set high goals and possess the determination required to achieve them. You're caught up in your work, giving it your all and gaining respect for your accomplishments. People admire you, even though you're hard to get to know well. Although driven by success, you share generously with those you care about.

You won't let others push you around but at your core, you're a soft-hearted romantic. There's nothing you wouldn't do for your loved ones, and you deeply enjoy knowing your efforts are appreciated.

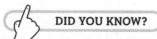 **DID YOU KNOW?**

As a Destiny Number 8, Soul Number 9, and Personality Number 8, you give everything your all, whether you're at work, donating your time to charity, or competing in a sport. Others respect your dedication and accomplishments.

Destiny Number 9, Soul Number 1, Personality Number 8

You're an energetic individual and accomplish your most when put in charge. Others respect how confidently you approach challenges.

At work, autonomy to set your own schedule is important to you. You have the vision to see the most efficient method to achieve your project's goals and don't waste any time in implementing that vision. You tend to take care of the coordination and the big issues while delegating the details to others.

You're a free spirit who refuses to be dominated. You often come up with original ways to accomplish philanthropic goals. Although you care about helping others, you look out for number one first.

Destiny Number 9, Soul Number 2, Personality Number 7

You project an air of confidence bordering on haughtiness that says that you're in control. This appearance of aloofness conceals a sensitive soul.

Sometimes you care so deeply that you come on too strong. As a consequence, you sometimes soft-pedal your feelings. Your pursuit of love and romance can result in overtures that are misunderstood.

Because you enjoy diversity, your friends come from all walks of life. Your interests are as broad as your circle of friends and include art, music, and travel. You're also happier working in a group than alone. Sometimes, in an effort to sell others on an idea, you embellish the facts.

You're generous and will help anyone who deserves it, but you expect your contributions to be appreciated. Unfortunately, people sometimes try to take advantage of your kindness and good nature.

Destiny Number 9, Soul Number 3, Personality Number 6

Friendly and outgoing, you can talk to anyone about any subject. Your enthusiasm is contagious, and people feel happier when around you.

Considered solid and responsible, people are surprised when they find that you sometimes take on more than you can handle. Because you have the best intentions and genuinely think you can do it all, you feel guilty when you can't fulfill your promises.

You put others at ease with your warm smile and winning personality. You excel in front of large groups and are a kind, compassionate teacher. You like to inspire people; when that's recognized, you feel like you've earned your gold star.

Destiny Number 9, Soul Number 4, Personality Number 5

You appear to others as full of life, but that conceals your conservative and somewhat rigid core. You value and practice honesty, which garners respect for your integrity.

By thinking things through in a clear manner, you're an effective problem solver. After careful planning, you work hard to achieve tangible results.

Your generosity is balanced by your pursuit of financial security. You hate waste and go out of your way to get value for your dollar. Although you're willing to spend for what you need or really want, you shun expenditures on things that are unnecessary.

You have a large social circle, enjoy travel, and cultivate your interest in the arts. Meaningful relationships are important to you, but even when feeling deep affection, you have difficulty expressing how much you care. Short of dishonesty, there isn't anything you wouldn't do for those you love.

Destiny Number 9, Soul Number 5, Personality Number 4

You have a humanitarian bent and are a keen student of human nature and behavior. Your family is the center of your world, and you will sacrifice anything for them and their well-being.

Quick to grasp new ideas, you excel at solving problems and puzzles. Your versatility in dealing with people and situations helps you compete effectively when faced with one of life's challenges.

Although you believe in a live-and-let-live approach, you give the impression of discipline and conservatism. People see the results of your efforts but don't always realize that you can play just as hard as you work.

You strongly believe in exercising to relieve stress. Always on the lookout to kill two birds with one stone, you often pack a tennis racquet or your golf clubs when traveling on business.

Destiny Number 9, Soul Number 6, Personality Number 3

You often involve yourself in good works and other charitable causes. In your personal life, you give freely of yourself, your home, and your talents, often making your contributions in the arts. A gifted conversationalist, you have the talent to make people laugh.

Your loved ones are the primary beneficiaries of your generosity—you delight in showering them with gifts. You also enjoy creating beautiful surroundings, and your family and home are testament to your taste. While your home is your haven, you're willing to open the door wide to let others in and enjoy your company.

Destiny Number 9, Soul Number 7, Personality Number 2

Although outwardly cooperative and sensitive to others' feelings, you do all you can to avoid superficial company and idle chitchat. You're fussy in choosing friends, often preferring to keep your own company.

You go along with almost anyone who can present a good, logical case. A perceptive analyst, you achieve many successes by following your hunches. Carefully considering all options and information first, you watch and listen before venturing an opinion. Even though politeness is your policy, an insatiable curiosity compels you to ask questions in pursuit of knowledge.

The disparity between your very private side and your interests in public causes can confuse others. These mixed messages and a reluctance to share your opinions make you a mystery to casual acquaintances.

Destiny Number 9, Soul Number 8, Personality Number 1

You have the will to meet any challenge, putting all possibilities within your reach. You're not one to stand on the sidelines or be part of a team—you crave power.

You project a larger-than-life image, and your ability to communicate with others makes your influence felt. With a reputation for being broadminded and tolerant, others readily follow your lead.

Sharing your talent and expertise, you always seem to show a profit. The financial rewards of your efforts aren't enough, though; you also seek public recognition and appreciation. Any individual or group who doesn't express gratitude won't benefit from your generosity a second time.

 PYTHAGORAS SAYS

As a Destiny Number 9, Soul Number 8, and Personality Number 1, you can excel at a career in the self-help field. Not only would it satisfy your desire for financial and emotional recognition, you would relish in the power and influence of your position. The influence you have in such a role also sates your craving for power.

Destiny Number 9, Soul Number 9, Personality Number 9

You offer yourself, your time, and your talents freely without expecting recognition; however, you appreciate it deeply when your efforts are acknowledged.

You have musical or artistic talent, or at least a strong appreciation of them. Unprejudiced, you have unusual friends from all walks of life. Others trust you because of your broadmindedness. Your heart rules you, and that emotional approach has brought you your share of disappointments. If you let them, your feelings can tear you apart.

Despite your heart of gold and willingness to do almost anything for a friend, your spirit bristles when you feel too tightly bound by commitments. You don't want to hurt anyone, but you need the freedom to pursue your own interests as well.

You like to deal with grand concepts and leave the petty details to others. It's important to not let people take advantage of you, because you're prone to tell more than you should to anyone who shows an interest.

The Least You Need to Know

- Your Destiny Number is the sum of your Soul Number and Personality Numbers when reduced to a single digit.
- Each Destiny Number has nine possible combinations of Soul Numbers and Personality Numbers.
- The attributes, traits, and characteristics of your Soul and Personality Numbers influence how strongly your Destiny Number's characteristics shine through.

Elements Within Your Name

Your name is a treasure trove of numerologically meaningful elements. Whether it's the significance of your name's first vowel, how frequently letters appear, what letters are absent, and how many letters are present, all of these elements contribute to the numbers within your name and the meaning of those numbers. Additionally, combinations of the numbers attached to your name interact in a way that tells you more about who you are.

In this chapter, I show you the importance of the first vowel in your name and also discuss the Inclusion Table, which you can use to organize the various meanings hidden in your name. I wrap up the chapter with which letters show your type and traits and contribute to the physical, mental, emotional, and intuitive aspects of your persona.

In This Chapter

- The meaning of the first vowel in your name

- Organizing meanings of your name with the Inclusion Table

- Exploring the frequency of values with the Intensification Number

- What's missing: Karma Numbers

- Instincts and the Subconscious Response Number

- Seeing who you really are inside with the Point of Security Number

- Looking at the Type and Traits Chart

The First Vowel in Your Name

Each letter in your name is significant, but sometimes the location of the letter can be of special importance.

The first vowel in your name gives you a glimpse into your inner core and your first emotional reaction to events that affect you directly or indirectly. The number attached to that letter is a "secretive" number that few people wear on their sleeve—that is, it represents something that probably only you know. It's important because it is a glimpse of how you view the world around you.

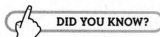 **DID YOU KNOW?**

It's important to note that I don't consider W and Y to be vowels, even when they appear to play that role or stand in for the sound of one. However, both still have significance in numerology: W in a name adds restlessness or difficulty to a person, while Y denotes being at a crossroads, a mystical quality, wisdom, or mystery.

In the following, I explain the significance of each vowel when it appears as the first vowel in your name.

A as the First Vowel

A is the letter of independence, action, initiative, activity, self-mastery, and originality. If you have A as the first vowel in your name, you're hardworking, loyal, and driven by positive feedback. You feel the need to work using your own methods and may be prone to rebellion if you feel questioned or unjustly scrutinized. You tend to reject the advice of others, even if it is good advice. When you make a mistake, you feel as if you have failed. You also thrive on honest feedback but are sensitive to criticism that lacks a gentle delivery.

A as the first vowel indicates you're reflective on the mental, physical, and spiritual planes and seek honesty, truth, and wisdom. Those with A as the first vowel also have a tendency to be impulsive.

E as the First Vowel

E is the letter of freedom, energy, excitement, enjoyment, wide-ranging interests, interest in the opposite sex, and—most of all—intuition. If you have E as the first vowel, you're especially instinctive and interested in many subjects. You're like a detective and researcher who can ferret out information; because your intuition is most often accurate, be sure to listen to your inner voice. You have a quick mind as well as an inner light that brings beauty and magic to the world.

In a conversation, you might jump from one subject to another without segue, leaving the other person thinking, "What just happened?" or "Is that what we were talking about?" Your first reaction to things may be an emotional one. If life seems boring, you're able to change your interest to something new. Although you enjoy hearing the stories and drama of others, you sometimes find it draining.

I as the First Vowel

I is the letter of intensity and the "I am" spirit, as well as the letter of research and responsibility. You're idealistic and at times impractical in emotional matters.

If you have I as the first vowel in your name, you're impossible to hold down. You're a law unto yourself and are admired and respected by others. You're also a born leader who's driven by perfection—whatever you do, you want to do it well. Patient by nature, you'll repeat activities over and over until you get them right.

I as the first vowel indicates you may have challenges or issues with your family. This means you either feel responsible for one or more family members (especially parents) or feel unloved. At times, you aren't realistic in romantic situations and sometimes regret your impulsiveness later.

O as the First Vowel

O is the letter of magnetism, reasoning, and protection. If you have O as the first vowel and don't have children, you may have a pet or someone else's child who you enjoy caring for. O is also a letter of contradiction—you appear modest yet independent or seem strong but helpless. Above all, you're communicative yet can internalize your emotions. So while you're able to hold in your emotions, you're also a magnetic personality whose mood can easily affect how others feel. Take care not to become drained by the emotional demands others place on you.

If you have O as the first vowel, you like to take the time to research and analyze problems and their solutions. You're at your best in a position of authority and need to excel in that role.

U as the First Vowel

U is the letter of energy and spontaneity. If you have U as your first vowel, you seek spiritual enlightenment. The U shape is like a cup for emotions; although you're emotional at times, you can hold in your emotions until they overflow with a fury.

U is also letter of the communicator—storytellers who lead a colorful life. Having U as the first vowel shows you're in touch with your inner child and could be a great stand-up comedian or comedic actor. You have a way of telling stories that can lighten up a room and have people on the edge of their seats. Known to exaggerate, you never let the truth get in the way of a good story!

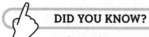

DID YOU KNOW?

If your first vowel is also the first letter of your name (such as in Anna, Edward, Isabel, or Oscar), you may take a while to make decisions. If required to give an instant answer, you may have a difficult time doing so.

Organizing Your Name's Meanings with the Inclusion Table

The Inclusion Table is like a graphic organizer of your name. It analyzes the numeric values that repeat more or less frequently in your name. When numbers appear more frequently, they have a higher vibration and indicate stronger characteristics. When they appear less frequently, they indicate things you need to learn. You will discover characteristics involving the letters in your name, including your Intensification, Karma, Subconscious Response, and Point of Security Numbers.

Intensification Number	1	2	3	4	5	6	7	8	9
Karma Number	1	2	3	4	5	6	7	8	9
Subconscious Response Number	1	2	3	4	5	6	7	8	9
Point of Security Number	1	2	3	4	5	6	7	8	9

If you're like most readers, you're probably curious about your own name. To begin the Inclusion Table, fill out your name.

R	A	U	L		A	G	U	I	L	A	R							
2	1	6	3		1	3	6	1	3	1	2							

2,
3,
4,
2,

Use this blank chart to fill in your name.

1. Using the full name on your birth certificate, print your name with one letter in each square. Leave a space between your first, middle, and last names for clarity.

2. In the square below each letter, place its corresponding value (refer back to the "Pythagorean Letter-to-Number Table" in Chapter 2 if you need a refresher).

In the following example, I've entered the name of my eldest daughter, Jamie Lynn Simpson. In each square, I placed every letter of her name exactly as it appears on her birth certificate, and below those letters I placed their numerical value based on the Pythagorean system of numerology (see Chapter 2 if you need a refresher on converting letters to numbers).

J	A	M	I	E		L	Y	N	N		S	I	M	P	S	O	N
1	1	4	9	5		3	7	5	5		1	9	4	7	1	6	5

Now that you've written your name and the values of each letter, check out the following sections, which break down each piece of the Inclusion Table and the meanings behind the numbers.

The Intensification Number Section

Intensification quantifies how many times letters and their number values repeat in a name. When someone has more than the average numbers of any given number value, this represents an intensification of certain characteristics. For example, if a person has an intensification of 5s, they are always on the go and may have a difficult time staying focused long enough to complete a task. Or if an individual has an intensification of 4s, they probably have the patience of Job and take joy in being frugal while hunting for bargains instead of paying retail.

You've probably noticed when looking at names over time that certain letters show up quite frequently, while others are found very rarely. The table that follows shows the average number of times letter and number values appear in most current U.S. and Western European names.

IT DOESN'T ADD UP

Average is just what the word implies. If you have more or fewer letters or number values than the average in your name, it's not a reflection of whether your name is "good" or "bad." In numerology, all names are good.

Number Value	Letters	Average Intensification
1	A, J, S	Three or more times
2	B, K, T	Usually once
3	C, L, U	Usually once
4	D, M, V	Usually once
5	E, N, W	Three or more times
6	F, O, X	Usually once
7	G, P, Y	Sometimes missing
8	H, Q, Z	Sometimes once or missing
9	I, R	Three or more times

When looking at this table, you'll notice that on average, people have three or more 1s (A, J, or S), 5s (E, N, or W), and 9s (I or R) in their name. These frequencies should not be surprising, since A, E, I, N, R, and S are the most commonly occurring letters in English (as Scrabble players and crypto-puzzle fans can attest).

Now it's your turn to count the various letters and their number values in your name as you wrote earlier and see how they compare to the average for the Intensification Number section. You can use the following to record your information.

Number Value	Letters	Average	Actual
1	A, J, S	Three or more times	
2	B, K, T	Usually once	
3	C, L, U	Usually once	
4	D, M, V	Usually once	
5	E, N, W	Three or more times	
6	F, O, X	Usually once	
7	G, P, Y	Sometimes missing	
8	H, Q, Z	Sometimes once or missing	
9	I, R	Three or more times	
Total			

Record the frequency of number values and the total of your name.

Intensification Number	1	2	3	4	5	6	7	8	9

Circle the number values that occur more frequently than average in your name, if any.

1. Refer to the earlier portion of this section, when you recorded your full birth name and placed the numeric values below the letters.

2. Count the frequency of each number value in your name and write the sum for each in the "Actual" column. If your name doesn't have a certain number value in it, simply write a 0 for it in the "Actual" column.

3. Add the numbers in the "Actual" column vertically, and write your total at the bottom.

4. Determine whether you have more than an above-average proliferation, or Intensification, of any letters and their number values in your name and circle the ones that apply. For example, if you have six 5s in your name, which is above the average, you circle 5.

IT DOESN'T ADD UP

In your excitement of getting to know the secrets in your name, it's easy to make a mistake. Remember, the total should be the same number as the number of letters in your name. If it's not, check your calculations.

To show you this process in action, I used the number values of Jamie Lynn Simpson's name to find out her Intensification Number.

J	A	M	I	E		L	Y	N	N		S	I	M	P	S	O	N
1	1	4	9	5		3	7	5	5		1	9	4	7	1	6	5

Number Value	Letters	Average	Actual
1	A, J, S	Three or more times	4
2	B, K, T	Usually once	0
3	C, L, U	Usually once	1
4	D, M, V	Usually once	2
5	E, N, W	Three or more times	4
6	F, O, X	Usually once	1
7	G, P, Y	Sometimes missing	2
8	H, Q, Z	Sometimes once or missing	0
9	I, R	Three or more times	2
Total			16

Notice that she has four 1-value letters, zero 2-value letters, one 3-value letter, two 4-value letters, four 5-value letters, one 6-value letter, two 7-value letters, zero 8-value letters, and two 9-value letters.

I then circled any letters that appeared with above-average frequency. In Jamie's name, she has an intensification of the letters values 1, 4, 5, and 7.

Intensification Number	①	2	3	④	⑤	6	⑦	8	9

Next, I totaled the amount of times the numbers repeat in Jamie's name in the Actual column (4 + 0 + 1 + 2 + 4 + 1 + 2 + 0 + 2 = 16). I then counted the letters in Jamie's name and found she has 16 letters in her name. The sum of the vertical column (16) and the amount of letters in her name (16) matched. Hooray! I correctly counted all of the numbers in her name.

What are your Intensification Numbers? That is, what letters and number values do you see repeated most? Let's find out what this information means to you!

Above-average 1 values (A, J, S): You have strong opinions and set ideas. You're quick to make decisions and are able to come up with original ideas. Happy to work independently, you can tune out distractions and single-mindedly see a task to completion. Because of your comfort with change and strong determination, you have great leadership qualities. You also aren't afraid to stand up for yourself and can be aggressive when you feel the situation calls for it. However, avoid becoming too arrogant or dogmatic in your approach.

Above-average 2 values (B, K, T): You're very cooperative and get along well with others. Because of that ease, you possess the ability to arbitrate situations when there is discord. Your feelings can be hurt easily, and you can at times be hypersensitive. In your desire to be liked, you may try to appease others beyond reason. You also can be overly dependent on others because you don't like to do things alone. You're very adaptable—perhaps too much so—and vacillate before making decisions.

Above-average 3 values (C, L, U): You can be extravagant, spending too much money on frivolous things in an effort to impress others, and may talk (or brag) about yourself too much. You're overly concerned with your appearance and may worry about how old you'll look someday. You may also have a tendency to be childlike, to the point of being childish. In terms of focus, you can be irresponsible, scattering your forces and not sticking to the task at hand.

Above-average 4 values (D, M, V): You have great self-discipline and find it easy to stick to a schedule, to the point of possibly getting too detail oriented and fixated. You can also get too set in your ways and be stubborn in your viewpoint. You prefer to be overly prepared and spend too much time getting ready. You may even arrive too early at parties or appointments out of fear of being late. When it comes to family, you find that your in-laws are a source of both pleasure and problems.

Above-average 5 values (E, N, W): You can adapt easily to change. You like to throw caution to the wind in your desire to have fun, which can leave you prone to impulsive or irresponsible actions. Restless in nature, you have difficulty sticking to a schedule and are unable to commit due to your need for freedom. You tend to be sensually overindulgent and seek carnal pleasure. You also may be interested in too many things, possibly making you a Jack of all trades and a master of none. While you're apt to be critical of others, you have a gift of salesmanship that makes others come around to your viewpoint.

Above-average 6 values (F, O, X): You're flexible and find it easy to adjust to situations. You also try too hard to make people like you, to the point that you forget your own needs and wind up a slave to theirs. You're prone to self-righteousness and tend to place your high ideals on others. However, you must avoid being judgmental and learn to not be hurt when others aren't as loyal and responsible as you are. Also, you must try not to get so involved in your desire to help others that you smother them.

Above-average 7 values (G, P, Y): You tend to overanalyze things, asking questions to the point you annoy others. You enjoy your alone time, which could lead to you isolating yourself to the point you live a hermitlike existence. Prone to fear, depression, or melancholy, you should avoid using alcohol or drugs as an escape, as you can be affected by them differently than other people. Also, you may experience false pride, or a pride that comes from approval from others rather than genuine self-satisfaction. Learn to stay away from get-rich-quick schemes or secretive undertakings.

Above-average 8 values (H, Q, Z): Overly organized, you possess an intense drive to accomplish work or plans in an effort to secure money and position. Be careful to not dominate others and abuse your authority—you may become frustrated or bossy with those who don't have your abilities. Also, you must realize you can only change yourself; it's not up to you to change the world. When it comes to money, avoid being greedy in your desire for monetary success.

Above-average 9 values (I, R): You may be musical or artistic, with a tendency to move between emotional extremes. You need to be more balanced in your feelings, thoughts, and actions. You should also avoid dissipating your resources trying to save the world. Because you're overly solicitous and helpful to others, you may get taken advantage of; be more discerning about who you help. Also, avoid emotional eating when you're disappointed.

 DID YOU KNOW?

> Combinations of Intensification Numbers also have an impact. When both 1s and 8s abound, you might be geared toward business, don't get overly emotional, and can be the rock around which others anchor. A lot of 2s, 3s, and 6s mean you're blessed with artistic ability and an inspirational quality that could make you a good teacher. When 4s and 7s dominate, you tend toward mechanical, mathematical, or scientific fields—often the hallmark of an engineer or architect. When you have an above-average number of both 7s and 9s, it indicates you have skill at research or literary pursuits.

The Karma Number Section

The next section of the Inclusion Table looks at Karma Numbers. Without getting too philosophical, I find the Karma Numbers very enlightening, as do most of my clients. Some people believe they have to do with our past-life experience, while others see them as insight into our opportunities to learn more about our hidden talents. Understanding your Karma Numbers will explain the kind of situations or experiences you did *not* have in your previous existences and may need to develop during your current visit on Earth. Or, if you don't believe in past lives, they show you skills and attributes you may need to cultivate to better help you handle the situations you will likely find yourself in throughout your life.

How do you find your Karma Numbers? Go back to the previous section on Intensification, where you entered the frequency of letters and number values in your name in the "Actual" column. Any number values with a zero next to them are Karma Numbers. If you have any Karma Numbers, circle them in the Karma Number section.

Karma Number	1	2	3	4	5	6	7	8	9

Circle the number values that don't appear in your name.

In our earlier example, Jamie had no 2s or 8s in her name, so her Karma Numbers are 2 and 8.

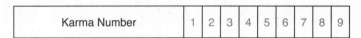

Now that you know how to find Karma Numbers, here's a rundown of what each Karma Number means:

No 1 values: You should develop leadership qualities and take the initiative. Learn to be strong and courageous, with value for your own ideas. You could find yourself in situations where you may need to develop more self-reliance and work independently of others. Pay more attention to yourself than you do to others. Form opinions and don't be afraid to express them; at the same time, don't let yourself be swayed by the opinions of others. Learn to stand up for yourself by not saying "yes" when you really mean "no"—don't be a doormat for others.

No 2 values: Develop more attention to detail. You can enjoy your independence, but make sure you know how to cooperate with others. Be more considerate of others and their feelings, wants, and needs. Learn to be a good friend to others and attract them for yourself by demonstrating more patience and tact. Also, be more adaptable and easygoing—don't be negative, petty, or picky. Put yourself in others' shoes in the interest of getting along better with others. Show others you respect their time and keep appointments.

No 3 values: Be more flexible and less structured, with a concentration on being more imaginative and developing your talents. Try to be more trusting and joyful, and take more chances on new things. Bolster your self-confidence so you're not as bashful. Improve your communication skills in social situations and enlarge your circle of friends. Be willing to express your feelings and share facts about yourself with others. Also, spend some time working on your appearance and updating your wardrobe.

No 4 values: You should try to be more self-disciplined and pragmatic, with better focus on details. Develop a systematic way of doing things so you can be more meticulous in your daily life—that means developing routines, making a schedule, and sticking to it. Realize that shortcuts don't always save time, and that everything has a price. In money matters, watch your spending and stick to a budget.

No 5 values: Look at situations and the big picture with a more open mind. You should not only accept change, but also embrace it. Be more flexible and open to new ideas and experiences—discover the joy of travel and participate in more activities that will keep you busy. When it comes to others, look at them with more tolerance and avoid getting restless or impatient. Know when to release or let things go.

No 6 values: You need to develop more of a sense of responsibility. This means taking relationships more seriously and seeing commitments through to their conclusion. Care more about the needs of your friends and family. Discover the joys of entertaining by inviting people to your home more often. When it comes to other people, try to be more charming when working with them. Be a friend and a teacher, sharing your knowledge and giving advice when asked. Also, spend more time beautifying yourself and your surroundings.

No 7 values: Be less fearful and more open-minded; have faith in yourself and let go of any false pride. Learn to be alone without being lonely. Enjoy books and study things that interest you, and discover the joy of being outdoors in nature. Have more faith in yourself, and let go of any false pride. Also, work on being more analytical. Look under the surface of situations to discover what's really going on, and consider things carefully before asking questions. When it comes to money, develop skill handling and managing it.

No 8 values: Develop more self-control and sound judgment on all levels. Weigh decisions carefully before making them and taking action. Whatever you decide to do, take charge, and don't pass the buck. When it comes to finances, be more careful of your spending and learn how to handle money—don't be too generous or too stingy. Health-wise, pay more attention to your diet and avoid talking about aches and pains.

No 9 values: Let yourself experience and adapt to sudden changes in your life readily—don't hold onto people and possessions too tightly. Be more generous and giving in all areas of your life, with great tolerance, compassion, and empathy. Expand your frame of reference from your personal sphere and learn the meaning of "universal love." Develop an interest in art, music, beauty, and world affairs. Also, try not to isolate yourself from the feelings of the past.

The Subconscious Response Number Section

The next section of the Inclusion Table is about the Subconscious Response Number. The Subconscious Response Number indicates the way you instinctively act or react in times of emergency or crisis. Do you stop and call 911 when you see a stray dog running on the side of the freeway, or do you forge ahead, not wanting to be late for your appointment? Are you calm and reserved in a crisis, or do you panic and pray that someone else will take charge? Are you the first one to board the lifeboat, or do you help others climb in first? These are things that reveal the fundamentals of your inner workings.

To get your Subconscious Response Number, determine the number of Karma Numbers you have and subtract that number from 9. Here's a quick breakdown of missing numbers and their related Subconscious Response Numbers for reference:

Missing Numbers in Your Name	Subconscious Response Number
0	9
1	8
2	7
3	6
4	5
5	4
6	3

Once you have the result, circle that value in the Subconscious Response section.

Subconscious Response Number	1	2	3	4	5	6	7	8	9

Circle the number you get when you subtract how many Karma Numbers you have from 9.

For example, Jamie has two Karma Numbers (2 and 8). To determine her Subconscious Response number, I subtracted 2 from 9 (9 − 2 = 7), which revealed her Subconscious Response Number is 7. I then circled that value in the Subconscious Response section.

Subconscious Response Number	1	2	3	4	5	6	⑦	8	9

IT DOESN'T ADD UP

If you get a Subconscious Response Number of 1 or 2, that means you have eight or seven number values missing from your name, which is impossible. If you get one of these answers the first time around, recheck your calculations.

Now that you know your Subconscious Response Number, here's how to interpret it:

Subconscious Response Number 3: You tend to be uncertain when confronted by urgent matters. While you can readily handle challenges one at a time, you can have difficulty prioritizing when confronted with multiple issues.

Subconscious Response Number 4: You have a tendency to find multiple solutions to a problem, but may run around in circles unable to decide which one to pursue.

Subconscious Response Number 5: You tend to exercise caution and focus on details rather than the big picture.

Subconscious Response Number 6: You're very responsible and often place the welfare or wishes of others ahead of your own.

Subconscious Response Number 7: You approach situations analytically, weigh the evidence, and seek reasonable solutions. You tend to seek a meditative escape after a crisis passes.

Subconscious Response Number 8: You tend to be a take-charge type who delegates responsibility to find the most efficient way out of a dilemma.

Subconscious Response Number 9: You tend to be unfazed in a crisis, knowing from experience that you can deal with whatever comes your way.

The Point of Security Number Section

The last section in the Inclusion Table deals with the Point of Security Number. The Point of Security Number tells you what you have within you to be successful both personally and professionally, no matter what comes your way. Even in the worst-case scenario or when all your cards are on the table, your Point of Security Number will ensure you've got what it takes to handle the highs, lows, and sometimes in-betweens in your life. If you lose a job or a loved one, have an accident and are injured, or are faced with a financial crisis, your Point of Security Number is the bottom line of the total *you* inside.

The Point of Security Number is determined by simply counting up the total number of letters in your name (see the total on your Intensification table) and reducing to a single digit. You can then circle the number in the Point of Security section.

Point of Security Number	①	2	3	4	5	6	7	8	9

Circle the value you get from counting up the letters in your name and reducing to a single digit.

As you discovered earlier, Jamie has 16 letters in her name, so her Point of Security Number is 7 (1 + 6 = 7).

Point of Security Number	1	2	3	4	5	6	⑦	8	9

It's not the abundance of any particular letter that has significance—just the total number of letters used. Although there are exceptions at either end of the scale, most people have between 14 and 18 letters in their name. Longer is more common than shorter, though, primarily due to cultural considerations—longer given names, multiple middle names, and compounded or hyphenated surnames among them.

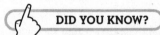

DID YOU KNOW?

Interestingly, some metaphysicians believe that the number of letters in your name indicates how many lives you have lived.

Here are the interpretations of the various Point of Security Numbers:

Point of Security Number 1: You're always able to stand on your own two feet. No matter what others may say about you, you can always count on yourself. You're inventive and can dream up imaginative ways of doing old things in new ways.

Point of Security Number 2: You're always able to work well with others. Your intuition and ability to tune in to the Universe and the feelings of others can serve you well throughout your lifetime.

Point of Security Number 3: You always have an optimistic attitude and the ability to express your thoughts and feelings. You can earn a living using words or in creative pursuits.

Point of Security Number 4: You're always on an even keel—not much can rock you. You also always have loyal friends or family nearby. You can earn a living organizing things or developing systems.

Point of Security Number 5: You're always active and able to roll with the punches to deal with change. You have the gift to adapt and accept whatever comes your way.

Point of Security Number 6: You always think responsibly and enjoy your family and friends. You're able to attract whatever you want in life with your random acts of kindness.

Point of Security Number 7: You're always able to analyze and think things through before making a decision. Your ability to enjoy spending time alone consistently restores you.

Point of Security Number 8: You're always able to take charge and control your life. Your ability to handle your emotions and be balanced in all you do serves you well.

Point of Security Number 9: You're always understanding of others because of your kind heart and generous spirit. Travel to various locations brings you pleasure.

Type and Traits Chart

In the 1930s, some research numerologists, led by Dr. Juno Jordan, claimed that man is fourfold, with a body, brain, heart, and spirit. They discovered that letters and their corresponding numbers can be grouped into four categories based on those "planes of expression," as Dr. Jordan called them: physical, mental, emotional, and intuitive.

Physical letters (4 and 5 number values) represent the body and are ruled by instinct. Concerned with the tangible and real, *common sense* is the keyword associated with the physical. The number of the worker and builder, 4 is economical and practical. The 5 value is less practical and suggests curiosity and security.

Mental letters (1 and 8 number values) represent positive states of mind, analysis, reasoning, facts, executive ability, and leadership qualities. *Determination* is the keyword associated with the mental. These letters also suggest only accepting things that are obvious and can be proved. On the mental plane, 1 is the number of imagination and strong will. The 8 value is about control of the mind via practicality and logical reasoning.

Emotional letters (2, 3, and 6 number values) represent the heart of man. *Feeling* is the keyword associated with the emotional—facts give way to inspiration, imagination, and vision. The letters aren't based on practical or logical foundations, but rather deal with sentiments over reason. They also represent feelings and imagination, as well as sympathetic and sensitive responses to human emotion. Sensitive to timing, 2 is the number of ideas and sharing love with others. The 3 value centers around imagination in relation to emotion, while 6 is the number of truth, beauty, and harmony.

Intuitive letters (7 and 9 number values) represent the spiritual part of mankind that uses intuition to delve into the unknown and uses the "inner guidance" to reach goals. *Metaphysical* is the keyword associated with the intuitive. Dealing with technical facts, 7 is about analysis and research. Deeply sensitive and imaginative, 9 works on a higher plane to impress the universe.

Think of the four categories as four levels of consciousness; the Type and Traits Chart delves deeper into those levels and shows how you are unique from others, looks at how you view life, and provides insight into your character. The Type and Traits Chart also looks at what talents and skills you were born with and what kind of work you might enjoy or be successful doing.

How to Use the Type and Traits Chart

Earlier in this chapter, in the "Organizing Your Name's Meanings with the Inclusion Table" section, you found out what numbers you have in your name. Now you're going to use those same numbers and place them in the Type and Traits Chart. The following walks you through the process, with a blank chart for you to fill out.

PYTHAGORAS SAYS

If you don't have any letters of a particular number, write a zero in the corresponding boxes. Having a zero doesn't mean you're lacking or devoid of those traits—rather, a zero simply means that they're not dominant traits.

Type			Traits				
Physical			4s				5s
Mental			1s				8s
Emotional			2s		3s		6s
Intuitive			7s				9s
Total							

Use this blank Type and Traits Chart to complete the steps.

1. Fill out the number of 4s and 5s in your name in the "Physical" row of the Traits portion of the chart. Count up the 4s in your name and print the sum in the empty box just to the left of the "4s" box. Likewise, count up the 5s in your name and print the sum in the empty box just to the left of the "5s" box. Add up the row and print the sum of 4s and 5s in the empty box to the right of "Physical" in the Type section of the chart.

2. Fill out the number of 1s and 8s in your name in the "Mental" row of the Traits portion of the chart. Count up the 1s in your name and print the sum in the empty box just to the left of the "1s" box. Likewise, count up the 8s in your name and print the sum in the empty box just to the left of the "8s" box. Add up the row and print the sum of 1s and 8s in the empty box to the right of "Mental" in the Type section of the chart.

3. Fill out the number of 2s, 3s, and 6s in your name in the "Emotional" row of the Traits portion of the chart. Count up the 2s in your name and print the sum in the empty box just to the left of the "2s" box. Likewise, count up the 3s in your name and print the sum in the empty box just to the left of the "3s" box. Count up the 6s in your name and print the sum in the empty box just to the left of the "6s" box. Add up the row and print the sum of 2s, 3s, and 6s in the empty box to the right of "Emotional" in the Type section of the chart.

4. Fill out the number of 7s and 9s in your name in the "Intuitive" row of the Traits portion of the chart. Count up the 7s in your name and print the sum in the empty box just to the left of the "7s" box. Likewise, count up the 9s in your name and print the sum in the empty box just to the left of the "9s" box. Add up the row and print the sum of 7s and 9s in the empty box to the right of "Intuitive" in the Type section of the chart.

5. Add your total physical, mental, emotional, and intuitive numbers to make sure you entered the information properly. The sum should equal the number of letters in your name.

As an example, I filled in a Type and Traits Chart for Jamie Lynn Simpson. Earlier, you saw that Jamie has four 1s, zero 2s, one 3, two 4s, four 5s, one 6, two 7s, zero 8s, and two 9s in her name. Here's how I filled out each part of the chart for Jamie:

1. I first filled out the "Physical" row. Because Jamie has two 4s in her name, I wrote 2 in the empty box to the left of the "4s" box in the Traits section. Jamie has four 5s in her name, so I wrote 4 in the empty box to the left of the "5s" box in the Traits section. I then totaled up the number of 2s and the 5s in her name: 2 + 4 = 6. I wrote the 6 to the right of "Physical" in the Type section of the chart.

2. I next filled out the "Mental" row. Because Jamie has four 1s in her name, I wrote 4 in the empty box to the left of the "1s" box in the Traits section. She has no 8s, so I put a zero in the empty box to the left of the "8s" box in the Traits section. I then added up the number of 1s and 8s in her name: 4+0=4. I wrote the 4 to the right of "Mental" in the Type section of the chart.

3. I then filled out the "Emotional" row. She has zero 2s in her name, so I wrote zero in the empty box to the left of the "2s" box in the Traits section. Jamie has one 3, so I wrote 1 in the empty box to the left of the "3s" box in the Traits section. She has one 6 in her name, so I wrote 1 in the empty box to the left of the "6s" box in the Traits section. I then added up the number of 2s, 3s, and 6s in her name: 0 + 1 + 1 = 2. I wrote the 2 to the right of "Emotional" in the Type section of the chart.

4. I next filled out the "Intuitive" row. Jamie has two 7s in her name, so I wrote 2 in the empty box to the left of the "7s" box in the Traits section. She has two 9s in her name, so I wrote 2 in the empty box to the left of the "9s" box in the Traits section. I then added up the number of 7s and 9s in her name: 2 + 2 = 4. I wrote the 4 to the right of "Intuitive" in the Type section of the chart.

5. Finally, I added the sums of each row vertically. The total is 16 (the amount of numbers in Jamie's name). Here's how Jamie's Type and Traits Chart looks in its final state.

Type			Traits			
Physical	6	2	4s		4	5s
Mental	4	4	1s		0	8s
Emotional	2	0	2s	1	3s	1	6s
Intuitive	4	2	7s		2	9s
Total	16/7					

But what do the values for each of these categories mean? The following walks you through what these values mean in relation to you.

Type and Traits Chart Meanings

Taking the entries one at a time, the following gives more insight:

Number of physical letters: Having zero physical letters denotes a lack of physical endurance or a tendency to be impractical. If you have one physical letter, you're apt to be active and enthusiastic about life. Having two physical letters in your name indicates that although you may be sensitive, you are charming and clever. If you have three physical letters, you are imaginative, creative, and talented. Four physical letters denotes hard workers who are tenacious and can carry out their ideas to fruition. Those with five physical letters lead an active life and can be good salesman. If you have six physical letters, you accept responsibility readily and enjoy helping others. Those with seven physical letters delve deeply into things; although you're friendly, you may not be very social. If you have eight physical letters, you're ambitious and able to handle big projects with ease. Those with nine physical letters have a natural flair for drama and can achieve success in publishing or large corporations.

Number of mental letters: If you have no mental letters in your name, you sometimes lack willpower and have difficulty making and sticking with your decisions. One mental letter indicates you can be witty and are an original thinker. Those with two mental letters are collectors of knowledge and things and are naturally agreeable and cooperative. If you have three mental letters in your name, you're popular but prefer to make decisions on your own. Those with four mental letters are determined and have the ability to concentrate. If you have five mental letters in your name, you're curious and enjoy having many irons in the fire simultaneously. Those with six mental letters are responsible and can be depended upon to follow through with promises. If you have seven mental letters, you're observant and introspective, and require proof before you're convinced of anything. Those with eight mental letters are ambitious and enjoy being in charge. If you have nine mental letters in your name, you enjoy working with people of diverse backgrounds and cultures.

Number of emotional letters: If you have no emotional letters in your name, you may have a difficult time expressing your emotions and may not be very empathetic of others' feelings. Having one emotional letter is apt to make you a bit high-strung yet capable of dealing with all kinds of people. If you have two emotional letters, you're an intuitive and generous person who's willing to share your possessions with others. Three emotional letters indicates you need an artistic outlet for your emotions and are gifted with words. Those with four emotional letters don't like feeling restricted in their work or personal lives and need to be appreciated and validated by others. If you have five emotional letters in your name, you enjoy learning how others think and feel about various subjects. Those with six emotional letters are honest, feel things deeply, and tend to worry about others. If you have seven emotional letters in your name, you're thoughtful and reserved, rarely expressing your emotions. Those with eight emotional letters have strong feelings and a strong need to excel. If you have nine emotional letters in your name, you enjoy receiving attention from others and may get pouty when you don't receive the attention you crave.

Number of intuitive letters: If you have no intuitive letters in your name, you're apt to lack interest in world affairs and prefer to see things in black and white rather than trusting impressions. Those who have one intuitive letter are inspired—solutions and ideas come to you quickly. If you have two intuitive letters in your name, you may be a bit extreme in your thinking but are sensitive to the feelings of others. Three intuitive letters indicate you may get psychic hunches, have the ability to inspire others, and are good with words. If you have four intuitive letters, you tend to enjoy the ceremonies connected with religion or tradition and like facts more than fiction. Those with five intuitive letters can think outside the box, are curious, and like to know "why." If you have six intuitive letters in your name, you have high ideals and could succeed as a minister or in a creative profession. Those with seven intuitive letters are perfectionists and sometimes want to mold others the way they think they should be. If you have eight intuitive letters in your name, you have intuitive instincts and can excel as a researcher or historian. It is not only unlikely, but almost impossible, to have nine intuitive letters in your name; however, if you're the one in a million who happens to have nine intuitive letters, you're a very unique person. You dwell in the abstract, are highly impressionable, and are a dreamer rather than a doer.

 DID YOU KNOW?

In most names, the intuitive letters are lacking—or at the very least, not found in abundance. Why? Intuition is a dynamic quality, and only a touch of it is generally needed in a person's life.

The Least You Need to Know

- The first vowel in your name is a good indicator of the inner you.
- The Inclusion Table organizes the meanings associated with your name.
- The number values you have an abundance of in your name are called Intensification Numbers. Your Intensification Numbers tell you about your special gifts and talents.
- The number values you are missing from your name are called your Karma Numbers. Your Karma Numbers tell you what qualities you have not as yet developed and the lessons you need to learn in your lifetime.

- The number of letter values you are missing, when subtracted from 9, yields your Subconscious Response Number. This number tells you how you act instinctively in an emergency.

- The Point of Security Number is simply the number of letters in a name. It tells you what characteristics will lead to your ultimate success.

- The Type and Traits Chart breaks down into physical (4s and 5s), mental (1s and 8s), emotional (2s, 3s, and 6s), and intuitive (7s and 9s) letters.

Progression of Letters and the Hidden Essence and Essence Numbers

As you learned in previous chapters, the letters in your name can be used to help you understand everything from your purpose in life to your inner and outer self. Now, I want to take it a step further and show you how your name can tell you what happens during every year of your life and the duration of those occurrences.

In this chapter, you learn how to progress the letters in your name and the significance behind those progressions. I then teach you how those progressed letters can help you calculate your Hidden Essence and Essence Numbers.

In This Chapter

- Progressing the letters of your first, middle, and last names
- The meaning of the progressed letters and progressed double letters
- The significance of Hidden Essence and Essence Numbers
- How to calculate the Hidden Essence and Essence Numbers
- Understanding the meaning behind your Hidden Essence and Essence Numbers

What Is a Progressed Letter?

A progressed letter is a letter that's repeated the number of times represented by its numeric value on your Life Chart (see Chapter 18). For example, if you have a D in your name, which has a numeric value of 4, you write that letter four times. The following table shows you the correspondence between letters and how many times you must repeat them.

Times to Repeat Letter	Letters
1	A, J, S
2	B, K, T
3	C, L, U
4	D, M, V
5	E, N, W
6	F, O, X
7	G, P, Y
8	H, Q, Z
9	I, R

Progressing the Letters in Your Name

Your first, middle, and last names should be progressed separately. If you have more than one first, middle, or last name, progress all your names exactly as they appear on your birth certificate. The following is a chart you can use to practice progressing your name. Before you start, write in the years associated with your respective ages. Note that this chart only goes up to age 32; when filling out your Life Chart, you'll progress your name all the way up to age 98.

Year																																	
Age	0	1	2	3	4	5	6	7	8	9	10	11	12	13	14	15	16	17	18	19	20	21	22	23	24	25	26	27	28	29	30	31	32
First Name																																	
Middle Name																																	
Middle Name 2																																	
Last Name																																	

To begin, progress your first name. As an example, if your first name is Jonathan, the progression would be JOOOOOONNNNNATTHHHHHHHHANNNNN, because J has a numeric value of 1, O has a numeric value of 6, N has a numeric value of 5, A has a numeric value of 1, T has a numeric value of 2, H has a numeric value of 8, A is (once again) 1, and N is (still) a 5. If necessary, repeat the progression process until you have a letter for every age. If your first name is actually two names but used as one (for example, Lee Ann or Billy Bob) and you have a middle name as well, progress your two-name first name together as one first name.

The following shows the First Name row for my daughter Jamie Lynn Simpson for the ages of 0 through 32.

Year	68	69	70	71	72	73	74	75	76	77	78	79	80	81	82	83	84	85	86	87	88	89	90	91	92	93	94	95	96	97	98	99	00
Age	0	1	2	3	4	5	6	7	8	9	10	11	12	13	14	15	16	17	18	19	20	21	22	23	24	25	26	27	28	29	30	31	32
First Name	J	A	M	M	M	M	I	I	I	I	I	I	I	I	I	E	E	E	E	E	J	A	M	M	M	M	I	I	I	I	I	I	I

Next, you should progress your middle name. Middle names are highly variable across the population—some people are no middle name, some have one, and some have more than one. Examples of this variability can be seen quite readily when you look at the British Monarchy. Queen Consort Anne Boleyn had no middle name; Queen Elizabeth II, the current monarch, was born Elizabeth Alexandra Mary Windsor; and George V was born George Frederick Ernest Albert Windsor.

Each middle name, if you have more than one, is treated as a separate entity and receives its own line on the chart. Because more than one middle name is uncommon and more than two is (barring royal birth) exceedingly rare, the chart I've provided has lines for two middle names. Some of you won't use either line, and only a few of you will find need for the second. If you do have three (or more) middle names, you'll need to make your own copy of the grid and add the extra lines. Then progress the letters of your middle name(s) just as you did your first name, repeating the progression as necessary.

Here's how Jamie's chart appears after her middle name has been progressed.

	68	69	70	71	72	73	74	75	76	77	78	79	80	81	82	83	84	85	86	87	88	89	90	91	92	93	94	95	96	97	98	99	00
Year	68	69	70	71	72	73	74	75	76	77	78	79	80	81	82	83	84	85	86	87	88	89	90	91	92	93	94	95	96	97	98	99	00
Age	0	1	2	3	4	5	6	7	8	9	10	11	12	13	14	15	16	17	18	19	20	21	22	23	24	25	26	27	28	29	30	31	32
First Name	J	A	M	M	M	M	I	I	I	I	I	I	I	I	I	E	E	E	E	E	J	A	M	M	M	M	I	I	I	I	I	I	I
Middle Name	L	L	L	Y	Y	Y	Y	Y	Y	Y	N	N	N	N	N	N	N	N	N	N	L	L	L	Y	Y	Y	Y	Y	Y	Y	N	N	N
Middle Name 2																																	

Finally, progress your last name. Unlike middle names, which are distinct, a hyphenated or compound last name is still a last name. For example, the composer Ludwig von Beethoven lacked a middle name, but had a two-word last name—von Beethoven. Similarly, world champion boxer Oscar De La Hoya lacks a middle name but has a three-word last name. As you did for your first and middle names, write down the progression, repeating as necessary until you have a letter for each age.

Jamie's progression, now including all three names, is displayed in the following chart.

	68	69	70	71	72	73	74	75	76	77	78	79	80	81	82	83	84	85	86	87	88	89	90	91	92	93	94	95	96	97	98	99	00
Year	68	69	70	71	72	73	74	75	76	77	78	79	80	81	82	83	84	85	86	87	88	89	90	91	92	93	94	95	96	97	98	99	00
Age	0	1	2	3	4	5	6	7	8	9	10	11	12	13	14	15	16	17	18	19	20	21	22	23	24	25	26	27	28	29	30	31	32
First Name	J	A	M	M	M	M	I	I	I	I	I	I	I	I	I	E	E	E	E	E	J	A	M	M	M	M	I	I	I	I	I	I	I
Middle Name	L	L	L	Y	Y	Y	Y	Y	Y	Y	N	N	N	N	N	N	N	N	N	N	L	L	L	Y	Y	Y	Y	Y	Y	Y	N	N	N
Middle Name 2																																	
Last Name	S	I	I	I	I	I	I	I	I	I	M	M	M	M	P	P	P	P	P	P	P	S	O	O	O	O	O	O	N	N	N	N	N

DID YOU KNOW?

The Germans seem to be particularly adept at complicating the letter progressions. For example, the politically popular German Minister of Defense at the time of this writing has a hyphenated given name, eight middle names, and a four-word surname—Karl-Theodor Maria Johann Jacob Phillipp Franz Joseph Sylvester von und zu Guttenberg. That must be really difficult to fit on a driver's license or credit card—especially if you include the title Freiherr (Baron), which precedes the surname!

Progressed Letter Meanings

When you progress a letter, its value determines the length of time that its influence is felt. The following looks at the meaning behind the progression of each letter and details the special significance of double letters in a name.

Progression of A

The letter A has a progression value of 1, meaning things begin and end within one year. During this period, you're going to encounter new opportunities, ideas, and contacts.

This time period may bring a change in living conditions—either a move or trips—often without much notice. You may also have visitors or welcome a new baby into your immediate or extended family.

If you're action-oriented and determined during this time, you can expect success and advancement. Take initiative, but always use good judgment before taking the first step. Bite your tongue and avoid sarcasm for now.

During this one-year period, you have a newfound sense of determination and increased mental agility. Though it's difficult, take the time to think things through and be patient. You likely have important decisions to make and may need to make some type of sacrifice because of them.

Progression of B

B indicates a two-year period filled with professional and personal accomplishment and advancement. Art and science may be at the forefront during this period. While attention to details is critical to your success, you likely don't have the inclination to deal with minutiae. Delays are also inevitable, so factor extra time into any plans.

Family and home are important now. This is the time to make your surroundings comfortable and beautiful. Keep your bags packed, as you may take multiple short trips during this period. It's also possible that a short-term move is necessary for career gains.

Emotions are running high now, so try not to take things personally, and listen to others who may not have an emotional investment in matters. Take extra care of your health during this period of stress and tension.

You may feel a strong emotional connection to someone during this period. Be careful, as that person may be involved with someone else. Although you may experience a strong desire to marry right now, you're feeling incredibly misunderstood by those around you.

Progression of C

During this three-year span due to the letter C, you're going to focus on personal and financial improvements. It's a time of optimism, confidence, drive, and determination. There may be legal papers, written notices, and letters to deal with right now. You may feel a bit impulsive, but patience and willpower pay off in the end.

You have a strong need to change something in your life right now. This could be a new career path, home renovations or a move, or the end of a relationship. While marital differences are indicated, they can be averted with a strong commitment to the relationship and selfless behavior. The grass isn't always greener, so think carefully before pursing an extramarital affair. Gossip and scandal surround you during this period, so avoid anything that could set tongues wagging.

This is an excellent time to pursue intellectual or artistic interests. Success springs from your newfound creativity and inspiration, so consider attending a lecture or signing up for a painting class.

While you're in the mood to pamper yourself, your extravagance will likely lead to buyer's remorse. You may also find your social calendar brimming with activities and new friends, so be careful not to overcommit yourself.

Progression of D

Work and responsibility consume you during this four-year period for the letter D. This is the time to put your nose to the grindstone and take care of property issues, financial affairs, and family interests. You're building a foundation for your future right now, and your hard work and practicality will pay off down the road.

During this period, you're going to be faced with challenges and problems that need to be tackled head-on. Avoidance of these difficulties will only lead to disagreements. Resist any sense of limitation and restriction and work toward following through with the opportunities that come to you right now.

Be sure to pay careful attention to all legal documents to ensure that all Ts are crossed and Is are dotted. You also may have a tendency to misplace things related to money, so keep an eye on your purse, wallet, and financial documents at all times.

Although there may be small quarrels, family and friends bring you great pleasure during this period. Partnerships bring money to you now, helping you gain a new attitude toward life. This time is filled with travel and lots of activity, so be sure to establish a healthy lifestyle to keep your energy levels high.

PYTHAGORAS SAYS

During the four-year progression of the letter D, you may feel burdened by work and family responsibilities. Now is the time to get your financial house in order to ensure security down the road.

Progression of E

During this highly social and intellectual five-year period due to the letter E, you learn a great deal from many types of experiences—expect constant change, opportunity, and excitement.

You're particularly analytical and intellectual now, and these talents may be helpful in working with the public. But this isn't just a time for helping others; allow yourself to accept help from others during this period.

There may be a sense of dissatisfaction or confusion around your home now. For example, children and neighbors may present more challenges than usual. Renew your commitment to your home and family to dissuade any difficulties. Getting away through travel can help bring fun during this period.

You have a strong desire for freedom right now and may have a tendency to break rules and regulations. To prevent disagreements and legal troubles, sidestep any arguments with business associates, neighbors, or loved ones. If governmental or legal issues arise, face them head-on.

This is a time for you to walk the straight and narrow. If you're careless, your marriage can suffer, so this is not the time to enter into a sudden marriage or separation.

Progression of F

This six-year period for the letter F centers around love, marriage, home, and the community. During this time of growth and development, you experience financial gain through your dealings with the community.

Your sense of domestic responsibility drives you to repair or even renovate your home, making it a more beautiful place to enjoy with your family. There may also be unusual circumstances surrounding loved ones—for example, marriages, separations, or adoptions may not go as planned. This is a time to make sure loved ones know they are important to you; any selfish behavior could lead to a loss of an important relationship.

You also feel a strong sense of responsibility to others, driving you to help those less fortunate or in need. Associations with corporations or businesses can result in large and wide-reaching contracts or projects. Be careful not to overburden yourself now—enjoy the scenery on your road to success.

Money is on your mind right now, so be careful to avoid a materialistic outlook on life. Focus on charity endeavors, and the money will find its way to you.

Progression of G

During this seven-year period due to the letter G, you experience firsthand that knowledge is power. Using your intellect and training, you can carry out large business arrangements on a broad scale. You are highly influential now and have a deep understanding of others' motivations and desires.

Money is in the forefront now, and the first five years of this period bring financial gain. Luck is on your side, so expect to win the lottery or some type of raffle. It's important at this time to be responsible to ensure the long-term enjoyment of your home and improved finances.

This is a time of careful evaluation to avoid unexpected developments that could bring confusion and turmoil. Take the time to consider all available options, and don't overestimate your ability to deliver on your promises. You may find that others may unexpectedly oppose your plans, which could lead to slight disappointment in the last two years of this period.

Although this is a time of pleasure and happiness, you may be faced with the illness of a loved one. While you may experience occasional feelings of "Why me?" this is a time of strengthened love and friendship.

Progression of H

During this especially busy eight-year period indicated by the letter H, you advance professionally, financially, and socially and your hard work, excellent judgment, and skills are rewarded.

In this period, you likely find yourself in positions of leadership and increased responsibility, although challenges make it difficult to maintain this role. Keep your eye on the future and use your strong mental abilities to meet the position's many requirements. Your ability to recognize human nature comes in handy when evaluating individuals with whom you may enter into business arrangements.

Your executive skills may be helpful in community or civic activities or even politics. Projects and organizations are going to thrive under your direction, supervision, and organization; through these efforts, you have a chance to interact with people of importance and receive recognition for your efforts. This is also a time for writing, speaking, research, and membership in professional or philanthropic groups.

While you are likely to make money during this period, your expenses are going to typically match your income—so be careful to not overspend. Additional costs during this time may come from extra care needed by a loved one or home repairs.

Progression of I

This nine-year period due to the letter I is one of money, financial protection, and prosperity. You are the only thing in the way of your success! During this time, you attract people and opportunities that bring fortune your way.

Emotions run high now, so you must work to keep feelings under control. Otherwise, any moodiness can lead to a loss of opportunity, such as if you fail to make a good impression on a potential business associate. Demonstrate your strong character now to ensure your success.

During this period, you can use your creativity and imagination to beautify your home. You may even choose to move to a suburb in order to enjoy the spaciousness, slower pace, and quieter surroundings of "country" life.

Others may be jealous of your success during this period. No matter how others treat you, behave with love, tolerance, and compassion. Rather than fighting with those who are trying to bring you down, focus on inspiring those who are ready to hear your message, as your influence is very high right now. When it comes to romance, be especially careful with affairs of the heart; suitors may not really be who and what they purport to be.

While this is overall a happy time for you, there may be interludes of discord or opposition at work. It's possible that you may experience a loss, even if it's something small, like keys or a package.

Progression of J

During this one-year period indicated by the letter J, your life is going to take on a new direction. You're feeling especially daring and ready to create your own destiny now. This is a time for you to settle down, accomplish much, and progress in any area of interest or profession you choose.

In addition to an increased sense of initiative, you enjoy more authority at this time, possibly through a promotion at work. This may mean a change of office location or increased travel during this period. While you may feel increased pressure to perform, your strong will and fierce determination should open doors for you. Expect to head up projects and teams and deal with large corporations.

Your mind is on justice right now, and at this time, you work to ensure fairness for all at any cost. Someone around you may be dishonest, resulting in a change of your attitude toward this person.

This period may involve the birth or adoption of a child, while a loved one potentially deals with illness or even death. It's also possible that you may move to a new home or face some type of disruption, such as renovation or construction. While going through all this upheaval, be especially careful, as you are more accident-prone during this period.

Progression of K

During this two-year period of excitement and activity indicated by the letter K, you experience a series of unusual events. Whether you're the recipient of an inheritance or elope after a whirlwind romance, this is a time to expect the unexpected.

Emotions, particularly those dealing with love, are running high. During this period, you're prone to fall in love quickly. Be careful that the object of your affection has your best interests at heart and is honest and forthcoming. In either your professional or personal life, you may encounter an unscrupulous person who tries to swindle or take advantage of you. This is a time for extreme caution in financial matters; avoid signing over property or large amounts of money.

While others may share their opinions and advice with you, don't be afraid to stand on your own two feet. Your strong intuition during this period may save you heartache and disappointment down the road.

You're always willing to help others, so you may find yourself caring for a loved one during a brief illness and inevitable recovery.

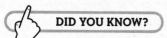

DID YOU KNOW?

During the two-year progression of the letter K, you may be traveling more as part of your family responsibilities. Fortunately, these occasional impromptu trips will be brief in duration.

Progression of L

This three-year period due to the letter L revolves around love, family, and friends. Others are attracted to your charm during this time, and your popularity and networking ability bring you advancement and enjoyment. You're apt to change your mind frequently during this period, so you should take care to avoid being impatient, critical, and selfish.

This is a time for self-improvement. Take time to study and research music, art, or other creative pursuits. Your life is well-balanced during this period. This is a time to enjoy the finer things in life, through an active social life brimming with entertainment and travel.

In areas of the heart, others turn to you as a confidante and for a soft shoulder to cry on. While you may make sacrifices for and possibly be separated from loved ones, you're going to be rewarded with appreciation and sincere thanks.

Progression of M

During this four-year period indicated by the letter M, you're going to be very active as you plan and build for the future. If you start planning in the first year, your goal will be realized by the end of the four-year span.

In addition to business affairs, you deal with property and financial matters at this time. Be responsible and tend to the details to ensure success.

When it comes to family, you're going to be surrounded by children—either yours or those of loved ones—during this period. Your in-laws or a mother figure may also figure prominently during this period and could require your assistance. Personally, you may have health matters during this time, so have a full physical during the first year to avoid problems down the road.

This is the time to hold your tongue—the less you say, the better. Use your quiet determination to move through any disagreements or opposition from family, friends, or business associates. Also, be honest and sincere in all your professional and personal dealings to ensure success in the long run.

Progression of N

Indicated by the letter N, this is a five-year period of progress on a mental and material level. This is a good time to study something of interest and gain position in the world with your new talents. With a strong desire to be constantly on the go, you may be spending more time away from home.

Financial interest is high right now, and money can be gained if you resist restlessness and keep your nose to the grindstone. This is a time to renew your interest in your career for long-term success.

If there's anything you've put off doing, now is the time to tie up loose ends. However, there may be some delays regarding legal or financial settlements.

You may be feeling somewhat unsettled at this time—perhaps you're unhappy with your relationship, or someone is pushing your buttons. This is a time for couples to focus on each other and grow closer.

Progression of O

Money, legal matters, and business surround this six-year period due to the letter O. This is a time to be very introspective and have a strong sense of responsibility.

This period involves the protection of children and loved ones; therefore, this is an excellent time to create or revise wills, trust funds, and other legal documents within the family. You're also enjoying your home and spending time with your family, and your quiet, happy home helps keep you healthy both emotionally and physically. In terms of your health, make sure to get enough rest. And if surgery is required during this period, it's likely that it won't be serious and recovery will be swift.

This is a time for sound investments, not speculation. So avoid lending or borrowing money right now. You may enjoy financial gain or gifts from a romantic interest. Secrets may be uncovered during this period, so look for what is below the surface.

You may be involved in your community right now, perhaps with a religious or artistic group. Participate in a club or join the company softball team. Use this time to help others, and you will be rewarded.

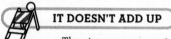 **IT DOESN'T ADD UP**

The six-year progression of the letter O can bring secrets, misrepresentations, or omissions in your personal or business dealings. Don't take anyone or anything at face value—with a little digging, the truth will be revealed.

Progression of P

During this seven-year period, P stands for power. You're going to have many opportunities in the area of science, education, or specialized skills. Patience, perseverance, and a positive mental attitude are essential to success during this progression.

This is an excellent time to develop new skills and discover hidden talents. Anything you undertake at the beginning of the cycle will be mastered by the end and may lead to financial gain, perhaps through the written word. Right now is also a time to read, observe others, study, and explore areas of interest. Mystical or spiritual studies may be of particular interest to you.

You may feel tired or overwhelmed by others and their problems. Any moodiness or fears you're experiencing now can inhibit your progress during this period, so cast aside those feelings and any hesitation and dare to use your talents. Avoid arguments and bitter words, as you'll inevitably regret what you've said.

Relationships may seem troubled during this period. Understanding and compassion are the keys to resolving any issues now. When it comes to your own well-being, this is the time to get plenty of rest, eat healthy, and give yourself time alone.

You may receive an inheritance or other financial gain from your mother's side of the family. Whatever you receive, it's possible that you'll pass it along to someone else.

Progression of Q

This eight-year period indicated by the letter Q is filled with unusual pursuits, methods, and occurrences. With hard work, you can excel at anything you take on at this time.

You may undertake a new activity during this time or go about your work through innovative methods. Children are important to you now, so you may find yourself teaching or speaking to youth groups. You're stimulated and energized to tackle old problems in new ways. You're an inspiration to others right now, so with careful planning and an eye on the future, you could turn your innovation into income.

Good judgment and a keen understanding of human nature are especially important right now. There may be misunderstandings at home that arise from your new areas of thought and interest. Use reason and compassion to work through any difficulties.

You're highly imaginative right now, which makes this an excellent time for writing. You may also pursue unusual interests or hobbies during this period. The mountains are calling your name right now, so enjoy the outdoors and fresh air.

Progression of R

During this nine-year period, you're going to experience many ups and downs as you gain a better understanding of mankind and life.

This is a busy time that brings you to a position of prominence. You feel a strong sense of self-confidence right now and are able to carry out large-scale projects at home or work. Because your responsibilities are great during this period, your character and principles are going to be called upon to accomplish your goals. Your efforts as you explore these great opportunities are rewarded with love, position, money, and recognition.

If you're married, your marriage brings you great enjoyment during this time. Give of yourself freely, as a selfish attitude limits your success. Also, be quick to forgive others.

You may experience difficulties when a business partner is dishonest or deceitful; it may involve legal matters that can continue over an extended period of time. Remember that honesty is the best policy in all dealings. Also, save for additional expenses that may arise toward the end of the nine-year cycle.

All things creative call your name right now, and you find great delight in art, literature, food, and the finer things in life. You may travel abroad to study cuisine or art during this time.

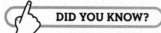

> **DID YOU KNOW?**
>
> During the nine-year progression of the letter R, you may experience emotional highs and lows. While business dealings may result in disappointment regarding a trusted partner, your personal life will bring you great joy.

Progression of S

Due to the letter S, this is a one-year period of suddenness and change. It also indicates a time filled with creative pursuits.

Because the only thing constant right now is change, it's difficult to make plans right now. Try to roll with the punches and adapt to your ever-changing circumstances. This could be the start of something big that won't realize itself until later in your life, so try to relax and avoid tension and nervousness this year.

In matters of love, you may experience some type of change of heart. There may be sudden relationships or a love-at-first-sight experience, likely resulting from feelings of loneliness during this period.

In your personal life, a family member may need your help now. You may also show an increased interest in religion during this time.

Progression of T

During this two-year period indicated by the letter T, you enjoy advancement in your career and an improved financial situation. Your mind is quick and you're especially disciplined right now, so use these skills to step into a new cycle in your life.

Partnerships are important to you right now, so you may find yourself working in groups toward a united goal. Others may try to disrupt your plans, but use self-control to stay the course. You may experience deception from a business partner or loved one. Therefore, do your due diligence to look into the background of anyone under consideration for a long-term partnership, whether it's in work or romance.

You may feel especially nervous right now. Take care of your health and try to keep your emotions on an even keel. Also, try to avoid arguments, as they will likely lead to disappointment. Friends can provide a great source of support and help for you during this period.

While you will likely feel a sense of relief at the end of this two-year period, the lessons learned will serve you well in the future.

Progression of U

Indicated by the letter U, this is a three-year period that focuses on career and intellectual pursuits. You are presented with multiple opportunities—both professional and social—during this time.

This is a time for expression both at work and through a creative outlet. You're also blessed in your personal life, where you're showered with gifts. Be warned, however, that love affairs entered into right now likely won't last.

Health issues, although minor, appear during this period. You have an increased risk of catching several colds right now, so be sure to get plenty of rest. A family member may also fall ill and call upon you for help and support.

Try to let your guard down a little, as you tend to be more self-protective and self-centered right now. Friends and associates bring you enjoyable changes and events during this period, so don't be afraid to let them in.

 PYTHAGORAS SAYS

Tap into your creativity during the three-year progression of the letter U. Although you may be a bit emotional, you can soothe your soul by finding enjoyment and inspiration in art, writing, music, or other creative pursuits.

Progression of V

During this four-year period due to the letter V, you're going to be especially introspective, giving great thought to life and business. There's also a lot of work to be done during this period, so establish a routine and hunker down.

It's possible that a new business venture will land in your lap during this period. While you may experience some type of disappointment in your career, a surprise (perhaps a promotion or opportunity) may bring added responsibility and reward. Be practical and tend to any pending financial, real estate, and legal issues now—you may have long-standing debts that should be cleared up during this period.

Caution is your keyword during this period. Allow yourself to analyze situations and people carefully before proceeding. Your intuition is high right now, so trust your gut. This is also a time to watch your spending more carefully, as regret over a large purchase is likely.

In your personal life, you have a strong desire for travel, luxury, and the finer things in life right now. Appearance is important to you at this time, making you especially fastidious about clothes and accessories. You may also pursue spiritual or philosophical interests during this period.

Progression of W

During this five-year period due to the letter W, you're going to experience peaks and valleys that may lead to a change in your life's path. Scattered in many directions, you have a difficult time focusing and making decisions. Set emotions aside and seek counsel from those you trust. This kind of communication is important to you now, so you may find that you're calling, writing, texting, and emailing more than usual.

There's a sense of surprise during this time. You may take a sudden trip, move unexpectedly, or change your career path. It's possible you may even retire during this cycle. There may also be real-estate opportunities now or something that involves underground work, such as mining, oil, or natural resources. Whatever you do, be honest in all dealings during this cycle, as any secrets or untruths will be uncovered otherwise.

Things are moving at a fast pace now, so resist the tendency to be nervous. You have an intense desire to rearrange your life right now, so seize the opportunity to mix up your routines and know that personal growth will come from this process. In the end, you'll see things in a whole new light.

Because you're protected by the Universe during this period, something or someone keeps you from making a big mistake. While it may be disappointing initially, it benefits you in the long run.

Progression of X

Family is everything to you during this six-year period indicated by the letter X. You feel especially close to your immediate family and experience a strong sense of loyalty and commitment. Be cautious of possessiveness, though, as someone may push back if they're feeling smothered. Parent-child relationships may also take on an unusual angle during this period. For example, there may be an adoption or a secret surrounding a child.

Business is good right now, especially for those involved in serving the public or manufacturing goods for everyday needs. Avoid arguments during this period, as they will be fruitless; take the high road now and hold fast to your strong values and ideals. You're courageous now, but remember to consider the needs and desires of others before acting.

Your memory is like a steel trap during this period, so this is an excellent time to enjoy music or take up an instrument. You may also crave quiet right now, but you'll have a difficult time acquiring it.

Progression of Y

Indicated by the letter Y, this is an eight-year period of spirituality, insight, and kindness. During this time, you have a strong need to learn about and gain insight into humanity. When it comes to your own life's path, you have a choice to make when faced with a fork in the road about which direction you should go.

You have a strong desire to elevate your existence and life on a more intellectual level. This is the time for you stand on your own two feet and face the world head on. If you're pursuing advancement in your career, a delay is likely. However, try to avoid feeling disappointed and understand that what's truly yours can't be taken away from you.

You may be experiencing a lack of interest in your romantic life right now. It's only because you're distracted by your own interests during this period. Also, because you're pursuing so many avenues, be sure to get enough rest, as you're likely to tire easily right now. Make sure your family stays healthy and well-rested, too, as illness may appear in the men in your life.

 PYTHAGORAS SAYS

During the eight-year progression of the letter Y, you may be at a crossroads in life and not sure which direction to turn. Instead of participating in hectic group events, allow yourself plenty of alone time to rest, read, and reflect.

Progression of Z

During this nine-year period due to the letter Z, you're going to be full of revelation. This is the time to start a new position or undertake a new activity or interest. You may also develop a new belief system during this period, as you have a strong ability to look below the surface to see what's really happening.

Through mental acuity, study, and good old-fashioned hard work, you can accomplish a great deal during this period. Your studies center around writing, and you're especially gifted in learning new languages right now. Whatever you decide to do, there are opportunities for advancement and recognition.

Your career may require travel during this period and will ultimately result in improved position and finances. If governmental work arises, stay level-headed and use your innate reasoning skills.

You may have an interest in spiritual or psychological studies right now. Because of this, you may bring together others who share your interest and pursue knowledge as a group. Mystery surrounds you right now, so be sure to look beneath the surface of others to uncover any possible deception.

Double-Letter Progressions

Letters that appear twice in succession (such as the "Aa" that begins the name "Aaron") are especially significant, with their period of influence doubled. Unfortunately, the double-letter progressions often carry twice the stress, pressure, and health issues of their single-letter versions. The following are the meanings behind double-letter progressions.

> **PYTHAGORAS SAYS**
>
> Additionally, later in this chapter, when you calculate the Hidden Essence Number and look at the letters in your name vertically, look for double letters repeated in the first, middle, or last names during the same year.

AA, JJ, SS: During this period, you're incredibly busy and feel as though nothing is coming of your extra effort. Because of this extra responsibility, you may feel tense. Make time to eat healthy, exercise, and get enough rest, as your physical and emotional health could be at risk now.

BB, KK, TT: This is a difficult time emotionally for you. You're extra sensitive to criticism and could possibly obsess about things over which you have no control. Your nerves are on edge, and you may feel as though you're carrying the weight of the world on your shoulders. A loss of a loved one or deception by others is also possible during this time.

CC, LL, UU: This is a time when you can be especially accident prone, so take great care in your everyday activities. Sensuality is important to you now, but be cautious about the possibility of sexually transmitted diseases. If you're a woman, you may experience some type of reproductive illness or surgery.

DD, MM, VV: This may be a time of health issues. Those with a DD may experience a longer recovery time than the MM progression. If you have a VV progression, make the time for a full physical, possibly including a full-body scan, to ensure that all internal organs are in working order.

EE, NN, WW: Health is an issue during this progression; if you're a woman, you may experience problems with reproductive organs. You may also be especially nervous at this time. Accidents are indicated, so take great care in daily activities and avoid any unnecessary danger.

FF, OO, XX: These progressions indicate coronary issues with yourself or a loved one. Take the time to have a full physical, including an EKG and a stress test, to identify any underlying issues. The XX progression may indicate extreme unhappiness and mental-health issues. Don't hesitate to speak with a professional if you're feeling despondent during this time.

GG, PP, YY: During this period, you or someone you love may suffer from long-term illness— use your research skills to uncover the best treatment and newest research. You may feel especially lonely right now, but take great care in choosing companions and confidantes, as treachery from others is likely.

HH, QQ, ZZ: This is a time of critical health issues. Pay attention to the smallest change in your physical well-being and see a doctor to address any concerns early. Tension and stress are high, so get plenty of rest to ensure your mental state.

II, RR: During this period of personal and emotional sacrifice, you may feel pulled in many directions. Accidents are indicated, and international travel should be avoided, if possible.

Now that you know the meaning of each progressed letter, let's move on to find the Essence and Hidden Essence Numbers determined by the progressed letters in your name.

What Are Essence and Hidden Essence Numbers?

Your Hidden Essence Numbers are determined by adding the numeric values of the letters in your given name. The numeric value of every letter determines how long each influence lasts. For example, the influence of an E lasts for five years because its numeric value is 5. Similarly, the influence of an O with a numeric value of 6 lasts six years.

Each year your Hidden Essence Number is based on the numeric values of the combination of letters progressing in your first, middle, and last names and is a yearly indicator of the possible influences in your life during that particular time frame.

If a person has a first, middle, and last name, the Hidden Essence Number is generally a double-digit number. For example, if you are progressing an E (numeric value 5) from your first name, an A (numeric value 1) from your middle name, and an R (numeric value 9) from your last name, your Hidden Essence Number for that particular year is 15.

Your Essence Numbers are the single-digit numbers derived by reducing the double digits of the Hidden Essence Number.

Calculating Your Hidden Essence and Essence Numbers

To calculate your Hidden Essence Numbers, you simply add the letter values in each "Age" column. To get the Essence Number, you reduce that Hidden Essence Number to a single digit, if it isn't already. If it can't be reduced, the Essence Number is the same as the Hidden Essence Number.

The following shows Jamie's chart through age 32 that includes both her Hidden Essence and Essence Numbers.

Year	68	69	70	71	72	73	74	75	76	77	78	79	80	81	82	83	84	85	86	87	88	89	90	91	92	93	94	95	96	97	98	99	00
Age	0	1	2	3	4	5	6	7	8	9	10	11	12	13	14	15	16	17	18	19	20	21	22	23	24	25	26	27	28	29	30	31	32
First Name	J	A	M	M	M	M	I	I	I	I	I	I	I	I	I	E	E	E	E	E	J	A	M	M	M	M	I	I	I	I	I	I	I
Middle Name	L	L	L	Y	Y	Y	Y	Y	Y	Y	N	N	N	N	N	N	N	N	N	N	L	L	L	Y	Y	Y	Y	Y	Y	Y	N	N	N
Middle Name 2																																	
Last Name	S	I	I	I	I	I	I	I	I	I	M	M	M	M	P	P	P	P	P	P	P	S	O	O	O	O	O	O	N	N	N	N	N
Hidden Essence Number	5	13	16	20	20	20	25	25	25	25	18	18	18	18	21	17	17	17	17	17	11	5	13	17	17	17	22	22	21	21	19	19	19
Essence Number	5	4	7	2	2	2	7	7	7	7	9	9	9	9	3	8	8	8	8	8	2	5	4	8	8	8	4	4	3	3	1	1	1

Hidden Essence and Essence Number Meanings

The following is a breakdown of the meanings of the Essence Numbers, grouped with the Hidden Essence Numbers that can reduce to that Essence Number.

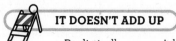

IT DOESN'T ADD UP

Realistically, you can't have a Hidden Essence Number of 1 because there are always at least two numbers to add—the one from a letter in your first name and the one from a letter in your last name.

Essence Number 1

This is a lucky time for new directions, new ideas, new contacts, new occupations, new enterprises, and new environments. Your leadership skills are important, and a change where your job is concerned (perhaps a promotion or other advancement) is likely during this time. You may also be called upon to make an important decision based on an event that's occurring in your life now. Perhaps you're offered a sizeable promotion but accepting it would require you to move to another state, or you're happy living in your home and a real estate agent knocks on your front door and tells you her client wants to pay you $1 million in cash for your home. Be sure to keep your bags packed, as this is a time for quick getaways or extended vacations.

Hidden Essence Number 10: This period brings improvement in all areas of your life. You're going to feel bolder and more confident, which corresponds to your new wave of ambition during this period. You also have more decisions to make, and are able to overcome difficulties and carry out your plans to fruition. During this period, remain open to new friendships—they may be beneficial down the road. Also, you may be separated from your loved ones for a short period of time due to personal or professional obligations. During this Hidden Essence Number, you may be hearing about or dealing with children, either your own or those of relatives or close friends.

Hidden Essence Number 19: This period likely brings some type of advancement for you. Although you may experience a bit of trouble or discord, money is going to find its way to you in some way. And while you're presented with multiple opportunities, it's best if you consult a professional before making a decision on your own. Marriage is involved under this number, so you may get married, improve your relationship, or part ways at this time. Your temper may run high during this period, so think of the other person, remember the Golden Rule, and avoid acting selfishly. Your character is also tested during this period; if you take the high road, Essence Number 19 brings honor, advancement, happiness, and success.

Hidden Essence Number 28: This Hidden Essence Number has many contradictions and involves the learning of important life lessons. This may be a period of legal difficulty, so be wary of trusting others you don't know well and entering into new business partnerships. You're especially prone to financial losses during this period, so this isn't the time to make investments. In your desire for change, be careful with whom you become involved. You may have to or choose to start your life over during this period with a new marriage, job, or home.

Hidden Essence Number 37: This is a fortunate number that promotes friendship and love. Partnerships of all kinds—whether business or personal—are favorable now. In your personal life, romance abounds. During a Hidden Essence Number 37, business profits should be plentiful, provided you use ordinary caution regarding the source of the profits. You also experience a sense of peaceful contentment; the outlook is good for a rosy future.

Essence Number 2

Cooperation and patience are essential to your success during this period—there's no need to rush. Don't hesitate to accept help from others when offered. It's also important for you to maintain a positive outlook and a good disposition at this time. Pay attention to the details now—there are a lot of loose ends to be tied up and many little tasks to be accomplished.

Hidden Essence Number 11: This is an important Hidden Essence Number that can bring many lessons to be learned. Patience needs to be used in all of your relationships and business affairs. Don't be surprised if there's a sudden break-up, crisis, or emotional shock to deal with during this time. For example, you may hear of an illness of a relative, so be prepared to lend a helping hand. There's a sense of suddenness in many of your dealings, which may lead you to unexpectedly enter or exit a relationship. Take the time to develop inner peace now—be still, listen to your heart, and know. Be careful of deceit, illusion, and delusion from others.

 PYTHAGORAS SAYS

It's rare to have a single-digit Hidden Essence Number because of the average number of letters in most names. However, Essence Numbers are always one digit because they are the double-digit Hidden Essence Number reduced to a single digit.

Hidden Essence Number 20: This is not a time for dreams or fanciful thoughts—this is a time for action. Keep your eye on the future as you progress through this period, and understand that you may face judgment, obstacles, and delays along your path. Relationships and companionship may also be on your mind now. Take the time to rest, and be especially aware of low energy or other symptoms that could signal a hidden illness. This is a period of change, with many ups and downs, making it a good time to study something of a mystical or religious nature. Keep your bags packed, because short pleasure trips are apt to be on your agenda.

Hidden Essence Number 29: During this Hidden Essence Number, you are cautioned to avoid deception, deceit, and dishonesty from others. Be careful of the friends and romantic companions you choose, because what appears on the surface may not be reality. Uncertainties and unexpected dangers come from dealing with romantic partners at this time, as there's a chance the love isn't genuine. You also may feel compelled to visit ailing friends or family members at this time, which likely leads to physical and emotional exhaustion. Try to dissipate your nervous energy during this period through exercise or a hobby.

Essence Number 3

This is a period filled with social activities, friends, and the problems of those friends. Inclined to expand your horizons now, you're apt to take a trip to study history or cultures. You may have an increased desire to work—not because you have to, but rather because you desire the company of others. A little extra income to improve your surroundings won't hurt, though. Be cautious of your finances during this time, and avoid reckless spending of money. During this period, you may be especially focused on the immediate rather than the future, which could lead to a hasty marriage. Be conscientious and fulfill all obligations during this period, as doing so could garner you a raise or put you in a position of authority. Not only do you give orders during an Essence Number 3, you also expect others to follow your orders, which may or may not happen.

Hidden Essence Number 12: This Hidden Essence Number is a peculiar number, in that it involves a woman a little bit older and a little bit smarter than you. Unfortunately, you struggle in your dealings with her. This isn't a time to acknowledge past regrets and mistakes—move on and let old feelings go. To avoid feeling anxious, use your creative imagination and plan for your future. While you may take trips for pleasure, be careful when choosing your traveling companions to avoid gossip or scandal. Also, be cautious when choosing confidants and avoid false friends—look below the surface and listen to what's not being said. While you may be inclined to make amends now, be sure the other party is willing to listen and accept your apology with the spirit in which it is given. You're able to express your ideas in writing or speaking during this period, and doing so may lead to career advancement. Hearing about or dealing with children—either yours or those of someone close to you—may be involved during the Hidden Essence Year Number 12.

Hidden Essence Number 21: This Hidden Essence Number is a mystical number that represents the highest goal to which people aim. You have a happy-go-lucky attitude during this period, in spite of the emotional ups and downs and disappointments that appear here and there. During this time, you need to correct any mistakes you've made in your recent past. It's time to stand on your own two feet and be courageous and determined in whatever you undertake. Also, be generous yet businesslike in all of your affairs. You're apt to yield to your business partner or spouse, setting aside your own desires to keep the peace. During this time, focus on yourself and what you're doing, rather than being concerned with what others are doing. This is also an excellent time to follow artistic or creative pursuits, whether it's studying plants for making perfume or preparing and presenting food.

Hidden Essence Number 30: This Hidden Essence Number brings opportunities for advancement in your career and romantic life. During this period, you're going to have many irons in the fire on a mental level, allowing you to pursue many business opportunities simultaneously. Also, if you've been advised to have surgery, this is the perfect time to do so. If a health issue arises, it's likely not a serious problem and usually involves the mouth, throat, or tongue. You feel superior to others around you during this time and are apt to put any desires for monetary gain aside for the time being.

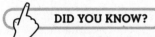 **DID YOU KNOW?**

In a Hidden Essence Number 30, others find you especially attractive. If you're married or in a committed relationship, you'll experience a deepening of your love. If you're single, you'll enjoy multiple romantic prospects.

Essence Number 4

This is a time to be conscientious and get your life and affairs in proper order. During this period, unknown facts come to light regarding a situation that has been puzzling you. Even though your life may seem to be moving at a snail's pace, be responsible and keep your nose to the grindstone to see positive results near the end of this period. Even if you feel restricted or limited, there's work to be done, so do it! Also, be aware that relatives or in-laws may make demands on your time and pocketbook during this period. Now is a good time to schedule a checkup and maintain good health habits. Even if you feel melancholy or lonely during this time, try not to be too sensitive or get your feelings hurt.

Hidden Essence Number 13: This Hidden Essence Number brings complications that can be solved by responsibility and hard work. It's a period of change, both big and small. On the job front, you could be transferred to a higher position with more responsibility. At home, you could have an extended visitor or even move. You're also faced with many demands from relatives, including lots of tasks for you to complete for them, during this period. Law prevails now, making it probable that you're going to receive a settlement of some kind or that you need to go to court. Don't despair if the settlement isn't as much as you wanted or expected—everything will work out for the best in the long run. You may also feel as if you're being held down by someone or something beyond your control at this time—have patience.

Hidden Essence Number 22: This Hidden Essence warns of illusions and delusions. Be cautious of false friends and bad advice. In your desire to help others, you may find yourself dissatisfied or upset. Take great care in making decisions during this period, because you'll likely regret your poor choices later. If you're required to work in a way that you feel is beneath you, try to avoid resentment. You may also experience some form of disappointment where money is concerned during this time. Practice moderation and financial responsibility—for example, by paying your bills on time. You're apt to hear of the usual run-of-the-mill illness of a child around you, which is nothing to be worried about. This is also the time to improve yourself and not be concerned with the activities and actions of others.

Hidden Essence Number 31: During this period, you may be inclined to spend time alone and isolate yourself more than usual. Also, finances are important now—you could receive money through the sale of land, real estate, or other material property. You may even collect from some sort of settlement, such as an inheritance, insurance claim, or legal matter. Even though you're self-contained and self-content now, make sure to avoid being selfish.

Essence Number 5

This is a busy period, with lots of activity; you may feel as if you're being pushed in one direction and pulled from another. There may be a tendency to leave things unfinished and procrastinate during this time, as you often drop or defer uninteresting responsibilities for something more enjoyable and exciting. You also have a strong desire to be constantly moving and are inclined to take short trips during this period. Follow the laws of the land at this time. Heed the speed limits and pay particular attention when preparing your taxes; otherwise, you're likely to get caught!

Hidden Essence Number 14: This Hidden Essence Number is the number of transition and continual excitement. When you have nervous energy, slow down and don't run around in circles, accomplishing nothing. Also, avoid quarrels that could lead to legal troubles and separations. Now is an excellent time to use your progressive ideas to create new projects and pursue new interests. When you're honest, investments and sound entrepreneurial ventures can be especially fruitful during this time. Use sound judgment when choosing companions and friends, because you may be especially trusting and even gullible now.

> **DID YOU KNOW?**
>
> The Hidden Essence Number 14 is a time when someone may try to sweep you off your feet. Be careful to not let your romantic fantasies cloud your good judgment or you could be led astray.

Hidden Essence Number 23: You're filled with cleverness and quickness of thought during this period; you should find that learning comes easily now. Things happen suddenly during this time, so be ready for love at first sight, a marriage, or other quick impulses and actions. Be on the lookout, as some unexpected happenings may be quite unusual. Also, you receive help from people in high positions during this period. While there's much talk about changes you'd like to make, it's more talk than action right now. You're tuned in to the Universe at this time, and many things seem interesting to you. Be sure to keep your bags packed during Hidden Essence Number 23, as you may take long journeys.

Hidden Essence Number 32: During this period, you find yourself working with groups to better mankind. Listen carefully to your inner voice and make your own plans. Be careful to keep your plans to yourself so the naysayers can't discourage you. You're going to meet fascinating people who bring you many advantageous social connections during this period. Able to move easily from one occupation to another, you may even conduct business in a foreign land. At this time, avoid becoming involved in scandalous love affairs or a love triangle.

Essence Number 6

This time focuses on family, loved ones, and small animals. After years of hard work, your interest turns to love, home, family, and the appearance of your home surroundings. This is not a time for arguments or disagreements of any kind—rather, it's a time for peace and quiet, being surrounded by beautiful things, and being considerate of others. Your business and financial matters improve during this period and some form of financial gain will come from a member of the opposite sex. During this period, you may be saddled with unexpected expenses for medical, dental, or even veterinary care for your family, whether human or pet. Also, beware of an overly dominant, inconsiderate, and possessive person who's sure to bring you unhappiness at this time. Popularity, recognition, standing in your community, and a pleasant social life is your reward for service to others now.

Hidden Essence Number 15: This is a time of finance; money often comes easily right now, but you have unexpected expenses that require you to spend what comes in. Although you have many admirers, you may experience some difficulties when dealing with the opposite sex. During this period, you also may find that you or your partner is overly interested in family and not paying attention to the spouse. If you've helped someone in the past, this is the time to collect favors in return. Climb the career ladder of success now by giving 100 percent of yourself and accepting more than your share of responsibility.

Hidden Essence Number 24: This is a number that signals good fortune. Because you're spending so much time helping your family, you may find less time and freedom for yourself. There's also a chance of inheritance during this time; it may come from a grateful relative whom you have helped in the past or through the appreciation or kindness of others. Not one to be a social climber, you likely profit from your associations with influential members of the opposite sex. Be especially careful and alert so you can avoid accidents during this period.

Hidden Essence Number 33: This Hidden Essence Number is a beautiful period filled with love, kindness, friendship, understanding, and peaceful relationships. You likely welcome many visitors to your home during this period and may experience household upheaval, such as a change of residence or someone leaving your home. Being dignified and trustworthy now will reap you rewards in the future.

Essence Number 7

This is the time to delve into the mysteries of life, psychic experiences, or metaphysical studies. During this period, you experience many serendipitous experiences that cause you to reevaluate your beliefs about life. Open your intellectual interests to new experiences that employ a finer use of your talents. Literary or educational pursuits can bring much success and advancement in your career. During this time, you should also give very careful consideration to the chance for long-term happiness with your prospective mate before walking down the aisle. If you're married or in a relationship, a period of trouble and struggle may arise at this time. This is a good time to take control of your thoughts and emotions to ensure more happiness in your life.

Hidden Essence Number 16: This is a period of change for you, so be ready for your plans to change on a whim. If you feel as if your life is falling to pieces during this period, rest assured that it's actually falling into place. This is a time of karmic tests and mental reevaluations. You may find that scientific work, technology, research, law, or other fields of study are of particular interest to you now. If you experience disappointments in love or marriage, rest assured that any trouble experienced under a Hidden Essence Number 16 never lasts long—this, too, shall pass. This is also a time to tend to your health and pay special attention to avoid careless accidents or slip-and-falls. If you happen to be around people who have had too much to drink during this time, offer to be the designated driver. Expect to hear unusual news during this period, as you are a confidante to many at this time.

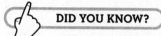
DID YOU KNOW?

The Essence Number 7 (Hidden Essence 7, 16, 25, and 34) is one of great intuition and mystical or psychic experiences. You're tuned into the Universe and will gain greater understanding of life's mysteries.

Hidden Essence Number 25: During this Hidden Essence Number, you're able to read the minds of those around you and are especially in tune to psychic experiences. You also find this is a period of strange occurrences. Powers of keen observation and imitation are yours now; you acquire inner knowledge that can help you solve any difficulties that you may encounter. Also, be ready to take a trip over or near the water at this time—at the very least, you could learn to swim.

Hidden Essence Number 34: This period is surrounded with mystery, as is everyone you welcome into your existence at this time. Staying in the background and shunning publicity is advisable now. Following the rules and acting in a conventional manner can bring you more success during this time. It may seem as if something interrupts your plans or that there's an obstacle to everything you undertake now. You also may need to deal with the illness of your parents or some member of your family, or may be separated from them for a period of time. Take extra care during this period to prevent accidents. You may be involved in discussions or disagreements about religion now. Also, this period is excellent for musical pursuits—especially singing—or other educational studies.

Essence Number 8

This number is one of power and authority. Expect to find yourself in leadership positions or financial affairs that use your executive skills to organize activities or be in control of situations. This number also is involved with buying, selling, exchanging, or renting of property. Money can be earned during this period, but be advised that expenses usually are similar to your income, so be sure to balance the budget before writing checks. Monetary gain could also come through some form of sports. During this time, better results are gained when working in groups rather than by yourself.

Hidden Essence Number 17: During this period, you are going to rise above petty differences in life and be poised, powerful, and prosperous. This is a time to pay great attention to detail and use your powers of intuition. Now is also a time to be wise in all of your decision-making. Expect money to come to you via checks, either from a pay increase, insurance, stocks, or bonds that pay good interest. This is a time for secret investigations or being a super sleuth to gather the information you need. Take care to avoid being judgmental of others right now. Also, be ready to take important journeys either near or on water.

Hidden Essence Number 26: During this Hidden Essence Number, you have many small duties to attend to but can make gains in business through networking and association with others. You have executive ability and can manage multiple projects during this period. Able to speak with power and conviction, you can reach others with your words and messages now. Birds of a feather flock together, so take care when choosing your companions. Also, be cautious about any get-rich-quick schemes—if something sounds too good to be true, it probably is. It's probable that you're going to be paying out financially for others right now, leaving less for you to be self-indulgent. This is a time to keep your emotions on an even keel.

Hidden Essence Number 35: During this time, you're going to ride the wave of all the good in your life. Success comes easily to you now and may even bring a monetary inheritance your way. This is a period of social opportunities, activities, and help from friends. On the business side, you're presented with money-making opportunities, new work, ideas, interests, and investments now. Also, expect to travel for both business and pleasure during this period.

Essence Number 9

This number provides many blessings in disguise, as long as you possess a tolerant, compassionate frame of mind during this period. These years are a time of deep feelings and drama, where you must avoid being possessive. But on the flip side of the coin, you may enjoy love affairs or romance of some sort. You may experience a loss during this time, but rest assured that it will make way for something bigger and better in your life. Remember that everything happens for a reason. Big business, government dealings, and the acquisition of money can be yours during this time. To avoid being involved in legal matters, strict honesty is essential in all transactions. Quarrels, arguments, or legal matters can be long and drawn out, so it's best to avoid them altogether.

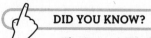 **DID YOU KNOW?**

The Essence Number 9 (Hidden Essence 9, 18, 27, and 36) can present extreme emotions—both highs and lows—in addition to disagreements and strife. If you can keep an open mind about others, you can enjoy numerous blessings during this period.

Hidden Essence Number 18: This Hidden Essence Number is interesting, because you're dealing with big corporations, lawyers who may straighten out a will or inheritance, doctors, or dentists for yourself or a family member. Money acquisition to the point of greediness shouldn't be your sole purpose in life during this period. Although others may be bickering or arguing around you, avoid getting involved in petty disagreements or bitterness. Be careful of your emotions and friendships now—there's someone who isn't worthy of your friendship, time, or good-natured personality. Be on guard and pay attention to your intuition to detect the motives of others. During this period, be sure to watch traffic lights and follow all rules of the road, or you're sure to get a ticket. Also, be careful of accidents caused by the carelessness of others.

Hidden Essence Number 27: During this period, use your strength and reasoning to plan for yourself rather than listening to the opinion of others. This is the time to work with the public, give speeches, and create literary triumphs. Art, music, beauty, peace, and justice are part of your world now, so avoid intolerance and bigotry in all forms. If you're unable to do or accomplish all you want to do right now, avoid feeling disappointed. It's also best to sidestep extra work at this time to protect your good health. If you experience disappointments in love affairs, pick yourself up, dust yourself off, and realize that there are more fish in the sea. Short and long journeys are especially beneficial during this time.

Hidden Essence Number 36: During this Hidden Essence Number, you have the power to overcome ordinary obstacles and experience eventual success. You may be especially generous and sympathetic now, with a strong desire to help those less fortunate. Use all of your talents in a constructive manner at this time, and you'll receive many benefits in return.

The Least You Need to Know

- Progressing the letters of your birth name can tell you what's happening during certain ages in your life and for how long.
- The Hidden Essence for each age is the unreduced total of the progressed letters in your birth certificate name for that year.
- Reduce the Hidden Essence Number to a single digit to obtain that age's Essence Number.

What You Were Born With

In Part 3, I walk you through how to use your date of birth to calculate your Birthday Number and discover the influences in your life.

You also learn to calculate your Life Path Number, which gives you clues about the opportunities and lessons you'll encounter during your lifetime. After that, you learn to determine your Pinnacles and Challenges, which foretell important peaks in your life and potential bumps in the road along the way.

I also show you how you can determine your strengths and weaknesses over different stretches of time with the Personal Year Number, Triad Numbers, Personal Month Number, and Personal Day Number. These exciting numbers provide guidance about what you might do, should do, and probably shouldn't do based on the time frame.

The Birthday Number

Many metaphysicians and some numerologists believe your soul selects your birthday. The day you were born supposedly indicates what you need to help you achieve your life's goals. In numerology, you use what's called the Birthday Number to get a better understanding of your day of birth.

In this chapter, I discuss what the Birthday Number is, show you how to calculate it, and walk you through the meanings of each one.

In This Chapter

- The significance of the Birthday Number in numerology
- Calculating your Birthday Number
- Meanings of the various Birthday Numbers

What Is the Birthday Number?

The Birthday Number focuses on the day you were born and what impact that has on your life. While the Life Path Number (see Chapter 10) is focused on the big picture of your life, your Birthday Number indicates one or more special talents that will serve you on your journey through life.

Your Birthday Number points out characteristics and traits you share with others born on the same day of the month, as well as those common to people whose day of month reduce to the same value. By knowing your Birthday Number and its meaning, you can accentuate your positive traits and minimize or even eliminate the negative ones.

 PYTHAGORAS SAYS

You can combine the knowledge obtained from your Birthday Number with the possibilities revealed by your Destiny Number (see Chapter 3) to see the best way to achieve the positive aspects of your destiny and how to mitigate the challenges your Destiny Number discloses.

Calculating Your Birthday Number

This is, without a doubt, the simplest calculation in all of numerology. To get your Birthday Number, you do the following:

1. Write down the day you were born.

2. If necessary, reduce to a single digit.

So if you were born on one of the first nine days of a month, you're already finished. If your birthday is on the 10th or later, just keep reducing until you get a single digit. For example, if you were born on the 13th: $1 + 3 = 4$.

Birthday Number 1

Your Birthday Number is 1 if you were born on the 1st, 10th, 19th, or 28th. As a 1, you have an independent streak and like to be the leader of the pack. All those who have a Birthday Number of 1 are innovative and can dream up new methods of doing things. Energetic and creative, 1s are the inventors and pioneers—in fact, it's likely that many of those on the first wagons heading West were Birthday Number 1s.

1st

Famous people born on the 1st: singer Justin Bieber, Revolutionary patriot Paul Revere, Princess Diana, TV personality Dr. Phil

If you were born on the 1st, you're a leader who paves the way for others using your ingenious ideas. Charming, original, and inventive, you put a unique twist on old things and do them in a new way, all the while seeking praise for your way of thinking. You're qualified to assume the leadership role and have the dynamic energy necessary to carry out your plans. With your creative ideas and inventions, you're truly a money-making machine.

It's no wonder you arrived on this day—you hate to wait and always want to be first. With your nervous energy, you're seldom idle and need to keep busy. You also like to be the boss; failing that, you prefer to work alone (which is like being your own boss). On the surface, you may seem aloof and are apt to give others the cold shoulder if they try to give you advice. When talking to others or responding to their advice, make sure to watch the tone of your voice.

When it comes to your personal life, you're often found outdoors soaking up the sunshine, as you enjoy breathing in fresh air. In affairs of the heart, you're accustomed to success. Honest, strong-willed, and with definite likes and dislikes, you're able to think and change your mind quickly.

10th

Famous people born on the 10th: singer Rod Stewart, actress Judy Garland

If you were born on the 10th, you have the ability to reinvent yourself when times get tough. You're blessed with the gift of intuition and are most successful when you listen to your inner voice. You're also a dynamic idealist who's able to inspire others with your optimistic outlook.

Even though you have nervous energy, you're a clear thinker who experiences good health. Ambitious and independent, you're gifted in business thanks to your creative mind. You enjoy starting a project, but you tend to leave the finishing to others because you detest the details. Your originality and creativity truly shine when you're able to work alone, though.

You dislike clichés in work and in expressions of love. When it comes to your personal life, you have hundreds of acquaintances but few friends. You're also envied by others, so you tend not to tell anyone your plans to avoid them raining on your parade. When it comes to money, you're apt to have a wide fluctuation in your finances.

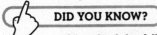 **DID YOU KNOW?**

If your birthday falls on the 10th, you'll have many interesting experiences during your lifetime. You may even live in a foreign country for a short period.

19th

Famous people born on the 19th: former president Bill Clinton, actor Bruce Willis, chef Paula Deen, singer Dolly Parton

If you were born on the 19th, you're a pioneer who's willing to take chances and start new things. Competitive by nature, you possess a strong will to win and don't like to come in second. You also have executive ability and are able to handle leadership roles naturally and easily. Ambitious, you work best alone to reach your goals.

You're energetic with strong personal magnetism. However, it's difficult for you to see yourself as others see you. You often feel lonely, even when you're in a congenial group.

A peacemaker who has a knack for always saying the right thing, you're determined and handle bumps in the road with apparent ease. Because of your tendency to do everything quickly, you're sometimes impulsive—for example, you may respond with an automatic "yes" or "no" without giving a matter much thought.

It takes a lot for you to get angry, but when you do, your icy words can cut like a sharp sword. However, your anger tends to be short-lived; you get over it quickly and may even forget an hour later what made you angry in the first place.

28th

Famous people born on the 28th: singer Lady Gaga, former first lady and icon Jacqueline Kennedy Onassis, singer Kellie Pickler, TV personality Kate Gosselin, actor Vince Vaughn

Pioneering, strong-willed, and clever, as someone born on the 28th, you aren't afraid to stand out in a crowd. Living by the rules and playing by them aren't your idea of fun. Determined and independent, you refuse to allow the opinions of others to discourage you and feel limited when anyone tries to interfere with your plans.

Although you're practical, you're also analytical. With your keen understanding of human nature, you have the know-how and ability to get what you want (lucky you!). Courageous in your approach to life, you're not afraid to try anything once.

A perfectionist, you're always searching for new ways to improve on your ideas. With your clever thinking and reasoning skills, you rarely know defeat—if you fall down seven times, you'll get up eight.

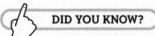 **DID YOU KNOW?**

Because of your fierce independence as sometime born on the 28th, you not only crave but require freedom like others need air to breathe.

Birthday Number 2

You have a Birthday Number of 2 if you were born on the 2nd, 11th, 20th, or 29th. Those born with a Birthday Number of 2 like partnership, teamwork, and harmony. You're considerate, sensitive, and cooperative and enjoy an aesthetic lifestyle.

2nd

Famous people born on the 2nd: talk show host Kelly Ripa, singer Jon Bon Jovi, singer Sting, model Christie Brinkley

As someone born on the 2nd, you're the proverbial juggler who's able to handle many projects simultaneously and somehow keep all of the plates spinning. Above all, you seek balance and harmony in your life.

Usually humble, you're most successful when you're not afraid to let your ambitious side show. Because you're always cooperative and diplomatic (to the point you could be nominated for a Nobel Peace Prize!), you're happiest when working in tandem or a group.

Loved ones and family are essential to your happiness. To truly be content, you need to choose your life companions very carefully. On the home front, you do your utmost to have beauty in your surroundings and enjoy taking care of it.

When it comes to your emotions, you have to curb the urge to not take things personally. Also, don't underestimate yourself and try to change—you inspire others just the way you are.

11th

Famous people born on the 11th: actress Jennifer Aniston, singer Harry Connick Jr., former vice presidential candidate Sarah Palin

If you were born on the 11th, you're idealistic, intuitive, and innovative. You work unceasingly to turn your unique ideas into a reality. You have the potential of a master, so don't linger at the bottom of the mountain when your place is standing at the top inspiring others.

Because you have highly charged energy and tend to get nervous easily, you require a balanced lifestyle. Others less illuminated than you drain your batteries, so it's essential for you to get enough rest.

You love creatures great and small, and you're happy when spending your time enjoying nature. You also desire love and companionship with others—just remember that you have to give as well as receive.

You have a tendency to dwell on past hurts and disappointments. Work to put the past in the past and close the door behind you. You're one of a kind, so develop your self-confidence and believe in yourself more.

20th

Famous people born on the 20th: television weather forecaster Al Roker, soccer star David Beckham, actress Nicole Kidman, legendary coach Pat Riley

If you were born on the 20th, you're the epitome of tact and diplomacy, choosing your words with the utmost care when talking with others. Always adaptable and with great empathy for others, you feel at home and can easily fit into any group.

You find happiness and joy in partnerships with kindred souls. However, because you're sensitive to the feelings of others, you can be indecisive or fickle in your desire to please them.

While you work best as part of a team, you sometimes may allow others to take advantage of your good nature. You also tend to get your feelings hurt and take things personally. You require peace and quiet, so don't hesitate to insist upon your "me" time.

PYTHAGORAS SAYS

If you were born on the 20th, you should learn to heed your intuition. Your instincts could lead to money-making ideas.

29th

Famous people born on the 29th: entertainer Michael Jackson, TV personality Oprah Winfrey, former President John F. Kennedy

As someone born on the 29th, you're a sensitive soul who excels when speaking to others. You have a strong character and the ability to inspire others. Philosophical and idealistic, you're a natural leader who's destined for greatness.

You are most successful in life when you select a career that emulates your talents. Often in the limelight, you tend to mask any shyness with a scintillating personality. You're also strongly influenced by power and money, but you're generous with those less fortunate when you've acquired that financial success.

You're less interested in the mundane and more interested in a higher dimension of life. Because of this, it would be wise for you to walk on a straight and narrow pathway—any other route will get you in trouble and is bad for your karma. You must also work to keep your emotions on an even keel to avoid dramatic mood swings.

When it comes to your personal life, you're cautious about trusting others; you desire love deeply but don't always feel secure enough to seek it. Often secretive, you don't express your feelings for fear of being ridiculed. You also may not have many children based on your intuitive knowledge that your negative memories from childhood may influence your parenting abilities. You should seek a spouse who's a kindred spirit and shares your outlook on life.

Birthday Number 3

If you were born on the 3rd, 12th, 21st, or 30th, you have a Birthday Number of 3. Recognized for your creativity, good sense of humor, and ability with words, you're enthusiastic, friendly, and fun, with a childlike spirit.

3rd

Famous people born on the 3rd: master crafter Martha Stewart, actor Mel Gibson, actor Eddie Murphy, actor Tom Cruise, actress Lisa Kudrow

As someone born on the 3rd, you're a natural showman who needs outlets for your creative abilities. A consummate entertainer who possesses the gift of gab and a genuine ability to wax eloquent, you're comfortable on center stage or as the center of attention. However, be careful about always being on the run; with your intense social calendar, you need to know when to take time to slow down and get some rest.

Because of your magnetic personality, you're very popular and sought after by others, especially in a romantic way. But you also may seem elusive or even remote to others, who have difficulty "placing you." That's not an uncommon feeling for you, either; often, you don't fully understand yourself.

You're quite lucky and seem to have blessings come to you from nowhere. Rarely upset or depressed, you quickly snap out of it when you feel stressed or blue. You're also able to deal with problems handily, as you've discovered the easiest route is to admit when you're mistaken.

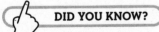 **DID YOU KNOW?**

A birthday on the 3rd indicates you aren't easily fooled. Because of this, you may find metaphysics or spiritual pursuits especially fascinating.

12th

Famous people born on the 12th: gold medal gymnast Cathy Rigby, late-night television host David Letterman, radio personality Howard Stern, businessman-turned-politician Mitt Romney

As someone born on the 12th, you live to be of service to humanity. A child at heart, you're happiest when surrounded by children. Because of your friendly and sociable personality, you also have unusual friends from all walks of life. When it comes to those you love, you feel deeply and are willing to suffer for them. However, when it comes to your own needs and feelings, you prefer to hide from others, which can make you seem mysterious.

Striving to be creative in all aspects of your life, you're competent and skilled in whatever you undertake. You're blessed with a large vocabulary and use your power with words to express yourself, making you a fascinating speaker and natural teacher. Because you're interested in many subjects, you should be careful not to spread yourself too thin. However, if you do find yourself in a jam, you have the power to draw on the help you need when necessary.

21st

Famous people born on the 21st: actress Goldie Hawn, reality star Kim Kardashian, actor Matthew Broderick

If you were born on the 21st, you seem to be blessed with luck and opportunity, and you enjoy sharing your good fortune with loved ones. Loveable and popular, you're a sought-after companion who likely has a social calendar booked far in advance. A joy to be around, you can talk to anyone about anything and know how to brighten the lives of others with your endless optimism.

An individualist with a capital "I," you use your power of words to get on your soapbox and express your thoughts to others. You also add your artistic flair to everything you do. Because you're interested in many different things, it sometimes makes it difficult for you to decide which interest to pursue.

When it comes to your well-being, you can feel edgy or have nervous energy when constantly on the go. Make sure you should curb your tendency to overcommit, lest you spread yourself too thin.

30th

Famous people born on the 30th: journalist and television host Piers Morgan, singer Celine Dion, actress Cameron Diaz, professional golfer Tiger Woods

If you were born on the 30th, you're a born entertainer with boundless creativity and endless charm. You're able to achieve success in life through your creativity, often due to your skill with words—in fact, you have a keen ability to talk your way out of jams. While you're capable and versatile, you sometimes have stops and starts when putting your plans into action.

You enjoy the finer things in life and have rather exclusive tastes. When you're flush with money, you enjoy lavishing your loved ones with gifts, to the point of being overly generous. Still, even with your champagne tastes, you're very good at handling money.

You believe that friendship and romance are keys to your happiness. Charming and fun to be around, you shine in social settings and attract people from all walks of life. But even with your outgoing and magnetic personality, some may find it difficult to get to know you intimately.

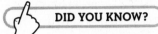

> **DID YOU KNOW?**
>
> As someone born on the 30th, you have the ability and proclivity to embellish the truth. In other words, you never let facts ruin a good story!

Birthday Number 4

If your birthday is on the 4th, 13th, 22nd, or 31st, your Birthday Number is 4. You have a strong desire for security and want to build solid foundations to secure your future. You're reliable, honest, self-disciplined, and fair, with a streak of practicality.

4th

Famous people born on the 4th: president Barack Obama, actress and humanitarian Angelina Jolie, actor Matthew McConaughey, "The Yankee Doodle Boy" songwriter George M. Cohan

As someone born on the 4th, you're very proud, conventional, and reserved. Practical and systematic in the way you do things, you're Rock of Gibraltar for those around you. You know how to get what you want and can intimidate the lazy with your steadfast determination. Because you're capable of forming your own opinions and have definite likes and dislikes, you may find it difficult to change your thinking.

In affairs of the heart, you may find it difficult to express your emotions and thoughts, which may make it hard for others to get to know you. But while you appear quite serious most of the time, you're actually very warm once your reserve is penetrated.

When it comes to taking care of yourself, you'll find you're happier if you try to have fun and enjoy life more. You also need to set aside 15 minutes of alone time every day to restore your vitality, as you tend to need lots of rest and relaxation.

13th

Famous people born on the 13th: singer Elvis Presley, singer and songwriter Taylor Swift, actor William Macy, actor and producer Tyler Perry

As someone born on the 13th, you have definite opinions and aren't afraid to share them. You're also complex—there are no limits to the heights (or depths) you can reach. Intellectual and with excellent reasoning powers, you can sense when something is about to happen. Because you're right most of the time, it's not always easy on others around you. You may never be fully understood because your thinking is ahead of its time.

Energetic and a hard worker, you'd do well in a profession that brings you in contact with the public. Because you're highly skilled in nature, you can do almost anything you set your mind to. You especially have an eye for design, with a keen sense of rhythm and balance. While you're usually organized, you occasionally allow yourself to kick up your heels and have fun.

You treasure tradition and adore love, home, and family. In matters of the heart, you tend to learn a lot about yourself (and others). You also believe that the atmosphere of your home is important to your success and happiness.

 IT DOESN'T ADD UP

If you were born on the 13th, you should be careful to avoid stress. High levels of stress can lead to possible health issues for you.

22nd

Famous people born on the 22nd: actress Reese Witherspoon, former president George Washington, best-selling author Ray Bradbury

As someone born on the 22nd, you're pragmatic and excel at organizing, which means you often find yourself leading large projects. Curious and inquisitive, you love to ask questions. You're also able to work well with others, despite your independent streak. You have an enthusiasm for life and feel proud of what you have accomplished.

You're competent and have the potential to reach the highest pinnacle, but you need to create balance in your life to avoid letting yourself sink to the lowest depths. When it comes to problems in your life, you're often required to find practical solutions. As someone who's highly intuitive, you should strive to follow your instincts.

You have many unusual friends and strive to make them happy. High strung, you have a strong personality that may have caused you minor difficulties in your childhood. You also work hard at hiding your sensitivity from others.

31st

Famous people born on the 31st: former vice president Al Gore, singer and actor Justin Timberlake, news commentator Jane Pauley

If you were born on the 31st, you travel frequently and often amass a fortune. Because you're often on the go with your suitcase packed, be sure you can follow through before you make more commitments.

You're strong-willed and determined to be successful. You tend to have artistic talent and need an outlet to express your creativity. You also have original ideas and are blessed with the ability to build and rebuild. Practical and grounded, you have the capacity for hard work. You're a good organizer of others and strive to better the conditions under which people live and work.

At some point, you'll be recognized for your honesty and high ideals. However, that can sometimes lead you to get set in your ways. Try to be more flexible—learn to see the gray areas rather than just viewing things in black and white.

Birthday Number 5

If you were born on the 5th, 14th, or 23rd, you have a Birthday Number of 5. As a 5, you share an inner sense of adventure and a desire for constant change and stimulation. You're not always patient, making freedom a must for you. Forward thinking, you're resourceful, curious, and quick in all you do.

5th

Famous people born on the 5th: entrepreneur and reality star Kris Jenner, singer Adele, former secretary of state Colin Powell

If you were born on the 5th, you'll never be thought of as traditional. You have a unique outlook on life and require freedom to do things on the spur of the moment. With boundless enthusiasm and energy, you're always on the go. Because you don't always follow the rules, you sometimes show a rebellious streak when adherence is required.

Clever and optimistic with a magnetic personality, you make a fascinating companion. You're quite a catch for a potential partner (if he or she is clever enough to get your attention), but you have a tendency to struggle with commitment.

When it comes to finances, you learn the value of money through your own experiences. You think quickly on your feet and know how to drive a hard bargain, making you excellent in sales.

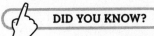 **DID YOU KNOW?**

As someone born on the 5th, you enjoy being self-reliant and self-sufficient. You're not afraid to take a gamble on a calculated risk and live by the motto, "Nothing ventured, nothing gained."

14th

Famous people born on the 14th: actress Halle Berry, fashion designer Ralph Lauren, former NBA star turned businessman Magic Johnson

As someone born on the 14th, you exemplify innovation and are interested in what's new and trendy. With your inherent sense of genius, you can think outside of the box. You like to take calculated risks, but you must avoid passing the buck if something goes wrong—handle things yourself.

Blessed with a good memory, you remember events from your past; however, that memory can lead to you to dwell on past hurts. You should learn to avoid holding grudges and forget the past. You must also strive to be adaptable and more flexible.

You enjoy indulging your five senses, and food and drink can be your friend or foe. Generous, you're adored by your many friends. However, you may get emotional now and then, stemming from your strong feelings and sense of being misunderstood.

23rd

Famous people born on the 23rd: NBA star Kobe Bryant, NBA star Jeremy Lin, singer Miley Cyrus, Renaissance painter Leonardo da Vinci, numerologist Jean Simpson (me!)

As someone born on the 23rd, you have a variety of interests and are skilled at many of them. Versatile and quick thinking, you add a creative touch to everything you do. You have a complete supply of curative remedies and know how to treat anything from a bee sting to the common cold. Because you're intuitive and possibly have psychic gifts, be sure to follow your hunches and listen to your inner voice.

Your determination and focus are second to none. Fueled by boundless energy, you enjoy being surrounded by excitement. You're also apt to be restless and want to search out what's new and different, which often leads you on many adventures. You rarely know defeat and always seem to land on your feet.

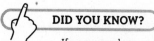

DID YOU KNOW?

If you were born on the 23rd, you have the power to attract whatever you want due to your social and friendly nature. This attitude can also lead you to be blessed with loyal employees.

Birthday Number 6

If you were born on the 6th, 15th, or 24th, you have a Birthday Number of 6. Devoted to those you love, you dislike arguments and strive for harmony. In fact, when others bicker, you feel physically ill. You're artistic, magnetic, and idealistic, with an enjoyment of comfort and quality. Your humanistic nature can attract whatever you want in life.

6th

Famous people born on the 6th: NBA star Shaquille O'Neal, NBA star Chris Paul, actor George Clooney, journalist Maria Shriver

If you were born on the 6th, you have striking features and an artistic flair. Creative and charming, you always add a touch of pizzazz to whatever you do and reap rewards when you put your good business sense to work. You also have an innate ability to rise above any challenges or hardships that may come your way. In those trying times, you find comfort and joy in music.

Idealistic and nurturing, you place importance on love, home, family, and helping those less fortunate. When it comes to your home life, you have strong ties to your family. Outside the home, you have great interest in community affairs and gladly work on projects to help those less fortunate. You also feel deeply and are apt suffer for those you love. This is seen in both your work and your personal life, where you shoulder responsibilities and always seem to take on more than your fair share.

You absorb knowledge from those in your social circle. Even though you're good at giving advice, you should be wary of meddling in others' affairs. You also find it hard to accept criticism, especially when it's delivered harshly.

15th

Famous people born on the 15th: actor and director Ben Affleck, shipping magnate Aristotle Onassis, chef and entrepreneur Emeril Lagasse

Those born on the 15th are emotionally sensitive and take love seriously. Sympathetic to the feelings of others, you often pitch in to help those who need it. You always think of others, take on their problems, and have a hard time letting go, making you generous almost to a fault. You also seem to struggle with commitment, even though love and family are important to you.

You have a sense of responsibility for others yet are independent. For example, you have a knack for getting people to change their annoying habits without them even realizing what you're doing.

While you've had difficulty choosing your path in life, you're well respected in business dealings and seem to attract influential people. You achieve financial success during your thirties, forties, and fifties.

When it comes to relaxation, your home is your haven. Travel is also something you enjoy, when you have the time. Listening to music or playing cards may be a good way for you to unwind.

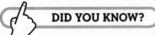

DID YOU KNOW?

As someone born on the 15th, you have strong intuition. When it comes to making decisions, you should act on your first instincts.

24th

Famous people born on the 24th: Apple co-founder Steve Jobs, singer Barbra Streisand, singer Neil Diamond

As someone born on the 24th, you're fair, sensible, and willing to work hard to reach your goals. You possess a practical approach to life that will be your key to success. When it comes to accomplishing your goals, perseverance is your middle name.

You are finely tuned and have an acute sense of rhythm, design, and balance. You believe in fairness and expect others to carry their share of the load and work as hard as you do. You pick up the pieces when others drop the ball. You can be reasoned with but not controlled. You should curb your proclivity to stubbornness.

When it comes to your personal life, you're adored and often surrounded by animals and children. To soothe your soul and unwind, you treat your home as your sanctuary and like to listen to good music.

Birthday Number 7

If were born on the 7th, 16th, or 25th, your Birthday Number is 7. A profound thinker who's private and reflective, you look for the deeper meaning in life. You may take a while to make a decision, but it's because you don't like to be wrong. Nature restores and rejuvenates you.

7th

Famous people born on the 7th: television journalist Katie Couric, actress Charlize Theron, actor Liam Neeson, singer Prince

If you were born on the 7th, others see you as intensely private. You appear aloof, but you may in fact be covering up the shyness. You also may just be secretive and prefer not to share your true feelings. Because of your love of privacy and inability to open up readily, only a fortunate few get to see your sensual side.

Inquisitive, you dig deep until you get to the bottom line. You need proof and often say, "Show me" or "I'll believe it when I see it." Even though you like asking questions, you resent being questioned by others. When it comes to finding answers, you need to trust your highly refined intuition.

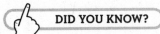

DID YOU KNOW?

As someone born on the 7th, you crave harmony in your life. You dislike conflicts and confrontations.

16th

Famous people born on the 16th: basketball star Blake Griffin, entertainer Madonna, comedian Will Ferrell

If you were born on the 16th, you're perceptive and can spot a phony arriving a mile away. Naturally inquisitive, you have highly developed intuitive skills and enjoy asking questions.

You dislike having loose ends and want to finish whatever you start. You also desire proof in an effort to meet your analytical nature. Because of this, your interests may be as mundane as computers, as technical as science, or as profound as metaphysics or spirituality. Whatever you decide to focus on, you tend to be a perfectionist or specialist in that area.

When it comes to your well-being, you should strive to see the bright side of life and avoid mood swings. Also, expect the unexpected—you tend to have more than your fair share of surprises throughout your lifetime.

25th

Famous people born on the 25th: entertainer Elton John, Oscar-winning actress Renee Zellweger, gymnast Aly Raisman, singer Aretha Franklin

As someone born on the 25th, you require tranquility and solitude. You dislike people talking too much or too loudly, which requires you to be alone to recharge your batteries. You thrive in nature—the beach is your particular favorite.

You live by the motto "for every problem there is a solution." You have an amazing knack for finding varied solutions to situations and challenges. You're also very curious about things and like to know how and why they work. You have strong intuition, so you should try to follow your instincts.

You're very interested in spiritual or metaphysical matters. Introspective and sensitive, you pick up on the feelings of others. When it comes to interacting and engaging with others, you should strive to avoid stubbornness.

Birthday Number 8

If were born on the 8th, 17th, or 26th, your Birthday Number is 8. Those born with a Birthday Number of 8 need to be the boss in most areas of their lives and have an authoritative air. Ambitious, capable, and confident, you're driven by success and material security.

8th

Famous people born on the 8th: business mogul John D. Rockefeller, actor/director Dustin Hoffman, singer Bruno Mars, actor Matt Damon

If you were born on the 8th, you have a presence so powerful that it may be intimidating. You like to make decisions yourself and not be told what to do. You also have common sense and know how and when to use it.

Success is important for your happiness. You have an uncanny ability to organize and are happiest when in charge or working alone. You also possess executive abilities that, when combined with your innate ambition, will bring you material success. You find happiness and security in having money and are skilled handling large amounts of it.

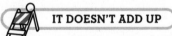

IT DOESN'T ADD UP

While you may enjoy having a lot of money, as someone born on the 8th, you should also strive to find balance between generosity and thrift. Don't be stingy!

17th

Famous people born on the 17th: actor Robert DeNiro, actor Sean Penn, actress Betty White, *Dancing with the Stars'* Derek Hough, singer Janet Jackson

As someone born on the 17th, you are ambitious, have an original approach, and are successful in business. You're blessed with a good mind and a terrific memory. While you're apt to be a bit self-centered, you have great intuition and a knack for imitating others. Not one to rely on hearsay, you need concrete proof.

Very systematic and organized, you may have great success in the economic field. You're a natural boss and leader who can shoulder responsibility easily—when faced with two alternatives, you're able to make a decision. You're also adept at managing large sums of money.

26th

Famous people born on the 26th: television host Ellen DeGeneres, singer Kenny Chesney, singer Keith Urban, former secretary of state Hillary Clinton

Those born on the 26th have strong feelings and desire harmonious relationships. You are loved and often surrounded by animals and children. You appreciate home and family but are often too busy to enjoy either one.

Able to accept responsibility, you were put on this Earth to lead and direct. You're an organized individual who should have financial success in your chosen field. To find success, make sure you stay level-headed when stressed.

You're proud of what you own and what you have accomplished. Because of this, you have a tendency to boast about possessions.

IT DOESN'T ADD UP

As someone born on the 26th, you tend to feel very strongly, to the point you get overwhelmed. You should strive to find balance when it comes to your feelings and emotions.

Birthday Number 9

If you were born on the 9th, 18th, or 27th, your Birthday Number is 9. You're a humanitarian who wants to make this world a better place. Able to see the big picture, you're very broadminded in your thinking and care about world affairs and politics. You also have the ability to understand people of divergent cultures and customs.

9th

Famous people born on the 9th: Duchess of Cambridge Kate Middleton, singer Whitney Houston, singer and songwriter John Lennon, basketball star Derek Fisher

As someone born on the 9th, you're a citizen of the world. You have a lovely disposition and a kind and compassionate heart. Idealistic, you want to help those who are less fortunate or are unable to care for themselves. However, even with your worldly attitude, you're also a very private person.

You're talented—often in music, writing, or art—and have universal appeal. You draw others to you with your friendliness. You also can be a dreamer and strive to inspire others to be the best they can be. But you should avoid always focusing your energy outside and strive to take better care of yourself.

18th

Famous people born on the 18th: business icon Richard Branson, singer and actress Queen Latifah, actor Brad Pitt, astronaut John Glenn

If you were born on the 18th, you have potential to achieve financial success. You have strong artistic interests and need creative outlets. You also instinctively know your strengths. Independent but able to work well with others, you're a born leader and a pioneer in your field.

Because of your good nature, you're admired by all. You live for others as much as you do for yourself. You also have refined tastes and aren't interested in what is common or mundane.

27th

Famous people born on the 27th: author Caroline Kennedy, performer and famed dancer Mikhail Baryshnikov, ice-skating gold medalist Peggy Fleming, baseball star Alex Rodriguez

If you were born on the 27th, you're intensely private and tend to keep your feelings to yourself. You're protective and will stand up for your family or employees in public, but you're apt to give them a piece of your mind in private.

With your many and varied interests, the world is your oyster. You also have a gift for communication and are able to express your emotions. You may be gifted in the humanities as a composer, author, or politician. Whatever your professional direction, you'll be successful at your choice.

The Least You Need to Know

- It's believed your soul selects the day you're born.
- Your Birthday Number is the simplest number to compute—you simply write down your day of birth and reduce it to a single digit, if it isn't already.
- Each Birthday Number shares various characteristics, but there are gradations for the various days that reduce to the Birthday Number.

The Life Path Number and the Hidden Cross

The month, day, and year you were born are an important part of numerology. Life is a long journey, and knowing and understanding the numbers related to your path in life and your mental, emotional, and physical traits can guide you to the appropriate lessons and greatest opportunities.

In this chapter, I discuss the Life Path Number, including how to calculate it and what it means to you. I also walk you through a graphic aid called the Hidden Cross, which offers further insight into your skills and abilities.

In This Chapter

- The significance of the Life Path Number
- How to calculate your Life Path Number
- Meanings of the Life Path Numbers
- Learning about the Hidden Cross
- How to fill in your Hidden Cross
- Interpreting the Hidden Cross

What Is the Life Path Number?

Many metaphysicians believe that you came onto this plane of expression that we call Earth already knowing what you need to know. But more often than not, there are things you need to learn. Some of these lessons are easy, and some take a bit of work. This is where the Life Path Number comes in.

Also known as the Birth Force or Lesson Number, the Life Path Number refers to the signpost you should follow through your life to achieve the most success. The advice you receive via your Life Path Number will save you time, energy, and even money along the way. Because your Life Path Number is derived from your birth date, it remains consistent throughout your life.

Calculating Your Life Path Number

To calculate your Life Path Number, you need the month, day, and four-digit year of your birth.

Before you begin the calculation, find out the numerical value for your month. As you can see in the following table, January through September apply to numbers 1 through 9. But what about October, November, and December? Because they are double-digit months, you need to reduce those months to a single digit. So October (month 10: $1 + 0 = 1$) is a 1, November (month 11 = $1 + 1 = 2$) is a 2, and December (month 12 = $1 + 2 = 3$) is a 3.

Month-to-Number Table

Month	Number	Month	Number
January	1	July	7
February	2	August	8
March	3	September	9
April	4	October	1
May	5	November	2
June	6	December	3

You can refer to this table to help you in this chapter and in Chapters 12 through 15, where I'll be discussing other numbers that come from your birthday or the current date.

Calculating your Life Path Number is, pardon the expression, as easy as 1-2-3.

1. On a piece of paper, print the month, day, and four-digit year of your birth date.

2. Write the numbers associated with them above the date.

3. Add and reduce the values to a single digit.

DID YOU KNOW?

A Life Path Number that doesn't need to be reduced indicates a very simple life with limited challenges and few lessons to be learned. Although it doesn't apply to anyone born between 1502 and 1999—and to only a very few birthdates outside that range—it does apply to a slightly larger (but still very small) number of birthdates in the twenty-first century. Two such birthdates are March 1, 2000, which produces a Life Path Number of 6, and April 2, 2010, with its Life Path Number of 9.

So, for example, if your birth date is November 19, 1998, you'd first print the month, day, and four-digit year.

> November 19, 1998

You'd then write the number values for each above your birth date.

> 2   19   1998
>
> November   19   1998

You then add and reduce the numbers to a single digit. Here's how it would look if you cast out extraneous 9s and any values that add to 9:

> 2   19   1998
>
> 2 + 1 + 9 + 1̶ + 9 + 9 + 8
>
> 2 + 1 = 3

And here's the long version:

> 2   19   1998
>
> 2 + 1 + 9 + 1 + 9 + 9 + 8 = 39
>
> 3 + 9 = 12
>
> 1 + 2 = 3

However you decide to do it, you should get a Life Path Number of 3 for the birth date of November 19, 1998.

PYTHAGORAS SAYS

Unless you're using an abacus or its modern equivalent, the calculator, you'll generally make fewer arithmetic errors if you simplify as you go. Until you get comfortable with doing the summations (or use a mechanical aid), consider doing the totals both by traditional addition and by the casting out nines method to make sure you get the same result.

Life Path Number Meanings

Now that you've done the calculation, it's time to find out the meaning of your Life Path Number. Because this number is the same throughout your life, you might view your Life Path Number as both an opportunity as well as a challenge. You also have the luxury of free will, so you can choose to either heed the advice of your Life Path Number or ignore the signs offered to you. It's completely up to you.

Life Path Number 1

If you have a Life Path Number of 1, you should believe in and value yourself more. Learn to stand on your own two feet and retain your individuality, especially when others don't agree with you. Remember, you can stand up for yourself and still express your different viewpoint in a nice way. Stop waiting for approval from others—validate your own parking ticket in life.

Avoid feeling possessed by other people, your job, your commitments, and so on. As a 1, you need to take control of situations as well as your life. Be more decisive and make up your mind faster. You should also learn to be courageous and not give in to others when you believe you're right. However, keep your temper in control and try not to fly off the handle when you feel stressed or cornered—this is a particular concern if your Life Path Number is 19 before it's reduced to 1 (1 + 9 = 10 and 1 + 0 = 1). Be content with your place in life without wondering if the grass is greener elsewhere.

Be creative and put your personal stamp on whatever you do. If your Life Path Number is 1, your ideal career may be at a university or one similar to a software development or research position, where thinking outside the box is encouraged and respected. Work on your executive abilities and assume leadership roles so you can develop new ideas, initiate projects, and promote unique concepts. Also, work on your innate talents of mental agility, quick thinking, and business acumen to set yourself apart from the rest of the crowd. To stay motivated to do this, keep your ideas to yourself so others can't burst your bubble before you've had the chance to execute them.

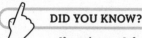 **DID YOU KNOW?**

> If you have a Life Path Number of 1 and a Destiny Number of 1, you already are what you need to learn. In other words, you're almost perfect just the way you are and only need to fine-tune your life lessons.

Life Path Number 2

If you have a Life Path Number of 2, you should work to develop your powers of persuasion. Be less blunt by becoming more diplomatic and tactful. Before you speak, gather the facts and weigh all decisions. You should also work on your skills of compromise by searching for win-win solutions. With others, adopt the role of negotiator and mediator, helping both sides agree on a solution. Always make sure you tell the truth without embellishing the facts.

As a 2, work on asserting yourself so others don't take advantage of you. However, avoid being sensitive and taking everything personally—listen to and learn from constructive criticism.

When it comes to your personal life, be adaptable and roll with life's punches. If you need help, ask for it. Also, take time to discover the joy of having a special friend or partner.

For Life Path Number 2, your ideal career may be one where you work with the public, machinery, or equipment. Inspirational to others, you excel in work involving the handling of details, researching, collecting, medicine, metaphysics, or religion. Overall, be a perpetual student who gathers facts and knowledge. Also, be willing to share your knowledge by cooperating fully when working with others.

Life Path Number 3

If your Life Path Number is 3, you must work on developing self-confidence and believing in yourself. Overcome your shyness by working on your social skills and the art of small talk. To help you in your interactions, increase your vocabulary and use words to express your feelings. You can even adopt the art of flirting! When it comes to your appearance, try to look more youthful.

You need to have fun and enjoy life more by harnessing your emotions and being more optimistic. Look at the glass as being half full instead of half empty. Also, notice the special and charming things about yourself. When it comes to others, toss aside your childish ways and be less critical and more observant of them.

Because you can make the dreams of others come true, you excel in work where feelings or emotions are involved. As a 3, your ideal career may be one where success likely comes from doing something in the artistic, literary, or entertainment fields. Be creative and find outlets for your artistic or musical talents. Also, concentrate on doing one thing at a time and doing it well—force yourself to focus without scattering your forces.

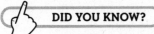 **DID YOU KNOW?**

When your Life Path Number is the same as your Destiny Number, it means you've learned your life lessons and you're perfect just the way you are.

Life Path Number 4

If your Life Path Number is 4, learn to be the architect of your own life, not somebody else's. Be steadfast and loyal in relationships, keep your commitments, and meet deadlines. Take control of your life, but pay attention to the rhythm of it—sometimes your tide is in and other times it's out.

As a 4, you should try to appreciate the value of things. Buy what you need, not just what you want. Money doesn't grow on trees, so curb spending habits while still getting value for your dollar—after all, a penny saved is a penny earned.

Realize that everything requires knowledge, even if learning bores you. Success is a product of planning and lots of work, so be more tenacious and develop the follow-through needed to finish what you start. Also, develop practical systems of getting things done and stick to a schedule. It's the little things that add up to big things, so take care of them right away rather than procrastinating.

If your Life Path Number is 4, your ideal career may be one developing projects from start to finish and putting the plans into concrete form. You excel in detail-oriented careers, such as event planning, project management, movie or television production, document handling, or anything involved with rules and regulations.

Life Path Number 5

If you have a Life Path Number of 5, you should realize that change and adapting to it are a part of life. Be flexible, bend when necessary, and be willing to take a risk now and then. And remember to kick up your heels and have more fun once in a while. Realize that freedom has a price and often requires giving up something else in your life.

Become more interested in current events and have a more liberal and open-minded way of thinking. Also, show a willingness to adapt to diverse situations or groups. When it comes to romance, heed your hunches.

As a 5, you need to focus on keeping your commitments and not being irresponsible. Focus and stick to one thing at a time. If you need help increasing your attention span, try doing some crossword puzzles or Sudoku.

Be more resourceful and grab various opportunities when they come your way. Take some time to develop your sales skills by not only asking questions but being willing to answer them as well.

If your Life Path Number is 5, your ideal career may be one where success comes from activities that are unique and buck routine. You excel in careers that center on change and variety, such as marketing or advertising, sales, entertainment, or anything that keeps you on the go and constantly moving.

PYTHAGORAS SAYS

If you have 5s (Es, Ns, or Ws) in your name and have a Life Path Number of 5, your lessons to accept change will be easier for you. If you marry someone with lots of 5s in their name or with a Destiny Number 5, be sure to give them plenty of space or expect to experience Newton's Third Law (which paraphrases to be "for every action, there's an equal and opposite reaction") firsthand.

Life Path Number 6

If you have a Life Path Number of 6, you should work on being more responsible around the house, attending to chores, and checking things off that "honey do" list. Pitch in to give extra help at work, even if you aren't being paid overtime. When it comes to taking care of yourself, pay more attention to your clothes and general appearance.

Be aware that others, both young and old, need you. Avoid selfishness in any form and give loved ones your affection. Also, try to take a more liberal and open-minded approach to life and let your idealistic trait show.

As a 6, you need to understand that even though you have your own way of doing things, not everyone else has to do things your way. Avoid being unreasonable or stubborn.

As for your role in the community at large, volunteer and give counsel and advice to others (but only when they seek it). Play the role of harmonizer and smooth ruffled feathers when others don't get along.

If your Life Path Number is 6, your ideal career may be one where success comes from making the lives of others more comfortable, luxurious, or beautiful. You'll excel in careers that involve counseling, working with animals or children, art, interior design, or catering.

Life Path Number 7

If you have a Life Path Number of 7, you should delve into life's metaphysical mysteries. Seek a higher plane position in life and the reason for the cause behind the effect. Also, make sure you ask questions and avoid taking things at face value. As you gain more wisdom, be willing to share it with others.

In your personal life, learn to be alone without feeling lonely. Discover the beauty of nature, or take time to enjoy quiet evenings at home. Above all, remember to get some rest.

When it comes to work, develop your ability with words—either in written or spoken form—and take the time to become proficient with technology. As a 7, your ideal career is one where success in life arises from work requiring analysis or research, particularly in a technical field, such as nutrition, computers, engineering, religion, metaphysics, psychic studies, investigative reporting, or detective work may also appeal to you.

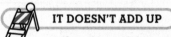 **IT DOESN'T ADD UP**

If you have a Destiny Number 7, a Life Path Number of 7, or many 7s in your name, be careful to not do anything to excess.

Life Path Number 8

If your Life Path Number is 8, you need to find more balance in all areas of your life. For instance, pay more attention to your health, diet, and exercise regime by joining a gym or, at the very least, starting to walk regularly. You should also become more aware of finances and your financial well-being.

Develop the ability to handle money, power, and success. That means working on your executive abilities and starting to delegate responsibilities to others. Be more authoritarian and earn the respect of others. Also, avoid rushing through tasks just to finish them—take the time necessary to do things well.

As an 8, you should avoid limiting yourself and find success on a grand scale. Your ideal career may be one that involves supervising, organizing, education, coaching, or dealing with finances. Careers in medicine, sports, real estate, and property management may also appeal to you.

Life Path Number 9

If you have a Life Path Number of 9, you should work to be a humanitarian and serve others. Show kindness and compassion, and be the inspirational light that sheds a beam on others to help them find their way in life. Remember the Golden Rule, "Do unto others as you would have them do unto you"—give without remembering and take without forgetting.

Develop an interest in world affairs and gain an appreciation for other cultures, customs, and religions. You should also take the time to explore your love of the arts, whether it's music, sculpture, paintings, theatre, or literature.

If your Life Path Number is 9, your ideal career may be one that involves helping others as a teacher, therapist, nurse, doctor, or lawyer. You may also like a career dealing with the arts, television, films, travel, big business, religion, or charity. When it comes to work, conceive grand-scale, moneymaking ideas and let others handle the details.

Master Life Path Number 11

If you have a Master Life Path Number of 11, many numerologists believe you came to Earth having few, if any, lessons to learn. However, understand that much is required of you as you travel along your special path in life.

You're happiest when inspiring and helping others, so become a messenger and share your energy, idealism, and philosophy. Accept others as they are, but inspire them with your good deeds as you take the high road in life. Stay humble and live with an attitude of gratitude.

Master Life Path Number 22

If you have a Master Life Path Number of 22, you need to let your inner light shine. Be open to messages from the universe, broaden your horizons, and expand your thinking.

You're happiest when you plan and organize for the benefit of mankind. Be the architect, as well as the builder, of things and ideas. Think big and develop international connections.

What Is the Hidden Cross?

Beyond your Life Path Number, your birth date can be used to reveal the connection between the three planes of your consciousness (mental, emotional, and physical) and how you react to others. This unique method is called the Hidden Cross and is typically used by only the most elite numerologists.

All of the horizontal and vertical lines on the Hidden Cross have meaning. The uppermost horizontal line represents the Mental (or spiritual) aspects of your life, including your nervous systems and all involuntary actions. The center horizontal line represents your Emotional (or astral) existence and includes bodily functions, circulation, and growth. The bottom horizontal line represents the Physical (or material) elements of your life and includes bones, muscles, and flesh. The vertical lines, moving from left to right, are the Self, the Many, and the All—these represent how you relate to yourself, others, and the masses.

Filling in Your Hidden Cross

How do you fill out the Hidden Cross? As you can see in the following grid, the Hidden Cross has a number assigned to each square. To fill out the Hidden Cross, you simply place each digit of your birth date in the correct square (see the "Month-to-Number Table" earlier in this chapter if you need a refresher on the numbers that go with each month). If you have one or more zeros in your birth date, place those at the side until you decide where you want to complete any row.

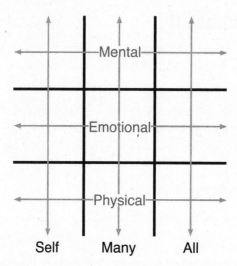

For the year of your birth, it's up to you whether you want to use the four-digit number or only the last two digits. I personally like to look at the Hidden Cross both with and without the first two digits of the birth year.

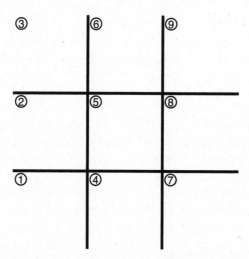

Use this grid to fill in the numbers of your birth date.

DID YOU KNOW?

While I, like some numerologists, use the four-digit year, some only use the last two digits of the year. One possible reason is that for a full century, all birth dates began with a "19," and anyone born during that century would all have 1 and 9 on their Hidden Cross. Another reason could be that the unchanging part of the birth year is possibly more accurate.

To show you how to fill out the Hidden Cross, I filled in three different Hidden Crosses using the birth dates of my daughters: Jamie, born on June 26, 1968; Brooke, born on July 19, 1969; and Chelsea, born on March 26, 1971.

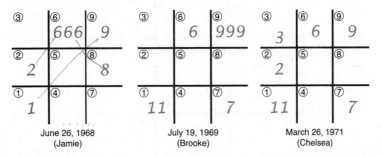

June 26, 1968
(Jamie)

July 19, 1969
(Brooke)

March 26, 1971
(Chelsea)

Jamie uses her mind in her work as a writer, which is shown by the majority of Jamie's numbers (three 6s and one 9) on the top "Mental" line of her Hidden Cross. In her career, she writes articles dealing with a wide variety of subjects that are of interest to "Many" and "All" people (as the lines and squares imply).

As for Brooke's Hidden Cross, you can see she has one 6 and three 9s on the "Mental" line. In the past, Brooke had a career that used her mental acuity as a personal-injury insurance claims specialist; however, she's now a busy stay-at-home mom who volunteers at school and through her work with the National Charity League. The 9s in her Hidden Cross, especially in her "All" line, show her humanitarian bent.

Chelsea's Hidden Cross has both a completed horizontal "Mental" line and vertical "Self" line. Chelsea is also a writer (she works from home, as shown by the Self line) and as the top "Mental" line denotes, she uses her mind to write educational curricula. In her free time, she uses her mind to help her very active children with their advanced homework.

To see a birth date with zeroes in it, let's look the Hidden Cross of someone born in the twenty-first Century: my grandson Jackson, born on March 24, 2003. As you can see, he has two zeroes in his birth date that he can place wherever he wishes in order to add emphasis to or fill in any particular line. He would probably choose to fill in his "Self" line because Jackson is always thinking about others and needs to think more about himself. The 3s at the intersection of the "Self" and the "Mental" lines show that one of Jackson's strong points are his common sense and reasoning abilities.

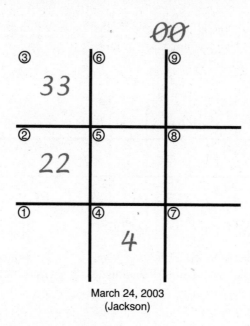

March 24, 2003
(Jackson)

Hidden Cross Square Meanings

Where do your numbers land? If your birth date included any zeroes, did you remember to allocate them on a line to possibly fill it in? Do you have any completed horizontal, vertical, or diagonal lines? In which squares do you have the most numbers? Check out the following to see the meaning of each square in the Hidden Cross.

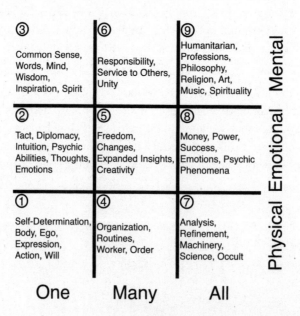

Here are the significant points that can come up in relation to the Hidden Cross:

- If you have a completed diagonal line from squares 1 through 9 or 3 through 7, the Hidden Cross indicates that you should have a relatively easy life.

- If you have a completed vertical line, you'll have many opportunities in life and be able to accomplish them all with ease.

- If you have a completed horizontal line, you'll be able to accomplish much in your lifetime.

- If you have no completed lines, you might meet your goal, but it may take some extra time.

- If your completed lines are all vertical, you may experience a few bumps in the road, but you will complete your goal.

- If squares 2, 4, and 8 have one or more numbers in them, you'll have money in your lifetime.

- If square 4 has more than one number in it, you have good physical strength.

- If have two 4s or two 8s on your Hidden Cross, you have super physical and mental strength.

- If you have two 2s in your Hidden Cross, you're very sensitive.

- If you have one or more 3s in your Hidden Cross, you have good common sense and know what to do and when to do it.

- If you have one or more 6s in your Hidden Cross, you have lots of common sense and know the easiest and most practical way to do things.

- If you have one or more 9s in your Hidden Cross, you have a touch of genius (lucky you)!

The Least You Need to Know

- The Life Path Number comes from your date of birth and gives indications as to the opportunities in life for you to learn your lessons that you can leverage to make your path through life easier.

- Use the month, day, and four-digit year of your birth to calculate the Life Path Number.

- The Hidden Cross is a graphic view into your birth date that tells you about your traits based on your three planes of consciousness (Physical, Mental, and Emotional). Any zeroes in your birth date are wildcards that you can use in any square to complete any line.

- Completed lines in the Hidden Cross indicate solidification of that line's characteristic.

Pinnacles and Challenges

Change isn't usually easy. Everything appears to be going along smoothly, until suddenly you encounter bumps in the road and nothing seems to be going your way. Yet change is the thing that takes us from Point A to Point B—it's how we progress. That's where Pinnacles and Challenges come in. Pinnacles are like blueprints that show you what's coming up in your life and when. Each Pinnacle indicates a period of growth and development. Meanwhile, Challenges are just what they sound like—obstacles that can appear in your path.

In this chapter, I take you through Pinnacles and Challenges, including how to calculate them and what they mean.

In This Chapter

- What are Pinnacles and Challenges?
- Calculating your Pinnacles and Challenges
- Interpreting each Pinnacle and Challenge

What Are Pinnacles?

Pinnacles give an overview of circumstances and events you may encounter during certain periods of your life. They are a time when you may be thinking of making life-altering decisions, such as switching careers, marrying or divorcing, or other major physical moves or changes. In addition to giving you ideas about what will happen during a certain time period, Pinnacles point to useful activities, opportunities, and outlets for your talents and capabilities. For example, Pinnacles may force you into a career or line of work that isn't obvious from your Destiny Number but is actually a good fit based on your personal strengths. In short, Pinnacles provide guidance on how to be successful and manifest your good.

You have four Pinnacles in your lifetime of varying length. Each Pinnacle has an overtone or theme that represents your thinking, goals, life events, what you're facing, and the atmosphere and general conditions during that particular period.

- The first Pinnacle is one of the longest and begins at birth. Your first Pinnacle is very personal and important and represents your formative and developmental years.

- The second Pinnacle is nine years long and deals with responsibility and circumstances when it comes to your career and family.

- The third Pinnacle, also nine years in length, deals with middle age. It represents a more mature manner of thinking and is a time to reap what you've sown during your first and second Pinnacles.

- The fourth Pinnacle, frequently a long one, starts at the end of your third Pinnacle and continues until your demise. It represents your older years and focuses on using past experiences to successfully deal with present events and circumstances.

The transition from one Pinnacle to another is felt for two years—one before the change and one after. During the first year of transition, you're preparing to shift from one Pinnacle to the next. During the second year, you are adjusting after making the transition.

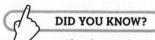 **DID YOU KNOW?**

The shortest first Pinnacle is from birth to age 27; this comes about if your Life Path Number is 9 (36 - 9 = 27). The longest first Pinnacle is birth to age 35, which happens if your Life Path Number is 1 (36 - 1 = 35).

Calculating Your Pinnacle Numbers

Your Pinnacles are calculated using the month, day, and four-digit year of your birth date, as well as your Life Path Number (see Chapter 10). If you'd like a quick reference for the ages you are at each Pinnacle in relation to your Life Path Number, check out the following table.

Pinnacles in Relation to Your Life Path Number

Your Life Path Number	The Ages of Your First Pinnacle	The Ages of Your Second Pinnacle	The Ages of Your Third Pinnacle	The Ages of Your Fourth Pinnacle
Life Path Number 1	0 to 35	35 to 44	44 to 53	53+
Life Path Number 2	0 to 34	34 to 43	43 to 52	52+
Life Path Number 3	0 to 33	33 to 42	42 to 51	51+
Life Path Number 4	0 to 32	32 to 41	41 to 50	50+
Life Path Number 5	0 to 31	31 to 40	40 to 49	49+
Life Path Number 6	0 to 30	30 to 39	39 to 48	48+
Life Path Number 7	0 to 29	29 to 38	38 to 47	47+
Life Path Number 8	0 to 28	28 to 37	37 to 46	46+
Life Path Number 9	0 to 27	27 to 36	36 to 45	45+

Using the chart I've provided, complete the following steps to get your Pinnacles. You can calculate the ages as in the steps, or refer to the "Pinnacles in Relation to Your Life Path Number" table.

When calculating Pinnacles, I do not use the Master Numbers 11 and 22. Reduce all of your calculations to a single digit.

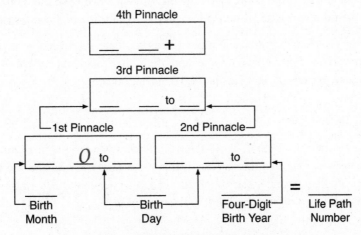

Use this chart to fill in the information for your Pinnacles.

1. Write down your birth month, birth day, and four-digit birth year on the lines provided.

2. If you don't already know it, calculate your Life Path Number (see Chapter 10) and write it down on the line provided.

3. Subtract your Life Path Number from 36; this gives you the age your first Pinnacle ends. Write that value in the "1st Pinnacle" box on the far-right line.

4. To find your first Pinnacle Number, add the single-digit version of your birth month and the single-digit version of your birth day and reduce, if necessary. Write the value in the "1st Pinnacle" box on the far-left line.

5. In the "2nd Pinnacle" box, write the ages your second Pinnacle starts and ends. The age your second Pinnacle begins is the same age as the end of your first Pinnacle. To get the age for the end of your second Pinnacle, you simply add 9 to the second Pinnacle starting age.

6. To find your second Pinnacle Number, add the single-digit version of your birth day and your four-digit birth year, and reduce to a single digit, if necessary. Write that value in your "2nd Pinnacle" box on the far-left line.

7. In the "3rd Pinnacle" box, write the ages your third Pinnacle starts and ends. The age your third Pinnacle begins is the same age as the end of your second Pinnacle. To get the age for the end of your third Pinnacle, you simply add 9 to the third Pinnacle starting age.

8. To find your third Pinnacle Number, add your first and second Pinnacle Numbers, and reduce to a single digit, if necessary. Write that value in the "3rd Pinnacle" box on the far-left line.

9. In the "4th Pinnacle" box, write the age your fourth Pinnacle starts. The age your fourth Pinnacle begins is the same age as the end of your third Pinnacle. Your fourth Pinnacle ends at your demise, so you don't have an end date to write down for this Pinnacle.

10. To find your fourth Pinnacle Number, add the single-digit version of your birth month and the single-digit version of your four-digit birth year, and reduce to a single digit, if necessary. Write that value in the "4th Pinnacle" box.

As an example, let me show you how I found the Pinnacles for the birth date of March 20, 1950.

The first thing I did for the birth date of March 20, 1950, was write the birth month (3), the birth day (20), and the four-digit birth year (1950) on the lines indicated on the chart. I then calculated the Life Path Number for March 20, 1950 (see Chapter 10). The Life Path Number is 2, so I wrote that down on the chart on the line provided.

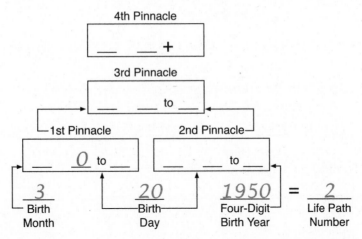

The first Pinnacle begins at zero, so I only needed to find the end age of the first Pinnacle. To get that value, I had to subtract the Life Path Number (2) from 36. This gave me a value of 34, so I wrote 34 in the "1st Pinnacle" box on the far-right line. To find the first Pinnacle Number, I used the birth month (3) and the single-digit version of the birth day (20; 2 + 0 = 2) and added them together: 3 + 2 = 5. I then wrote 5 in the "1st Pinnacle" box on the far-left line.

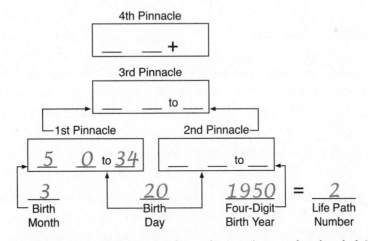

For the second Pinnacle, I needed to write down the ages it started and ended. The start age is the same as the end of the first Pinnacle, which is 34. The end age is the start age plus 9: 34 + 9 = 43. So in the "2nd Pinnacle" box, I wrote 34 and 43. I calculated the second Pinnacle Number by adding the single-digit version of the birth day (20; 2 + 0 = 2) and the four-digit birth year (1950) reduced to a single digit, if necessary: 2 + 1 + 9 + 5 + 0 = 17; 1 + 7 = 8. I wrote 8 in the "2nd Pinnacle" box on the far-left line.

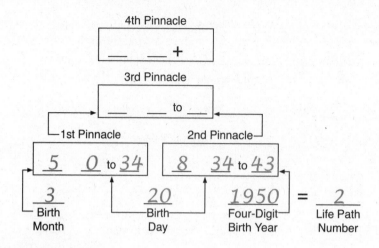

PYTHAGORAS SAYS

If it's easier for you, you can always use the "Pinnacles in Relation to Your Life Path Number" table to find all the ages with which each Pinnacle starts and ends. Because I used the birthday of March 20, 1950, which has a Life Path Number of 2, I could have looked at the line showing Life Path Number 2 to find the ages for each Pinnacle.

I next had to find the ages the third Pinnacle started and ended. The start age for the third Pinnacle is 43, or the same as the end age of the second Pinnacle. To get the end age, I added 9 to 43: 43 + 9 = 52. So I wrote 43 to 52 in the "3rd Pinnacle" box. To find the third Pinnacle Number, I added the second Pinnacle Number (5) and third Pinnacle Number and reduced to a single digit: 5 + 8 = 13; 1 + 3 = 4. I wrote 4 in the "3rd Pinnacle" box on the far-left line.

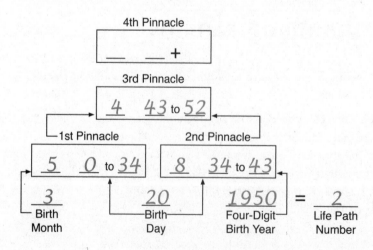

Because the end date is your demise, the fourth Pinnacle only has a specific start date—the same age as the age the third Pinnacle ended. Therefore, I wrote 52 in the "4th Pinnacle" box. Finally, I found the fourth Pinnacle Number by adding the birth month (3) plus the four-digit birth year (1950) and reducing to a single digit: $3 + 1 + 9 + 5 + 0 = 18$; $1 + 8 = 9$. I wrote 9 in the "4th Pinnacle" box on the far-left line.

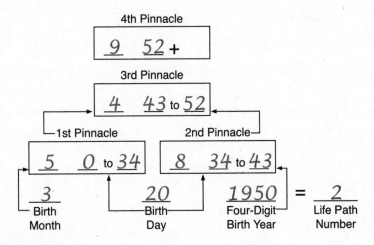

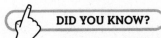

DID YOU KNOW?

You should always look at your Pinnacle or Challenge Numbers in relationship to your Destiny Number (see Chapter 3). Whenever a Pinnacle Number or Challenge Number is the same as your Destiny Number, you'll handle your Pinnacle or Challenge with ease.

Pinnacle Number Meanings

Pinnacle Numbers describe the circumstances you'll encounter during a Pinnacle. The following talks about both the meaning of each Pinnacle Number and how they apply to a particular Pinnacle.

Pinnacle Number 1

During Pinnacle Number 1, circumstances require you to do the following:

- Think of yourself and your needs and wants first.

- Be independent in your thinking and actions.

- Be confident and have the courage of your convictions.

- Be self-reliant and realize that when the chips are down, the only person you can ever really count on is yourself.

- Be a self-starter; take the initiative and don't wait for others.

- Be resourceful and innovative in your thinking—if Plan A doesn't turn out as you'd hoped, develop Plan B.

- Learn from the actions and mistakes of others.

- Be strong-willed and determined and forge ahead.

- Realize that every situation that presents itself offers you an opportunity to learn.

When Pinnacle Number 1 is your first Pinnacle: Your early years aren't always easy. While you're figuring out the ways of the world, you may not develop the skills necessary to stand up for yourself in a nice way. With Pinnacle Number 1 as your first Pinnacle, you may be headstrong and resistant to taking advice from others. By trying to do everything on your own, you may act self-important or egotistical.

When Pinnacle Number 1 is your second or third Pinnacle: You're afforded opportunities to be daring and utilize your own ideas. You can also use this time to develop talents you may not have previously realized you possess.

When Pinnacle Number 1 is your fourth Pinnacle: You have the opportunity to be courageous and use your determination to excel at whatever you undertake.

Pinnacle Number 2

During Pinnacle Number 2, circumstances require you to do the following:

- Be tactful, diplomatic, and fair when dealing with others on a personal or business level.

- Realize that two heads are better than one, and much can be accomplished working in pairs.

- Be patient; take your time working with details and avoid being careless.

- Develop your interests and talents.

- Be a student of life and gather facts and knowledge.

- Trust your intuition and read between the lines.

- Accept constructive criticism without getting your feelings hurt.

- Be a peacemaker and cooperate with others.

- Be considerate and helpful to others without meddling in their lives.

When Pinnacle Number 2 is your first Pinnacle: You're ultra-sensitive and get your feelings hurt easily. Learn to gather facts, develop skills, and get a good education. It's also important to cooperate with others and not be overbearing or aggressive.

When Pinnacle Number 2 is your second or third Pinnacle: You have opportunities for partnerships in both your business and personal lives. It's essential to learn the art of give and take and adopt a win-win approach in order to build successful relationships.

When Pinnacle Number 2 is your fourth Pinnacle: You can enjoy the comfort of knowing that any hurt feelings and relationship problems from your past are going to be resolved.

Pinnacle Number 3

During Pinnacle Number 3, circumstances require you to do the following:

- Use your creativity and imagination in all areas of your life.
- Be expressive without exaggerating—share your feelings in spoken or written form while avoiding gossip.
- Have an optimistic outlook; don't allow yourself to stay blue for very long.
- Strive to look your best and have a youthful view of life.
- Be genuine; avoid any form of superficiality.
- Develop the mindset to attract money and money-making opportunities.
- Be practical and remember to enjoy life's simple pleasures.
- Stay focused; don't scatter your energies.

When Pinnacle Number 3 is your first Pinnacle: You may need to learn to buckle down, realize that money doesn't grow on trees, and understand that success requires hard work. Artistic or creative outlets should be pursued early on purely for self-expression, even if they aren't used for a career later on.

When Pinnacle Number 3 is your second or third Pinnacle: You're blessed with opportunities to develop your talents. However, avoid get-rich-quick schemes or extravagance. Remain faithful to your spouse or partner, because over-the-top displays of affection could get you into sticky situations.

When Pinnacle Number 3 is your fourth Pinnacle: You experience joy and are able to enjoy life's great pleasures. Avoid getting swept off your feet. Also, be sure to control your emotions and finances.

PYTHAGORAS SAYS

Knowing your Pinnacle and Challenge Numbers helps you prepare for the times ahead. By making the most of or avoiding certain experiences during each period, you can maximize your assets while learning from your trials.

Pinnacle Number 4

During Pinnacle Number 4, circumstances require you to do the following:

- Be disciplined and work hard.

- Grasp the opportunities that come your way to secure your future.

- Be frugal—stick to a budget and know that pennies add up to dollars.

- Be methodical and precise in everything you do.

- Be trustworthy and know that honesty is always the best policy.

- Finish what you start, even if it bores you.

- Be responsible and keep your commitments.

- Be practical and down-to-Earth.

- Organize your life and prepare for success.

- Develop a "can-do" attitude.

When Pinnacle Number 4 is your first Pinnacle: You may be quite serious and feel the weight of your responsibilities. If you encounter financial limitations or concerns, you may find yourself working at an early age. It's important to be organized, realize the importance of a schedule, and stick to it.

When Pinnacle Number 4 is your second or third Pinnacle: You may have responsibilities to your immediate family or in-laws. Roll up your sleeves, get down to work, and wait for positive results to appear.

When Pinnacle Number 4 is your fourth Pinnacle: You can use a budget and transform your practical ideas into reality, even if problems arise along the way. A hobby may even bring tangible income.

Pinnacle Number 5

During Pinnacle Number 5, circumstances require you to do the following:

- Go with the flow, expect the unexpected, and adapt to life as it comes.

- Enjoy the freedom to come and go as you wish.

- Embrace all of the interesting experiences that come into your life during this time.

- Get enough exercise to dissipate your restlessness and nervous energy.

- Keep your suitcase packed, and always be ready for an impromptu getaway.

- The world is your teacher right now; open your mind and enjoy the adventure.

- Be open to meeting interesting people and making new friends.

When Pinnacle Number 5 is your first Pinnacle: You may feel restless and uncertain. Even though there's a lot of activity around you, this is the time to develop skills and apply yourself. Adapting to change early in life can be an asset later on.

When Pinnacle Number 5 is your second or third Pinnacle: You need to have faith that any financial concerns are fleeting and when you need money, it will be there. This period brings opportunities for advertising, civic interests, legal pursuits, or some form of public life. Don't enter into agreements without careful thought and evaluation.

When Pinnacle Number 5 is your fourth Pinnacle: You enjoy an interesting era of fun and freedom. It's doubtful that you retire during this time, but try to maintain roots somewhere. If you experience many changes or feel restless, avoid acting impulsively or making hasty decisions.

Pinnacle Number 6

During Pinnacle Number 6, circumstances require you to do the following:

- Feel responsible for love, home, and family.

- Put the welfare of others before your own and care for animals and children.

- Be a peacemaker—avoid arguments and make love, not war.

- Accept the responsibility to handle inheritances or trust funds.

- Pay more attention to love than anything else.

- Settle down and earn money.

- Be loving, loyal, and fair in personal and business relationships.

- Be kind, compassionate, and understanding when dealing with others.

When Pinnacle Number 6 is your first Pinnacle: You feel a sense of duty at home and may marry at a young age. You may even be responsible for your siblings or your parents. This can also be a time of financial stability and success.

When Pinnacle Number 6 is your second or third Pinnacle: You enjoy love and protection and feel a sense of duty and responsibility. If any disagreements arise, compromise with a loving heart.

When Pinnacle Number 6 is your fourth Pinnacle: You're surrounded by love. Others recognize you for the wisdom you've shared, the good deeds you've done, and all you've given to humanity.

> **DID YOU KNOW?**
>
> If you're single, widowed, or divorced, you may find a new love and build a new family during a Pinnacle Number 6. This is the time to listen to and follow your heart in matters of love.

Pinnacle Number 7

During Pinnacle Number 7, circumstances require you to do the following:

- Use your intuition and develop your ability to listen to your inner voice when it whispers to you.

- Don't take things at face value—dig deep into the hidden meaning of life.

- Cultivate your special talents and natural gifts.

- Be a perfectionist and demand the best from yourself.

- Investigate, study, and become a specialist in your field.

- Be introspective and enjoy spending time alone without feeling lonely.

- Be refined and gracious, even if others are boorish.

- Be content with what you have—the grass isn't always greener elsewhere.

When Pinnacle Number 7 is your first Pinnacle: You may feel misunderstood by others. If your feelings are hurt, you may withdraw and damage personal relationships. You may also have strict parents or health troubles. Receiving a good education is essential.

When Pinnacle Number 7 is your second or third Pinnacle: You attract money, as well as love, when you are patient. Be the epitome of integrity and honesty to attain your ultimate goals and success in life.

When Pinnacle Number 7 is your fourth Pinnacle: Use your inner power to understand hidden meanings by examining nonverbal cues and messages. Seek knowledge and share your wisdom with others. By leading an honest and honorable life, you can be very lucky.

Pinnacle Number 8

During Pinnacle Number 8, circumstances require you to do the following:

- Use your ability to judge the character of others.

- Be strong and courageous and take charge.

- Tackle challenges headfirst and persevere in your efforts.

- Be organized and efficient.

- Accept opportunities to manage and direct.

- Help friends and family if you're called upon to do so.

- Trust yourself and be your own authority.

- Reach your goals by using your mind rather than your heart.

- Live a balanced life, making sure to get enough rest.

- Realize you need to spend money in order to achieve financial success.

When Pinnacle Number 8 is your first Pinnacle: You may experience health issues that resolve themselves during this period. You're apt to select a career that you enjoy at an early age, but you may be required to support your relatives or family.

When Pinnacle Number 8 is your second or third Pinnacle: You're able to attain material success. During this time, you meet interesting people and have influential business contacts. Because of this, romance may take a backseat to your career.

When Pinnacle Number 8 is your fourth Pinnacle: You enjoy your many possessions and possible wealth. Your self-mastery brings you rich rewards.

Pinnacle Number 9

During Pinnacle Number 9, circumstances require you to do the following:

- Use compassion and tolerance in your relationships.

- Be aware that this is not a time for selfishness; rather, it's a time for sharing.

- Accept endings as a part of life and know when to release what's no longer useful to you and move on.

- Appreciate art, music, and beauty.

- Understand all the intricate facets of various cultures and their customs.

- Give more than you receive.

When Pinnacle Number 9 is your first Pinnacle: You may experience endings: the loss of a pet, a major move, or various disappointments. Learn to let go and don't look back. Realize that when one door closes, a bigger and better one opens. Something better is coming your way.

When Pinnacle Number 9 is your second or third Pinnacle: Your character may be tested. If money is lost, it can be made again. Be open-minded and listen to the opinions of others. And if you're tolerant, love will find you.

When Pinnacle Number 9 is your fourth Pinnacle: During this time, you enjoy recognition for your magnanimous acts. Travel and the arts bring you contentment.

 DID YOU KNOW?

Occasionally, some people have a 9 for all four Pinnacle Numbers. This applies to people born on September 9, 18, or 27 in any year that adds and reduces to a 9 (1981, 1998, 2007, 2016, and so on). Metaphysicians believe that this anomaly indicates old souls who have lived many lifetimes.

What Are Challenges?

Challenges foretell potential difficulties in reaching your Pinnacles. Think of them as the obstacles along the path you take to achieve your goals.

Challenges run concurrently with the Pinnacles and can't be avoided, even though you may want to! You must pay attention to your Challenges in the form of Challenge Numbers and not resist or bypass them. In fact, you must become them—otherwise, whatever you resist, persists.

Challenge Numbers are one of the few areas in numerology where you actually subtract numbers rather than add them. Because you subtract the reduced, single-digit value of your birth month from your birth date and birth year (both reduced to a single-digit), it's possible to come up with a Challenge Number of 0.

Calculating Your Challenge Numbers

While still a simple set of calculations to perform, the Challenge Numbers require a different skill set than what you used to calculate Pinnacles. Challenges involve subtraction. However, you've already done half of the work already; the ages at which each Pinnacle started and ended are the same start and end ages for each of your Challenge Numbers. If you'd like a quick reference for the ages you are at each Challenge in relation to your Life Path Number, check out the following table.

Challenges in Relation to Your Life Path Number

Your Life Path Number	The Ages of Your First Challenge	The Ages of Your Second Challenge	The Ages of Your Third Challenge	The Ages of Your Fourth Challenge
Life Path Number 1	0 to 35	35 to 44	44 to 53	53+
Life Path Number 2	0 to 34	34 to 43	43 to 52	52+
Life Path Number 3	0 to 33	33 to 42	42 to 51	51+
Life Path Number 4	0 to 32	32 to 41	41 to 50	50+
Life Path Number 5	0 to 31	31 to 40	40 to 49	49+
Life Path Number 6	0 to 30	30 to 39	39 to 48	48+
Life Path Number 7	0 to 29	29 to 38	38 to 47	47+
Life Path Number 8	0 to 28	28 to 37	37 to 46	46+
Life Path Number 9	0 to 27	27 to 36	36 to 45	45+

To calculate your Challenge Numbers, check out the following steps. You can use the chart provided to keep track of your information.

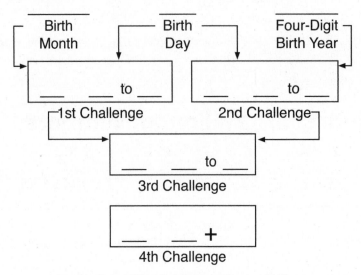

Birth Month   Birth Day   Four-Digit Birth Year

___ ___ to ___   ___ ___ to ___
1st Challenge   2nd Challenge

___ ___ to ___
3rd Challenge

___ ___ +
4th Challenge

Use this chart to fill in the information for your Challenges.

1. Write down your birth month, birth day, and four-digit birth year.

2. In the "1st Challenge" box, write down the ages your first Challenge starts and ends. Because they're the same as the ages for your first Pinnacle, you can simply refer to the Pinnacles chart you filled out earlier in the chapter, or check out the "Challenges in Relation to Your Life Path Number" table and look at the line where you see your Life Path Number.

3. To find your first Challenge Number, subtract the single-digit version of your birth month and the single-digit version of your birth day and reduce, if necessary. Write the value in the "1st Challenge" box on the far-left line.

4. In the "2nd Challenge" box, write the ages your second Challenge starts and ends. Like for the first Challenge ages, you can either check out the table or refer back to your Pinnacles chart for the age range.

5. To find your second Challenge Number, subtract the single-digit version of your birth day and your four-digit birth year and reduce to a single digit, if necessary. Write the value in your "2nd Challenge" box on the far-left line.

6. In the "3rd Challenge" box, write the ages your third Challenge starts and ends. Like for the first and second Challenge ages, you can either check out the table or refer back to your Pinnacles chart for the age range.

7. To find your third Challenge Number, subtract your first and second Challenge Numbers and reduce to a single digit, if necessary. Write the value in the "3rd Challenge" box on the far-left line.

8. In the "4th Challenge" box, write the age your fourth Pinnacle starts. The age your fourth Challenge begins is the same age your third Challenge ends. Remember, like your fourth Pinnacle, your fourth Challenge doesn't have an ending age, because your fourth Challenge ends at your demise.

9. To find your fourth Challenge Number, subtract the single-digit version of your birth month and the single-digit version of your four-digit birth year and reduce to a single digit, if necessary. Write the value in the "4th Challenge" box on the far-left line.

To show you how this works, the following walks you through how I calculated the Challenges for March 20, 1950, the same birthday I used to figure the Pinnacles earlier in this chapter.

The first thing I did for the birth date of March 20, 1950, was write the birth month (3), the birth day (20), and the four-digit birth year (1950).

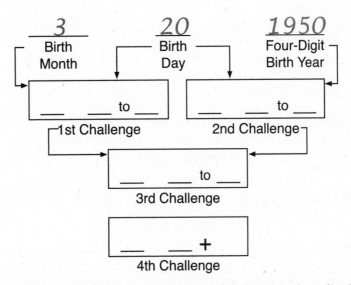

I then referred to the start and end ages in the Pinnacles chart I made earlier in the chapter and wrote them in their respective Challenge boxes. Remember, they are the same start and end ages as the Pinnacles.

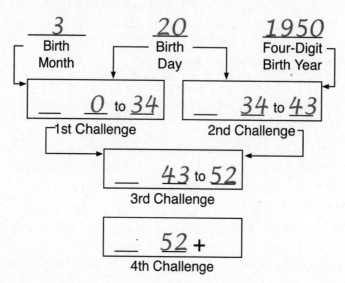

I found the first Challenge Number, which is the difference between the single-digit version of the birth month (3) and the single-digit version of the birth day (20; 2 + 0 = 2), reduced to a single digit: 3 − 2 = 1. I wrote 1 in the "1st Challenge" box on the far-left line.

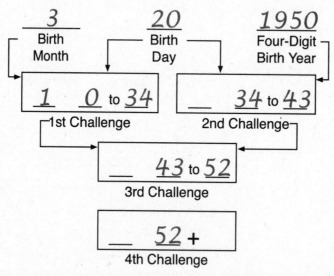

I next found the second Challenge Number, which is the difference between the single-digit version of the birth day (20; 2 + 0 = 2) and the single-digit version of the four-digit birth year (1950; 1 + 9 + 5 + 0 = 15; 1 + 5 = 6): 6 − 2 = 4. I wrote 4 in the "2nd Challenge" box on the far-left line.

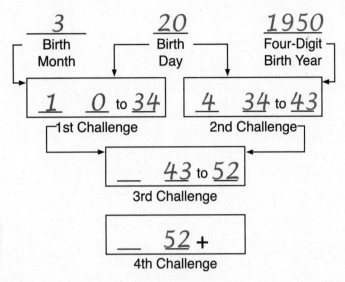

I found the third Challenge Number, which is the difference between the first and second Challenge Numbers: 4 - 1 = 3. I wrote 3 in the "3rd Challenge" box on the far-left line.

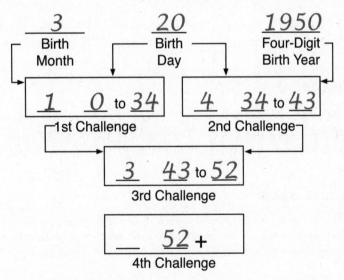

Finally, I found the fourth Challenge Number, which is derived by subtracting the single-digit version of the birth month (3) and the single-digit version of the four-digit birth year (1950; 1 + 9 + 5 + 0 = 15; 1 + 5 = 6) and reducing to a single digit: 6 - 3 = 3. I wrote 3 in the "4th Challenge" box on the far-left line.

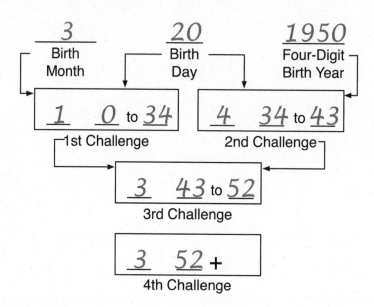

Challenge Number Meanings

Each Challenge Number, like each Pinnacle Number, holds sway during the entire period of the Pinnacle/Challenge. The following are the meanings behind the Challenge Numbers.

Challenge Number 0

If you have a Challenge Number of 0, metaphysicians believe you're an old soul who either has no challenges or has already experienced Challenge Numbers 1 through 8 in this and past lifetimes. So, in the words of Tony Soprano, "Fuggetaboutit"—you have it made in the shade.

PYTHAGORAS SAYS

The Challenge Numbers represent specific lessons you must deal with and overcome throughout your journey through life. The good news is that you should overcome your challenges significantly, if not entirely, by the end of your lifetime.

Challenge Number 1

Circumstances require you to be independent and stand up for yourself without being domineering. Don't be afraid to express your individuality. Learn to not only value but also voice your original ideas. Also, be self-reliant and don't expect others to help you. Avoid criticizing others simply because they are different from you. Accept responsibility for your actions, and don't pass the buck.

Challenge Number 2

Circumstances require you to avoid being jealous or fearful. Accept your sensitive nature, yet try not to take everything personally. Gather the facts and weigh decisions before you speak. Use precision when handling details, and be cooperative and diplomatic when working with others.

Challenge Number 3

Circumstances require you to use your imagination, creativity, and artistic or musical talents. Have more confidence in yourself and your abilities but temper your confidence with an ability to accept constructive criticism. Use your gift of words to express yourself but avoid using hurtful words when speaking with others. Be as interested in others as you are in yourself—don't hog the limelight.

Challenge Number 4

Circumstances require you to develop a code of ethics and a sense of values. Learn to focus on a project until it's completed. Realize you need to work to have financial security. Tone down your strong opinions, and allow others to voice theirs. Be more patient and use good judgment.

Challenge Number 5

Circumstances require you to be more curious and ask questions. Learn to be more flexible and less set in your ways. Enjoy your freedom without shirking your responsibilities. Avoid being so restless and impatient. Allow yourself to have more fun, try something new, and take a risk now and then.

Challenge Number 6

Circumstances require you to accept responsibility for your own actions. Learn to appreciate others more and enjoy giving without having strings attached. Be realistic in your idealism—don't set yourself up for disappointment by putting others on pedestals. Be honorable and learn to fulfill your commitments.

Challenge Number 7

Circumstances require you to overcome your feelings of loneliness and transform them into feelings of gratitude. Accept obstacles when faced with them—realize this is a time of inner growth and spiritual development. Don't allow false pride to get in the way of your happiness.

Challenge Number 8

Circumstances require you to be sincere and avoid being boastful. Learn to empower others instead of taking charge most of the time. Be willing to work for material success—there's more to life than a hefty back balance. Pay more attention to your health and diet and find balance in all areas of your life, especially where emotions are concerned.

IT DOESN'T ADD UP

Error! Having a Challenge Number of 9 is impossible. Because the largest digit you use in numerology is 9 and you're subtracting to get your Challenge Numbers, the difference between the two numbers must be between 0 and 8. If you end up with a 9, recheck your calculations.

The Least You Need to Know

- There are four Pinnacles and four Challenges in a person's life, and the Pinnacle and Challenge periods are concurrent.
- You use the month, day, and four-digit year of your birth as well as your Life Path Number to calculate your Pinnacles and Challenges.
- Pinnacles can be any number from 1 through 9. Pinnacle Numbers can have slightly different meanings depending on which Pinnacle the number falls in.
- Challenges can range from 0 to 8. A Challenge Number of 0 indicates no (remaining) challenges—either you had none or you've faced them all already.

The Personal Year Number

Knowing your Personal Year Number will help you answer the question, "What should I do now?" At birth, your Life Path Number (see Chapter 10) and Personal Year Number are the same. While your Life Path Number is constant, your Personal Year Number cycles through all the number values 1 through 9 and then repeats.

In this chapter, I detail what a Personal Year Number is, show you how to calculate your Personal Year Number, and provide the meanings for the different numbers.

In This Chapter

- What the Personal Year Number signifies

- How to calculate your Personal Year Number

- The meaning of each Personal Year Number

What Is the Personal Year Number?

Think of your *Personal Year Number* as a traffic signal. Some Personal Year Numbers are like a green light. In those types of years, it's time to put the pedal to the metal and move full steam ahead, as you can accomplish a great deal and be making important decisions. Other Personal Year Numbers are like a yellow light. At those times, you should use a little caution and take a wait-and-see approach for the year; do your research and think carefully before making any important decisions or changes. And some Personal Year Numbers are like red lights. These mean, "Whoa! Take your foot off the gas, pause, and stop to think things through"; it may be best to wait until the following year to make any major changes in your personal or professional life.

 **DEFINITION**

> A **Personal Year Number** tells you where you are and where you're going for the year. This number comes from the reduced sum of the day of the month on which you were born, the month in which you were born, and the year in which you last celebrated your birthday.

No matter whether it's a red, yellow, or green year for you, each Personal Year Number has its own vibration and gives you guidance and direction.

Calculating Your Personal Year Number

To find your Personal Year Number, you need your month and day of birth. Before you begin the calculation, figure out the number value for the month of your birth. If you recall, January through September apply to numbers 1 through 9, while the remaining months are added and reduced to a single digit, making October a 1, November a 2, and December a 3 (see the "Month-to-Number Table" in Chapter 10 if you need to jog your memory).

Now let's work through calculating your Personal Year Number using the following steps.

1. Write down your month and day of birth, and write the corresponding numbers below them.

2. Write down the year in which you last celebrated your birthday.

3. Add and reduce the numbers until you get to a single digit.

Let's work through an example. For a birthday of March 31:

March   31

3   31

8 − 21

2+1 =3   1956

If the calculations are being done in December 2013, the birthday has already been celebrated, so the year last celebrated is 2013:

March   31   2013

3   31   2013

Finally, the numbers are added and reduced to get a single digit:

3   31   2013

$3 + (3 + 1) + (2 + 0 + 1 + 3)$

$3 + 4 + 6 = 13$

$1 + 3 = 4$

So for people celebrating a birthday on March 31, their Personal Year Number for 2013 is 4.

Many numerologists use January 1 to December 31 as a Personal Year. However, there's really nothing "personal" about it when everyone's year spans the same dates. I believe that your Personal Year Number runs from your most recent birthday to the eve of your next birthday—after all, nothing is more personal than your birthday. Also, years of experience have shown me that working from your last birthday to your next birthday gives you the most accurate Personal Year Number. The following examples give you an idea of the difference in calculation.

Glen has a birthday of November 19. If he calculates his Personal Year Number on April 15, 2013, instead of writing down 2013, he'd write down 2012—the year he last had his birthday.

November   19   2012

2   19   2012

$2 + (1 + 9) + (2 + 0 + 1 + 2)$

$2 + 1$ (because $1 + 9 = 10$ and $1 + 0 = 1$) $+ 5 = 8$

So Glen's Personal Year Number is 8.

Madison has a birth date of May 28. If she calculates her Personal Year Number on July 24, 2013, she writes down 2013 as the year, as she's already celebrated her birthday in 2013.

May   28   2013

5   28   2013

5 + (2 + 8) + (2 + 0 + 1 + 3)

5 + 1 (because 2 + 8 = 10 and 1 + 0 = 1) + 6 = 12

1 + 2 = 3

So Madison is in Personal Year Number 3.

 PYTHAGORAS SAYS

In the relatively rare case that your birthday falls on February 29, use March 1 in nonleap years and February 29 in leap years.

Personal Year Number Meanings

Now that you've learned how to calculate your Personal Year Number, you're probably curious as to what you should glean from each number and how to deal with the events, joys, trials, and tribulations that year brings. The following provides information on each Personal Year Number and what you should consider from your last birthday to your next birthday.

Personal Year Number 1

Personal Year Number 1 is a time for fresh starts and new beginnings. Last year, in your Personal Year Number 9, you weeded your garden. Now, you're ready to plant new seeds you want to grow over the next nine-year cycle.

A 1 year is all about moving forward. Go out the exit door of your 9 year, lock it behind you, and don't look back! That was then and this is now; the slate was wiped clean in the 9 year you just completed. You may have ended something, changed friends, or even changed jobs or moved. Now is the time to cultivate new relationships, careers, and homes! If you feel stuck in a situation and didn't let it go when you were in year 9, it's time to get a new attitude about whatever bugs you. So a 1 year doesn't mean you have to get a new job, but at the very least, you should get a new feeling about it.

This year is the opportunity you've been awaiting for nine years, and you won't have this opportunity again for another nine years. So envision what you want and need now, determine how you are going to get it, and set your plans in motion. Start new projects and expand your horizons. Focus on the things you *do* want to accomplish in this new nine-year cycle that you have just started—not what you *don't* want. This is not a time to sit on your opportunities. Go out and find them!

Dream big, set some goals, and make plans to accomplish them. Have the courage of your convictions. To quote Yoda, "Do or do not. There is no try." Apply yourself, and don't waste a minute.

This is a year to take charge and use initiative in your affairs. Believe in yourself. Don't scatter your forces by talking about your ideas or asking the opinions of others, because people may try to discourage you from carrying those ideas to fruition. Instead, be courageous and take a leadership role. This means focusing on yourself and building up your self-confidence.

Personal Year Number 1 is a time to concentrate on the things you have, not on what you're lacking. And because your creativity is at an all-time high, you can see old situations or problems in a new light.

Make the most of your time, energy, hopes, wishes, and desires. Avoid scattering your forces by discussing your plans. Be decisive and go after what you want. Be sure to put yourself in the right place at the right time and make the most of every opportunity—don't be at the airport when your ship comes in!

PYTHAGORAS SAYS

In a Personal Year Number 1, remember the turtle: he accomplishes nothing until he sticks his neck out.

Personal Year Number 2

The seeds you planted in a Personal Year Number 1 are germinating now. Resist the temptation to dig things up to check on them. You may not see them growing, but have faith—they are.

This year may seem like you're at the ocean watching the current going in and out, or like you're saltwater taffy being pulled in two different directions at the same time. You may also feel as if you are taking two steps forward and one step back or that you're taking baby steps and not progressing as quickly as you would like. Be patient—this is a waiting time. You are like a sponge now, absorbing information, gathering facts, or studying something that interests you.

In a 2 year, your intuition is spot-on, so listen to the inner voice whispering to you now. Weigh all of the facts carefully and avoid making hasty decisions. If you find yourself in a sticky business or personal situation, use the natural tact and diplomacy that is yours now.

Togetherness and partnership are on your mind, and romance may be in your heart. Strengthen and renew old friendships and be receptive to finding new ones. Be open-minded and a good listener. Although you want to please others now, it's best to avoid your automatic "yes." You may be dealing with a female (or a persnickety male) who is irritating you now. Remember, patience is key this year!

Avoid taking things personally. Resist being petty. Stay positive and don't be fearful—remember, fear is (f)alse (e)vidence (a)ppearing (r)eal.

PYTHAGORAS SAYS

In a Personal Year Number 2, you may be feeling extra sensitive. It's important to develop a thick skin and not take things personally so you can enjoy the togetherness that's so vital to you now.

Personal Year Number 3

After planting in Personal Year Number 1 and waiting in Personal Year Number 2, Personal Year Number 3 is the time to reap what you've sown and make some choices!

This is the time to use your creativity and imagination. Do something you enjoy. Be optimistic, look on the sunny side of life, and practice the power of positive thinking.

In a 3 year, you're moving at a jet-set pace. Incredibly busy, you may feel as if you are a fireman putting out fires wherever you go. You also may be juggling many projects at once. Make sure you give yourself a break from your busy schedule by taking weekend getaways or short pleasure trips.

This is a good year to spruce up your living space. Colors are important to you now, and you may want things lighter and brighter. Lady Luck may also smile upon you this year (lotto tickets, anyone?), but be responsible about it. You may have unexpected expenses and need to spend more money than you planned on (or is wise).

Whether in spoken or written form, words are your magic wand in Personal Year Number 3. Socializing is on your mind, so like the TV ad, reach out and touch someone—reconnect with old friends, be spontaneous, and use your sense of humor. But with all of that socializing (and perhaps entertaining), be aware of your waistline. A 3 year represents expansion, so if you don't want to gain weight, you may need to pay attention to what you're eating!

In this year, it's best to practice restraint. Avoid getting carried away when you go shopping for the clothes you need to attend all of your social obligations this year. You may figure that if one pair of shoes fits you and feels good, you may as well purchase it in several colors! Instead of splurging on all new outfits, you can find a few accessories to liven up your outfits in different ways.

If you don't want to gain weight, don't eat your feelings. Think before you buy; if you use plastic to pamper yourself, you're going to have to pay for it sooner or later.

Personal Year Number 4

The keywords for Personal Year Number 4 are *order, form,* and *restriction.* This is a year filled with duty and responsibility, so roll up your sleeves and get to work. Now is the time to lay a firm foundation for your future.

This is a year to prepare and get organized so you can kick up your heels next year when you are in Personal Year Number 5. Concentrate on the tasks at hand and finish what you start. Because details come naturally for you now, you'll be able to clean out closets, organize your file cabinets, sort through papers, and tidy up in general.

Security is important to you now, so if you can, start saving. This is not the time to speculate, take chances, or extend yourself financially—stick to the tried and true. If you overspent in your 3 year, get on a budget and begin to pay things off. Also, tighten your belt on a personal level. If you gained weight last year, this is the time to fit back into your favorite clothes.

In the social realm, network and search out new contacts. Cultivate solid relationships, whether in business or your personal life. When making these connections, mean what you say and say what you mean (in a nice way, of course).

You may be tired from all of your running around last year; now is the time to get plenty of rest. Mull things over and learn from your past mistakes. Above all, be proud of your accomplishments!

Avoid the temptation to defer boring tasks; do them now to save time and money in the future. Count to 10 and don't fly off the handle.

 PYTHAGORAS SAYS

You're apt to be feeling overworked and stressed during a Personal Year Number 4. Because you're feeling tired, your patience may be running low. Try to avoid conflict and arguments right now, as they will only add to your pressures.

Personal Year Number 5

Last year in Personal Year Number 4, you hopefully got prepared. Personal Year Number 5 is the time to cut yourself some slack and give yourself permission to do things on the spur of the moment.

Get out of the rut! This is a year of fun, freedom, variety, changes, and travel. Be flexible and avoid monotony. If you're feeling stuck, you might consider a change of scenery, even if it means just rearranging the furniture. Keep your suitcase packed, expect the unexpected, and be open to new opportunities.

With your curiosity in high gear, a 5 year is a terrific time for you to search out fun new places to see. Take a chance when the opportunity arises and have fun, but don't be reckless about it.

This is a time to check home repairs. Check for leaks or dry rot. Seeking change and new horizons, you may also want to remodel, and what starts out small this year as a "honey-do list" may mushroom into a home makeover. And remodeling isn't just limited to the home. Full of energy and with pep in your step, this is the year to get onto a fitness regime.

Finish what you start. Keep commitments, and don't throw caution to the wind just to have fun. As you dash about at a high-speed pace, be careful driving or taking missteps this year.

Personal Year Number 6

You played last year in your Personal Year Number 5; this is the year to settle down and attend to your responsibilities. Personal Year Number 6 is about love, home, family, and responsibility.

It's a time of marriage and divorce, perhaps not on paper but in your mind and heart. Be harmonious, right all wrongs, and strengthen business and personal relationships. If you have issues with someone, this is the year to make the relationship better or decide to part ways.

A 6 year is also about catering to the needs of others. Be a magnet and attract people to you by being the kind of friend you'd want to have. If someone needs your help, experience the joy of lending a helping hand. Others may ask you for your advice, but be sure you first listen to the other person's idea before offering it. Called upon to be supportive, make sure you're willing to accept more than your fair share of the load. Be reliable, responsible, and, above all, keep your word.

You may be in the mood to try your hand at interior decoration this year by bringing the outside in, redoing the garden, or repainting and making the inside of your home lighter and brighter. You might also think more about your own appearance. Are your shoes shined, is your hair trimmed, and are your missing buttons replaced? These are things you'll consider at this time. Most of all, you want ease, comfort, and quality now. This is not the time to buy clothes that are made of scratchy fabrics. The softer the touch, the happier you'll be.

In your desire to be helpful and offer advice, be sure the other person wants to hear it. Allow others their freedom of thought and resist the temptation to smother.

Personal Year Number 7

Last year in your Personal Year Number 6, you had more than your fair share of responsibilities—in Personal Year Number 7, you're ready to cut the ties and allow others to stand on their own. Like a sabbatical year, this is a year of reflection and meditation.

At this time, you may be in desperate need of some quiet "me time" to do what *you* want and need to do. Recharge your batteries by spending time in nature, whether it's in the mountains, the beach, or your own backyard! You can also have some solitude and alone time by turning off your cell phone and giving yourself permission to curl up with a good book, play games such as solitaire or Scrabble, or do some sketching.

Your wisdom is at an all-time high this year, so get to know yourself better. Listen to your internal voice, and take time for yourself to analyze where you've been and where you want to go in life. However, don't brood too much about yesterday or tomorrow—be a today person. Dig deep and ponder. Even digging in the garden will put you in a meditative state. This is a year to not push things or seek new opportunities. Work with what you have and be patient, and new opportunities will come to you next year. Above all, rely on your intuition and allow your thoughts to guide your destiny!

Because you need to experience your emotions fully this year, you may want to limit or give up caffeine and alcohol. Avoid living in "should-itis" (would have, could have, should have)—stay in the present.

DID YOU KNOW?

In Personal Year Number 7, think, "Happiness is like a butterfly. It flies if we chase it, but when we sit quietly, it lands on our shoulder." This is a time to sit quietly and listen to your wisdom and intuition, which are at an all-time high this year.

Personal Year Number 8

In your Personal Year Number 7, you thought about it—now, in Personal Year Number 8, it's time to do it! This is a year of money, power, and success.

Your energy and enthusiasm can put you center stage, so don't rest on your laurels. This is the year to be the boss or take charge of a project. Get organized, put your systems in place, and hit it on all cylinders! Make a list and experience the fun of checking off your accomplishments. To advance your career, get to work early, stay late, and keep your nose to the grindstone. Time is money, so make every minute count. And speaking of money, an 8 year is a good time to stick to a budget and get your finances in order.

This year, trust your mind rather than your heart—common sense over emotional responses is the byword. Be balanced, and keep your emotions in check. Just deal with the facts, and avoid hearsay.

In Personal Year Number 8, be aware of health. It may not necessarily be your own, but someone close to you who may need monitoring. If you need to gain or lose weight, this is the perfect year to do it. Plan your meals ahead, shop the outside aisles of the market, and avoid going through the fast lane of the drive-thru!

Personal Year Number 9

Personal Year Number 9 is a year to tie up loose ends and finish what you started as your nine-year cycle comes to a close.

A 9 year is a good time to "clean house" and rid yourself of possessions, people, or situations that have served their purpose in your life. Look at things objectively in your personal and business life this year and get rid of unnecessary items or habits. What is it that you should give up and stop doing?

In Personal Year Number 9, you may be giving more than you are receiving and have unexpected expenditures, such as lending money to those in need. With your radar at full tilt in this year, you're picking up the feelings (both positive and negative) of others.

Get out your passport and call your travel agent in a 9 year. Faraway places with strange-sounding names are calling you! Long-distance travel or travel over water is enjoyable now.

As you get ready to celebrate your next birthday and move into an exciting Personal Year Number 1, formulate the new vision you want to create. This may be a year of endings, but with every ending in a 9 year comes the promise of a new beginning the next year.

Things are coming to their natural conclusion this year. Know that while you may be feeling some disappointment, bigger and better opportunities await you in your Personal Year Number 1.

The Least You Need to Know

- Personal Year Numbers run in a nine-year cycle, and knowing where you are in your cycle can help you plan for the future.
- The Personal Year Number runs from birthday to birthday.
- To get the most accurate calculation of the Personal Year Number, use the year in which the birthday was last celebrated.

The Triad Numbers

In Chapter 12, I told you about Personal Year Numbers, including how to calculate them and how to interpret the result of that calculation. But a Personal Year is just the Big Top that encompasses all the acts within it; you also have Personal Months (see Chapter 14), Personal Days (see Chapter 15), and this chapter's focus, the four-month cycles within the year known as Triads.

Using the information in this chapter, you will discover how to calculate and interpret your Triad Numbers to obtain more detailed information and guidance for each four-month segment of your Personal Year. Knowing your Triad Numbers will give you a deeper look into the activities and events you are apt to encounter during your Personal Year.

In This Chapter

- The significance of Triad Numbers
- How to calculate Triad Numbers
- Interpreting Triad Numbers and how Personal Year Numbers affect them

What Are the Triad Numbers?

Triads divide your Personal Year into three approximately equal four-month periods. I say "approximately," because in the Gregorian calendar, which is the primary calendar used throughout the modern world today, the months aren't all of equal length.

Your Triad Numbers, when read in concert with your Personal Year Number, will provide an added overtone of the circumstances and events you are likely to encounter in the corresponding four-month cycle. This gives you more detailed information on which to base your plans and actions. For example, you'll know when you will work well with others and when it's best to go it alone. Triads can also indicate times for avoiding big expenditures and periods when money will be made.

Calculating Your Triad Numbers

The pieces of information you need to calculate your Triad Numbers are your birth month, your birth day, the four-digit year in which you were born, the four-digit year in which you celebrated your last birthday, your age at your last birthday, and your Life Path Number. To calculate your Triad Numbers, follow these steps, using the blank worksheets and the table provided.

> **PYTHAGORAS SAYS**
>
> If you don't have your Life Path Number committed to memory at this point, or you are calculating Triads for someone else, refer back to Chapter 10 for how to get it.

$$\underline{\qquad} + \underline{\qquad} + \underline{\qquad} = \underline{\qquad}$$

Month   Day   Year Born   Life Path Number

$$\underline{\qquad} + \underline{\qquad} + \underline{\qquad} = \underline{\qquad}$$

Month   Day   Year of Last Birthday   Personal Year Number

$$\underline{\qquad}$$

Current Age

Use this worksheet to fill in the information requested in steps 1 through 3.

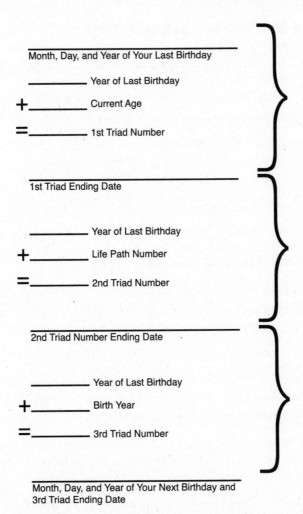

_____ Month, Day, and Year of Your Last Birthday

_____ Year of Last Birthday

+_____ Current Age

=_____ 1st Triad Number

_____ 1st Triad Ending Date

_____ Year of Last Birthday

+_____ Life Path Number

=_____ 2nd Triad Number

_____ 2nd Triad Number Ending Date

_____ Year of Last Birthday

+_____ Birth Year

=_____ 3rd Triad Number

_____ Month, Day, and Year of Your Next Birthday and
3rd Triad Ending Date

Use this worksheet to fill in the information requested in steps 4 through 10.

Triad Start and End Dates

Birth Month	First Triad	Second Triad	Third Triad
January	January–May	May–September	September–January
February	February–June	June–October	October–February
March	March–July	July–November	November–March
April	April–August	August–December	December–April
May	May–September	September–January	January–May

continues

Triad Start and End Dates (continued)

Birth Month	First Triad	Second Triad	Third Triad
June	June–October	October–February	February–June
July	July–November	November–March	March–July
August	August–December	December–April	April–August
September	September–January	January–May	May–September
October	October–February	February–June	June–October
November	November–March	March–July	July–November
December	December–April	April–August	August–December

1. On the first worksheet, write down the month, day, and four-digit year you were born. For your Life Path Number, you can either add all the digits together and reduce to a single digit, or retrieve your result from Chapter 10.

2. Write down the month, day, and four-digit year in which you celebrated your last birthday. For the Personal Year Number, you can either add all the digits together and reduce to a single digit, or retrieve your result from Chapter 12.

3. Write down your current age.

4. On the top line of the second worksheet, write down the month, day, and four-digit year you celebrated your *last* birthday. On the bottom line, write down the month, day, and four-digit year you will celebrate your *next* birthday.

5. To find the ending date of your first Triad, refer to the "Triad Start and End Dates" table or count four months from your most recent birthday. On the line above "1st Triad Ending Date," write down the month, day, and four-digit year your first Triad ends.

6. To find your first Triad Number, on the line next to "Year of Last Birthday," write down the four-digit year. Next, on the line next to "Current Age," write your age. Add the two values together and reduce to a single digit. On the line next to "1st Triad Number," write down your result.

7. To find the ending date of your second Triad, refer to the "Triad Start and End Dates" table or count four months from the end of your first Triad. On the line above "2nd Triad Ending Date," write down the month, day, and four-digit year your second Triad ends.

8. To find your second Triad Number, on the line next to "Year of Last Birthday," write down the four-digit year. Next, on the line next to "Life Path Number," write down your Life Path Number (see Chapter 10). Add the two values together and reduce to a single digit. On the line next to "2nd Triad Number," write down your result.

9. To find the ending date of your third Triad, refer to the "Triad Start and End Dates" table or count four months from the end of your second Triad; this date is your next birthday. If you completed step 4, you already wrote that information on the bottom line of the worksheet. If you skipped that step, though, write down that information now.

10. To find your third Triad Number, on the line next to "Year of Last Birthday," write down the four-digit year. Next, on the line next to "Birth Year," write down the four-digit year you were born. Add the two values together and reduce to a single digit. On the line next to "3rd Triad Number," write down your result.

11. As a reference, write down your Personal Year Number (see Chapter 12) to the right of the bracket.

 PYTHAGORAS SAYS

> But what do you do with a birthday on June 29 or 30 or October 29, 30, or 31 when the February date doesn't exist? The simple answer is that March 1 gets used. Similarly, if your birthday falls on March 31, the third Triad date should be December 1 because there's no November 31. Easy rule: If the date doesn't exist, jump to the first subsequent date that does exist.

To show you how the Triad calculation process is done, I'll use my daughter Jamie's birth date, June 26, 1968, as an example. First, I needed to find Jamie's Life Path Number. To do this, I added the birth month (6), birth day (26), and the four-digit birth year (1968) and reduced to a single digit: $6 + 2 + 6 + 1 + 9 + 6 + 8 = 38$; $3 + 8 = 11$; $1 + 1 = 2$. This provided a Life Path Number of 2. (You can see the detailed derivation of Jamie's Life Path Number in Chapter 10.)

To determine Jamie's Personal Year Number (see Chapter 12 for a refresher), I added the birth month (6), birthday (26), and the four-digit number in which she celebrated her last birthday (2013): $6 + 2 + 6 + 2 + 0 + 1 + 3 = 20$; $2 + 0 = 2$. Between June 26, 2013 and June 26, 2014, Jamie is in a Personal Year Number 2.

Finally, I found Jamie's age at her last birthday (June 26, 2013). She was born in 1968, so I sub-tracted 1968 from 2013, which gave me 45. That tells you she turned 45 on her last birthday. The following shows you a filled-in worksheet for Jamie's number for the first three steps of the process.

<u> 6 </u> + <u> 26 </u> + <u> 1968 </u> = <u> 2 </u>
Month   Day   Year Born   Life Path
                                   Number

<u> 6 </u> + <u> 26 </u> + <u> 2013 </u> = <u> 2 </u>
Month   Day   Year of Last   Personal
                    Birthday   Year Number

<u> 45 </u>
Current
Age

Next, I wrote down the start and end dates of each Triad.

June 26, 2013

October 26, 2013

February 26, 2014

June 26, 2014

With a birthday of June 26, Jamie's first Triad runs for the four months from June 26, 2013. Therefore, her first Triad ending date is October 26, 2013. To calculate her first Triad Number, I added the four-digit year she celebrated her last birthday (2013) to the age she turned on her last birthday (45) and reduced to a single digit. This gave me her first Triad Number: 6.

$$June\ 26,\ 2013$$
$$2013$$
$$+\quad 45$$
$$\overline{2058} = 15 = \textcircled{6}\ \text{1st Triad Number}$$
$$October\ 26,\ 2013$$

Jamie's second Triad will commence on October 26, 2013, and run until February 26, 2014. Therefore, her second Triad ending date is February 26, 2014. To calculate her second Triad Number, I added the four-digit year she celebrated her last birthday (2013) to her Life Path Number (2) and reduced to a single digit. This gave me her second Triad Number: 8.

$$October\ 26,\ 2013$$
$$2013$$
$$+\quad 2$$
$$\overline{2015} = \textcircled{8}\ \text{2nd Triad Number}$$
$$February\ 26,\ 2014$$

Jamie's third and final Triad begins on February 26, 2014, and continues for four months until her next birthday, June 26, 2014. Therefore, her third Triad ending date is June 26, 2014. To calculate her third Triad number, I added the four-digit year she celebrated her last birthday (2013) to her birth year (1968) and reduced to a single digit. This gave me her third Triad Number: 3.

$$February\ 26,\ 2014$$
$$2013$$
$$+1968$$
$$\overline{3981} = 21 = \textcircled{3}\ \text{3rd Triad Number}$$
$$June\ 26,\ 2014$$

This is how the second worksheet looks with all of Jamie's Triad Number information filled in, so you can get an idea of how yours should look when it's finished.

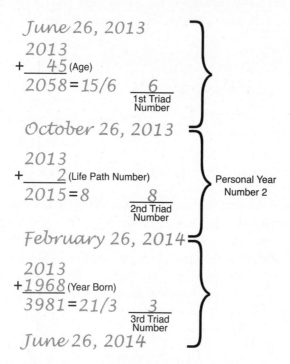

June 26, 2013

$$2013$$
$$+\ \underline{\quad 45\quad}\ \text{(Age)}$$
$$2058 = 15/6 \quad \underline{\quad 6\quad}$$
1st Triad
Number

October 26, 2013

$$2013$$
$$+\ \underline{\quad 2\quad}\ \text{(Life Path Number)}$$
$$2015 = 8 \quad \underline{\quad 8\quad}$$
2nd Triad
Number

February 26, 2014

$$2013$$
$$+\underline{1968}\ \text{(Year Born)}$$
$$3981 = 21/3 \quad \underline{\quad 3\quad}$$
3rd Triad
Number

June 26, 2014

Personal Year
Number 2

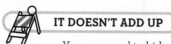

IT DOESN'T ADD UP

You may need to hide your credit cards during a Triad Number 3. You're apt to be in the mood to shop 'til you drop, especially if you're in a Personal Year Number 3.

Triad Number Meanings

Each of your Triad Number meanings is colored by your Personal Year Number. Therefore, along with the significance of each number, I also share special meanings based on the Personal Year Number it's paired with.

Triad Number 1

During Triad Number 1, you have more energy and may be in the mood to begin something new. You may also find a new solution to an old problem or get a new attitude about what's facing you. This is also a time to take charge of a situation and see tasks through to completion. All systems are go, so it's time to move ahead with your plans.

Personal Year Numbers in Conjunction with Triad Number 1

Personal Year Number	Meaning
1	Full steam ahead!
2	Cooperate while you delegate.
3	Make some new friends and socialize.
4	Practice patience and minimize your impulsiveness.
5	Bring newness into your life; expand your horizons.
6	Use a new approach to smooth ruffled feathers.
7	Look and think before you leap.
8	Consider new ways to make money.
9	Think of a new invention or project that would appeal to everyone.

Triad Number 2

During Triad Number 2, you may work in partnership with someone and learn something new by taking a class or personal study. This is a time to gather all the facts so you can get as much information as possible. Exhibiting more sensitivity than is your norm, you may also spend more time with friends and renew old acquaintances.

Personal Year Numbers in Conjunction with Triad Number 2

Personal Year Number	Meaning
1	You're torn—part of you wants to be tactful, while the other part of you just wants to speak your mind.
2	You want to work in tandem with another—anyone for a bicycle built for two?
3	You're sensitive and in the mood to do something creative.
4	Find a partner to get more accomplished in less time—after all, four hands can often do at least twice the work of two.
5	Go on a romantic getaway with someone you love.
6	Romance is on your mind.
7	This is definitely a time for research and study.
8	You'll encounter two different ways of making money.
9	You're in a humanitarian frame of mind and want to help the world.

PYTHAGORAS SAYS

Each Triad Number consists of an overriding theme. For example, a Triad Number 2 is all about partnership and digging for information. Your Personal Year Number will determine what aspects of the theme are applicable to you during the four-month Triad and will tell you how you can maximize the theme no matter what Personal Year Number you're in.

Triad Number 3

During Triad Number 3, you may be interested in a creative pursuit and use your verbal and written skill to express yourself or promote an idea. You either have an overabundance or a need of self-confidence. You also may want to get more sleep than you currently are. During this time, you may be spending more money than usual and entertaining friends or business associates.

Personal Year Numbers in Conjunction with Triad Number 3

Personal Year Number	Meaning
1	You'll be lucky in an unusual and unexpected way.
2	You may be spending money on others.
3	You have unexpected expenditures that pop up.
4	You're burning the candle at both ends.
5	It's time to promote your ideas, including through advertising.
6	You're using creative methods to help loved ones.
7	You should exhibit your verbal and written skills.
8	Your need to work and your desire to play are in conflict.
9	Your off-the-wall idea can bring you fame.

Triad Number 4

During Triad Number 4, you're able to build toward your future and are willing to roll up your sleeves and work hard. You should work toward meeting deadlines and finishing what you start. You may feel hemmed in or chafe at imposed restrictions. However, you should use this time to stick to a budget and to exhibit more patience and practicality.

Personal Year Numbers in Conjunction with Triad Number 4

Personal Year Number	Meaning
1	It's all work and no play.
2	You'll find it's more fun to work with someone else.
3	Follow your budget and curb your impulse to spend.
4	Don't allow yourself to get stuck in a rut.
5	You don't need to go first-class all the time—look for less-expensive options.
6	Try to seek out quality items that are on sale.
7	Be good to yourself and take some "me time."
8	Pull out all the stops and prepare for success.
9	You're giving someone the shirt off your back.

PYTHAGORAS SAYS

A Triad Number 4 may seem like all work and no play. Know that this time is building toward rewards that will be reaped during a Triad Number 8. And get your rest now; the Triad Number 5 will be filled with nonstop action!

Triad Number 5

During Triad Number 5, you're apt to be busy and involved in many activities. You're possibly feeling sensual as you enjoy your five senses. You may have a change in plans or direction and the opportunity to make a choice. You have the freedom to do what you want to do. This is a time you may also consider taking a trip or short getaway.

Personal Year Numbers in Conjunction with Triad Number 5

Personal Year Number	Meaning
1	Staying home is not an option—you have places to go and people to meet.
2	You're juggling several balls in the air in all areas of your life.
3	You have a jam-packed social calendar.
4	No matter how much you want to go, you know that you need to stay.
5	Holy Toledo! You're off and running.

continues

Personal Year Numbers in Conjunction with Triad Number 5 (continued)

Personal Year Number	Meaning
6	You're the toast of the town and in great demand at many social events.
7	You're compelled to rush around, but you crave rest.
8	You're busy making money.
9	It's time to ponder leaving on a vacation.

Triad Number 6

During Triad Number 6, you may be a peacemaker, helping others to get along with each other and offering advice. Practice your mediation skills and look for the win-win. You also carry more than your fair share of the load during this time. You attract others to you and may seek to change your appearance, whether through new clothes, a new hairstyle, or a makeover.

Personal Year Numbers in Conjunction with Triad Number 6

Personal Year Number	Meaning
1	You have a twinkle in your eye and pep in your step.
2	You have partnership and togetherness on your mind.
3	It's time to buy new clothes or change your appearance.
4	Look for beautiful things at bargain prices.
5	You have the urge to play but have too many responsibilities.
6	You're giving advice to or helping loved ones.
7	Someone wants or needs your help, but you want them to handle matters on their own.
8	You're in charge and want everyone to pull their weight.
9	It's time for candlelight, tender moments, and expressions of love.

DID YOU KNOW?

You may be feeling pulled in many directions during a Triad Number 6—everyone seems to need you right now.

Triad Number 7

During Triad Number 7, you may want to spend a little more time doing what you want, even at the expense of what you need to do. Consider the consequences before you act. You may also feel somewhat lonely and isolated. You should take more "me time" and get more rest than is your custom. This is also a time to analyze, evaluate, and think carefully before you speak.

Personal Year Numbers in Conjunction with Triad Number 7

Personal Year Number	Meaning
1	Check to see how deep the water is before you jump in.
2	You may be sensitive and feel misunderstood.
3	Express your feelings in words rather than actions.
4	Your life is going to improve soon, so don't get discouraged.
5	Be careful about overindulging.
6	You may feel a loved one is misunderstanding you.
7	You must bide your time.
8	Evaluate a situation carefully before offering to be in charge.
9	Don't cry over spilt milk—what's done is done.

Triad Number 8

During Triad Number 8, you may need to organize your finances. This is also a time to organize your finances and pay attention to your diet. You desire to make every minute count, but make sure your emotions stay balanced. You also should take charge when you feel the need, but avoid passing the buck.

Personal Year Numbers in Conjunction with Triad Number 8

Personal Year Number	Meaning
1	Get organized and proceed at full throttle.
2	Two heads can think better and faster than one, so join forces with someone working on a project.
3	Organize your finances.
4	Be aware that others may bristle at your bossy attitude.
5	It may look like chaos, but you know what's in every stack and pile.

Personal Year Numbers in Conjunction with Triad Number 8 (continued)

Personal Year Number	Meaning
6	Make sure you've got all the troops working together toward the same goal.
7	Delegate so you have some time for yourself.
8	Be careful not to let others load you down with too many projects and responsibilities.
9	Keep your emotions on an even keel.

Triad Number 9

During Triad Number 9, you may have some form of an ending—for example, completing a project or preparing to make a change. You may also experience conflict or a difference of opinion with a romantic partner, family, friends, or coworkers. During this time, you work with people from various walks of life and give more than you receive.

Personal Year Numbers in Conjunction with Triad Number 9

Personal Year Number	Meaning
1	Know that for every ending there's a new beginning.
2	Always remember to say "thank you."
3	Art, music, and beauty soothe your soul.
4	Organize humanitarian and charitable efforts.
5	Realize that change can be a good thing.
6	Love, home, and family are a big part of your agenda.
7	Take some deserved time off to just chill.
8	Don't give more than you can comfortably afford.
9	Be quick to forgive and forget.

The Least You Need to Know

- A Personal Year is divided into three four-month periods called Triads.
- Your Triad Numbers are calculated using your birth month, your birth day, the four-digit year in which you were born, the four-digit year in which you celebrated your last birthday, your age at your last birthday, and your Life Path Number.
- The Triad Number's influence is shaded by your Personal Year Number.

The Personal Month Numbers

In the previous two chapters, I taught you how to calculate your Personal Year and Triad Numbers, which give guidance for what to do during the year or during four-month cycles. If you want even a closer look at what's happening in your life's journey, you should check out your Personal Month Numbers. To me, this is one of the most exciting and impactful aspects of numerology because it gives you a microscopic view of what you're going to experience in any given month.

In this chapter, I show you how to calculate and interpret your Personal Month Numbers to learn your tendencies and challenges for every month in the year.

In This Chapter

- The significance of Personal Month Numbers
- How to calculate your Personal Month Numbers
- The meanings of each Personal Month Number

What Are the Personal Month Numbers?

Personal Month Numbers divide your Personal Year into 12 approximately equal month-long periods. Like with the Triad Numbers, they're only "approximate" because all the months aren't of equal length.

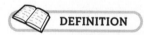 **DEFINITION**

> A **Personal Month Number** indicates the overall tone of the coming month and helps track how your feelings, attitudes, and circumstances change. It is the reduced sum of the number value of a certain month and your Personal Year Number.

When you know your Personal Month Numbers, you can track how your feelings, attitudes, and circumstances change during the course of a Personal Year. From this information, you can determine when it's a good time to take a vacation, start a project, or make like a turtle and keep your head down.

Each month has a unique and overriding energy or theme. For example, a Personal Month Number 2 is all about partnership, while a Personal Month Number 6 is about taking care of responsibilities and beautifying your surroundings.

Calculating Your Personal Month Numbers

To calculate your Personal Month Numbers, you only need to know the number of the months in question and your Personal Year Number (see Chapter 12). Using the blank table I've provided for you, follow the steps to get your different Personal Month Numbers.

Personal Month Start	Month Number + Personal Year Number	Personal Month Number

Use this table to fill in the information and calculations for your Personal Month Numbers.

1. Write down the month, day, and four-digit year of your last birthday in the top-left box.

2. Write down the month number (January = 1, February = 2, and so on; see Chapter 12 if you need a refresher) and Personal Year Number in the second column. Add the digits together and reduce to find your Personal Month Number.

3. Place the Personal Month Number in the third column.

4. Repeat the process, from left to right, for each successive Personal Month. If the date doesn't exist in the month, use the last day of the month as the transition day—so for March 31, for example, you'd write down April 30 for the next month.

You should now have the Personal Month Numbers for each month of your Personal Year.

IT DOESN'T ADD UP

Note that the Personal Month Numbers cycle between 1 and 9, with a break in the cycle at January, where you fall back by 2 (a 2 for December means an 8 for January, for example). If your Personal Month Number doesn't take two steps backward in January, check your arithmetic!

I'll use June 26, 1968, my daughter Jamie's birth date, as an example to follow. This birth date should be familiar to you by now, as I've used it in other chapters.

First, I found Jamie's Personal Year Number (see Chapter 12 for the calculation). Between June 26, 2013, and June 26, 2014, Jamie is in a Personal Year Number 2.

I next calculated Jamie's Personal Month Numbers. Her first Personal Month runs from June 26, 2013, through July 25, 2013. The number value for June is 6 and her Personal Year Number is 2, so I simply added the two numbers. This gave me her first Personal Month Number: 8. I repeated the process for each Personal Month to obtain the remaining Personal Month Numbers. The following table shows Jamie's Personal Month Numbers.

Personal Month Start	Month Number + Personal Year Number	Personal Month Number
June 26, 2013	6 + 2 =	8
July 26, 2013	7 + 2 =	9
August 26, 2013	8 + 2 =	10; reduces to 1
September 26, 2013	9 + 2 =	11; reduces to 2
October 26, 2013	1 + 2 =	3

continues

continued

Personal Month Start	Month Number + Personal Year Number	Personal Month Number
November 26, 2013	2 + 2 =	4
December 26, 2013	3 + 2 =	5
January 26, 2014	1 + 2 =	3
February 26, 2014	2 + 2 =	4
March 26, 2014	3 + 2 =	5
April 26, 2014	4 + 2 =	6
May 26, 2014	5 + 2 =	7

Personal Month Number Meanings

Each Personal Month Number has a message for you. Accompanying that message are some suggestions for how to make sure the message is delivered to best effect. The following detail the personal meanings for the Personal Month Numbers.

PYTHAGORAS SAYS

People born on the 2nd through the 18th of the month (due to the fact that two numerology values added together can't be less than 2 or more than 18) occasionally encounter especially strong Personal Month Number influences. These occur when the Personal Month Number, before reducing, coincides with the day of month on which they were born. At these times, because the numbers are the same, the same attributes are attributed, making them doubly felt.

Personal Month Number 1

Personal Month Number 1 is the time to plan and start new things. Make a plan for the month and put it in motion. For example, it's a good month to start and stick to a diet by adding new foods that are healthy and nutritious to your meals. Persistence will pay off in whatever you do this month.

Be active—don't sit at home. Take your life off hold and get a move on. Try new things like experimenting with a new restaurant or taking a different route to work. This month isn't a time to hesitate—just jump in and do it.

You've got what it takes to be noticed. If something needs changing about your appearance or you need to break a habit, this is the month to do so. You have the right to be proud this month, so accept the compliments you're getting and walk tall.

Act like the winner you are this month and focus on new possibilities. Rather than being satisfied with the crumbs and leftovers, you should enjoy the banquet. This is the month to chart a new course and be the leader of your own parade; use your dynamite personality to sweep people off their feet. If you take the lead, others will follow.

Take a fresh approach to whatever you do this month. This means trying to improve your attitude and getting a new lease on life. Attack an old problem from a new direction to come up with an innovative solution. Execute your plans; don't just think or talk about them. Stop straddling the fence and make decisions this month. Now is also the time to stand up for yourself and not let others sway you. Sit in your director's chair and call the shots.

Personal Month Number 2

In Personal Month Number 2, you need to stay on track to achieve your goals. You can be successful either working on two projects simultaneously or working with someone else. You may even decide to take a co-worker under your wing. Whatever the case, don't go solo this month.

This month is also a time for working on details and gathering facts while exercising patience. Label your files, straighten up your drawers, polish the silver, and sew on missing buttons.

Personal Month Number 2 is the time to spend time with those you care about. Seek harmony at work, at home, and in all of your relationships. Call up an old friend and renew old acquaintances.

You're sensitive this month, so work on trying not to take things personally. If you've been difficult or acting edgy, start making peace and make amends. Clear up differences of opinions and show loved ones that you understand their feelings so they will be more apt to listen to yours. Also remember to be thoughtful and say "please," "thank you," and "I appreciate you so much."

If you have the tendency to be very blunt or give too much information, this is the month to tone down your approach and soft-pedal your delivery a bit. You're ready, willing, and able to make a compromise, so make sure to be more tactful and diplomatic.

You're feeling idealistic this month, and your standards are high. Try not to feel disappointed if others don't measure up or aren't doing things your way. Be patient when others don't move as quickly as you do; they may be giving it their all and doing the best they can. Also work on forming an alliance with kindred spirits who share your high ideals and fast pace.

Your tactful diplomacy can help others achieve good compromises this month. Listen more and talk less, avoiding the urge to preach, mandate, or issue ultimatums. By listening and actually hearing what the other person has to say, you'll discover what's really going on. Your mind is ready to absorb, so learn something new.

PYTHAGORAS SAYS

Your personal radar is on a high frequency in Personal Month Number 2, so follow your hunches and listen to yourself think. However, don't make hasty decisions—do your homework, get the facts, and weigh decisions carefully.

Personal Month Number 3

Personal Month Number 3 is a time to exhibit your creativity. Figure out solutions to any problem that comes your way and use your imagination to put a new twist on the way you've always done things previously. Optimism is your goal at this time, so don't worry, especially about things over which you have no control.

This also is a very social month for you—say "yes" to life and have more fun. Accept all invitations, socialize, linger over lunch with friends, go to parties, meet new people, and renew friendships—basically, embrace spontaneity.

When you entertain this month, do it with flair. Have a fondue party or flambé cherries jubilee. Don't just give a birthday party for someone—plan a "This Is Your Life Party" and include a video commemorating their life in pictures and personal stories.

Embrace a more youthful side this month. This may be through doing things that require energy and excitement, such as rollerblading, ice-skating, riding a bike, or even taking a walk in the park. You may also be in the mood to pull out your favorite games from childhood, such as Scrabble or Monopoly.

In your swirl of activity this month, the tendency is to do too much. Exhaustion shows on your face, and because you're trying to look youthful this month, that's not a good thing. Don't overdo living in the fast lane.

When it comes to relaxation, give in to your vanity this month and schedule a beauty treatment, facial, or massage—even a pedicure or manicure will do. You may also decide to go to the theater, take in the art film that you've wanted to see, or see what's on cable or available on demand.

This month is also a good time for business or personal communication. Remember, it's not what you say but how you say it. You have a way with words this month, so don't just talk—communicate and really listen. This is the month to get out your joke books and have friends rolling in the aisles with laughter. However, remember to not hog the conversation and interrupt others. Your tendency this month is to be a motor mouth—put a governor on that motor. Also, focus on using your charm to get what you want—whining and pouting when things don't go your way doesn't work.

Personal Month Number 4

Personal Month Number 4 is a time to rest and take care of matters you've let slip. That means it's time to clean out rooms, straighten up your office, sort through your piles of papers, and put things in their proper place. This month is also a good time to get your worn-out shoes repaired or resoled and hem a skirt or slacks. You can use all this cleanup as a way to give back to others by donating to charity anything that's not the right size or that you're not using any longer—just remember to be organized and ask for a receipt.

Be responsible and finish what you've started. Look around your house. What projects did you start that you need to finish? Are there library books you need to put in a stack and return? What bills do you need to pay? Be like Santa Claus—make a list and check it twice. Stay on top of things and don't let things get out of hand this month.

This is the month to organize your finances and save for your future. Look into a 401(k) plan or an IRA or, if you're self-employed, find out about a SEP account. There's also no time like the present to learn a new computer program to help you save time and money. Wouldn't tax time be easier if you had entered things monthly on Quicken or in QuickBooks? You're a technical wizard this month, so learning how to save time and money through such projects will be fun for you.

Stick to your budget this month; look for bargains and avoid impulse spending. You could clip coupons or sign up for daily discount emails like Groupon. You may also consider joining a produce co-op or dinner co-op with families you know well. And yes, you can still go out to dinner, but when you do, why not share an entrée with a friend or take advantage of early-bird or happy-hour specials? You'll actually have fun saving.

Do what you say you will this month. Return phone calls, empty your inbox, and write your appointments in ink and keep them. If a project is due at work, turn it in on time (or early) and error free. This is also the month to do things you've neglected or put on the back burner. Procrastination is not a good thing this month, nor is passing the buck. Do what is expected of you (or more), and don't shirk your responsibilities.

> **PYTHAGORAS SAYS**
>
> In Personal Month Number 4, you have great inner strength and a heightened sense of duty. When it comes to your community, be a solid citizen and obey traffic laws. On the personal front, be a loyal friend; keep confidences to yourself and don't gossip.

Personal Month Number 5

In Personal Month Number 5, it's time to have some more fun, let down your hair a bit, and enjoy new experiences. This is not the month to take yourself or your life too seriously. After all of your diligence and hard work, you're entitled to some R&R.

What have you been wanting to do but haven't had time for? This is the month to do it. Instead of working on the weekends, take a quick getaway or plan a "staycation" and visit local museums, beaches, or attractions. Take a "mental health day" from work and play a bit. Or maybe give yourself some extra time before work to read the newspaper or check the computer for updates on news and activities to enjoy in your area. You'll be amazed at how refreshed and renewed you feel.

After the drudgery and the details last month, you're eager to get out of the rut and be on the go. You've had enough of sitting at home saving money and clipping coupons—this is the month to use all of those coupons you saved to get out and go to the 2-for-1 at the museum, or enjoy special pricing at your favorite restaurant. You may even decide to take the kids out on a Sunday for a change instead of staying home and having them help you with the laundry—after all, the dirty clothes will still be waiting for you when you get home. After enjoying a change of pace, you'll be more in the mood to tackle those household routines.

You have your fingers poised on the pulse of action this month, so take time to try new things. Whether it's a different car wash, the hottest restaurant, or a new theater or movie, it's time for change. Maybe take a new route when you go on errands. If you've been eating frozen vegetables or bought a warehouse-size bag of chips, seal it up and buy a new type. If you've been chewing red licorice, try black (or grape or apple). It can even be something as trivial as using a blue pen to check off your list instead of your normal black pen. Do anything where you can experience newness in whatever you do.

Because your mind is on fast-forward, this month is also a time to investigate fresh ideas. However, because of the speed of your thinking, you may get distracted and have to work to keep focused on the task at hand. To keep every Tom, Dick, or Harry from further distracting you, turn off your email and put your phone on "do not disturb." Also, because you're thinking so fast, you may have the impulse to interrupt if someone is taking too much time to make his or her point. True, you can finish others' sentences for them now, but you should resist that temptation.

In all your zipping about this month, you may tend to skip meals—the dieter's road to disaster. Because of this, you might want to check out the lower-calorie choices at your regular drive-thru or try to take food and snacks with you so you won't be ravenous and overindulge when you finally take time to eat.

Personal Month Number 6

Personal Month Number 6 is a time to be responsible and meet your commitments. Treat duties as pleasurable—write thank-you notes, fulfill promises, and meet social obligations. Who around you needs some help to make their life a bit easier? Does the older couple you live next to need a ride to the doctor or someone to help with their groceries or trash cans? This month, it's the little things you do for others that will give you—as well as them—much happiness.

This is also the month to put your family members first. Have your children been asking for more help with their homework? Clear your evening schedule and give them some extra time. Have they been asking you to spend some quality time with them? Do it now, maybe by preparing a family meal or baking cookies together.

Be objective this month and know that there are always three sides to every story—yours, theirs, and reality. Maybe they have a point, so stay open to others' comments or constructive criticism. When asked, freely share your experience and advice, but don't give it unprompted. You can provide a helping hand, but allow others to tell you what they want done or how they want you to complete the task. You won't win any popularity contests if you impose your will.

You may be called upon to settle squabbles around you this month. At those times, be sure to listen to everyone's point of view and ask questions rather than telling others outright what you think. Also, show others how to practice the art of give and take—after all, the best compromises mean there are no winners or losers.

Play fair and square this month. For example, if the server forgets to charge you for that extra dessert you ordered to go, bring it to his attention. Do the right thing, even if no one is looking. Honesty is always the best policy.

Put on your rose-colored glasses, or if you don't have any, at least be positive in your thinking—no one wants to be around a sourpuss. Attract people to you with your great attitude and smile. This month is a good time to focus on the positive aspects of others and not just on what bugs you. Go out of your way to be pleasant.

Happiness is on your mind this month. Your sense of love and romance is so strong that you'll be trying to keep the flames of love and the home fires burning. This is a time to attract new friends and business contacts and spend time with loved ones.

Make your home your haven this month. This is the month to see what sprucing up you can do (without spending a fortune, of course). Beautify your surroundings by doing something as simple as rearranging the furniture. Or look in the back of the linen closet, get out that set of sheets you've been saving for company, and enjoy them yourself! Cut some flowers from your garden or buy them at the grocery store and put them in a pretty vase where you can enjoy them; they will bring a smile to your face every time you walk past them.

This month is also a time to pay special attention to your appearance. Shop your own closet and put together some new outfits. You may also decide to take more time in the morning to shine your shoes or put on some accessories to brighten things up a bit. Whatever you do, you're bound to get compliments all day long.

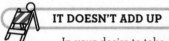

IT DOESN'T ADD UP

In your desire to take care of others this month, you may overcommit your time and neglect taking care of yourself. Don't forget to relax and have some "me time"!

Personal Month Number 7

This is the month to plan some quiet time so you can regroup, recharge your batteries, and do what you want to do. You may decide to visit the mountains or go to the beach, hang out at the library, listen to some music, or simply taking a walk alone. Or, if you can't do any of those, at least take the phone off the hook and enjoy some solitude and tranquility. You simply need some time to think, so don't feel guilty about claiming it in Personal Month Number 7.

This month, get inside your own head and think about your feelings as well as the facts. Visualize a mental picture in your mind and allow it to go onto autopilot to see where it leads you. You may think about where you've been, where you are now, and where you want to go. You can even analyze your goals and progress, looking for ways to improve your position. Because of your introspective frame of mind, this is also the month to ponder the mystical side of life.

Strive for high standards at home and at work this month. Be thorough and painstaking in your approach to any task, dotting all of your Is and crossing all of your Ts. And make sure the people around you are those you can trust and who share your high standards and sense of perfectionism—the last thing you need is someone who jumps the gun and tries to help you without getting your input and a game plan first.

Personal Month Number 7 is a time for beating around the bush. Don't rush after opportunities; instead, wait for opportunities to come to you. In business, you need to ask indirect questions to get the answers you seek. You hold the trump card in these and money matters, so keep your thoughts to yourself and don't speak until you're sure. This month, you have a knack for knowing what information to hold back and which to divulge—play your cards close to your vest.

Are you puzzled by your love life or lack thereof? Under that cool exterior this month beats a warm heart, and the mysteries of love may be absorbing your thoughts. In terms of family, make sure you spend quality time with your loved ones this month. Be calm, avoid gossip, and keep secrets.

IT DOESN'T ADD UP

Personal Month Number 7 is not the month to dash about and fill your social calendar. In fact, idle chatter and babbling voices are apt to drive you up the wall.

Personal Month Number 8

This is your month to step up to the plate and take charge. Obviously, don't take on any more than you can handle, but you can do a lot this month—in fact, in Personal Month Number 8, you can do it better than almost anyone else. Channel your energy and efforts—you have what it takes to achieve a lot. Also, organize your time and work efficiently by taking control of the situation and taking constructive steps to attain your goal. You can motivate others to pitch in when dealing with the details.

This is the month that you also want to get financial affairs in order. Balance your checkbook, make sure all of your revolving charges are up to date, and get your office organized. You should also purge those things you don't need for tax purposes or won't need at a later date. Use good judgment in finances, and don't overextend yourself.

Set up a filing system this month, if you haven't done so already. Doing so will eliminate the clutter from your mind as well as your desk. Remember, time is money, and knowing where everything is will help you find things you need faster.

In Personal Month Number 8, you're able to say how you feel in a direct way. If you have been carrying more than your fair share of the load at work, this is the time to have a heart-to-heart and discuss your feelings with your coworkers.

Dress for success this month—don't walk into a meeting with a grease spot on your tie, rundown heels, or unpolished shoes. It's the little things people are going to notice about you this month as you stand before them leading a meeting.

Your emotions may be like a rollercoaster this month, so work on staying balanced. Don't fly off the handle, and be sure to preface any criticism with some positive introductory comments. You can get your points across if you watch your words and are polite.

You should also be balanced in your scheduling this month—try eight hours to work, eight hours to rest, and eight hours to tend to the details and play. If you drag in the afternoon or after a stressful meeting, try taking a power nap.

Mind your diet and exercise regimen. You're apt to being busy going to business meetings and luncheons, not to mention dinners out, so try to avoid carbohydrates (and especially those high-calorie sweets) and concentrate on the protein and salads section of the menu. Also, get those endorphins going and get some exercise. If you don't frequent the gym, maybe a game of golf or taking a walk will help let off the steam. Eating well and exercising in Personal Month Number 8 will give you the energy to keep up with your schedule.

Personal Month Number 9

You'll experience endings often in Personal Month Number 9, but that doesn't have to be a bad thing. For example, you could end a bad habit, tie up loose ends on a project, or get rid of clutter that's been weighing you down. And if a relationship has run its course and you're going in different directions, this would be a good month to let it go. When we let something or someone leave our experience, something or someone new comes in to replace what has departed. Be willing to forgive, forget, and let things go.

Personal Month Number 9 is not the time to be selfish. If your mate wants to go somewhere and you could live without it, go ahead and go. It's the time to put your needs and wishes aside, help others, and let them have their way. You should also remember to express appreciation and give credit where due. What goes around comes around, so play by the rules, avoid pettiness, and keep the big picture in mind.

This is the month to put your needs aside and help others. If you have been considering volunteering, Personal Month Number 9 is a good month to do so. Perhaps you could help with Meals on Wheels, read to young children at your local school, help shelve books at the library, or volunteer at a hospital. At the very least, give your discards to charity. Make whatever you do count, and be generous with your time and effort.

Things you purchase this month won't always end up being something that you like and find useful. If you can, wait and make major purchases in another Personal Month, perhaps in Personal Month Number 1.

In Personal Month Number 9, you may take a trip across water (ocean, river, or lake) during business or personal travel. Strange as it may sound, you may be in the mood for exotic flavors and food this month. Perhaps Thai, Mongolian barbecue, Chinese Dim Sum, Tex Mex, or authentic Mexican food is calling your name.

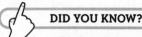

> **DID YOU KNOW?**
>
> Princess Diana got married in her Personal Year Number 9 as well as her Personal Month Number 9, and we all know how that marriage worked out. Sadly, she didn't find her Prince so charming after all.

The Least You Need to Know

- Personal Months divide a Personal Year into 12 parts.
- Personal Months run from the date of your birthday to the date of your birthday in the following month.
- Personal Month Numbers are the reduced sum of the month number and the Personal Year Number.

The Personal Day Number

While it's important to know what's happening on a yearly and monthly basis, you also make important decisions on a day-to-day basis.

By determining your Personal Day Numbers, you can investigate what particular days hold for you. Whether you're deciding when to buy a car or house, start a new job, or schedule a wedding, knowing your Personal Day Numbers can help you with important decisions.

In this chapter, I show you how to calculate and interpret your Personal Day Numbers to uncover what each day of the month may hold for you.

In This Chapter

- Learning about Personal Day Numbers
- How to calculate your Personal Day Numbers
- The meanings of Personal Day Numbers

What Are the Personal Day Numbers?

Your Personal Year has 365 Personal Days (366 in a Leap Year). Knowing your *Personal Day Numbers* allows you to schedule activities, big and small, for the appropriate days. Some examples are picking the right wedding date, scheduling medical and dental procedures, and planning parties and other celebrations.

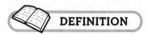 **DEFINITION**

> A **Personal Day Number** describes trends and influences that affect you on any given day. It is calculated by adding month and day numbers to your Personal Year Number and reducing to a single digit.

Personal Day Numbers can reveal tendencies for certain things to occur. For example, travel is most likely to occur on a Personal Day Number 5 and least likely to occur on a Number 4 Personal Day. You'll also see that you may be more confident on a Number 1 Personal Day and more prone to solitary introspection on a Number 7 Personal Day. Understanding the energy of each day can help you schedule important personal or business events based on your strengths on any given day.

Calculating Your Personal Day Numbers

To calculate your Personal Day Numbers, you need your Personal Year Number (see Chapter 12) and some months and days of interest to you. The following walks you step by step through the process; I've provided a table you can fill out.

Month	Day of Month	Personal Year Number	Add and Reduce	Personal Day Number

Use this table to enter your information. There's room for calculating six Personal Day Numbers, but you can always calculate more with a spare sheet of paper.

1. Write down the month and day of interest in the Month and Day of Month columns respectively.

2. Enter your Personal Year Number in the Personal Year Number column.

3. Add and reduce the numbers to a single digit in the Add and Reduce column.

4. Enter the result in the Personal Day Number column.

5. Repeat with the process, from left to right, for each successive Personal Day.

Congratulations! You now have your Personal Day Numbers.

As an example of how to calculate Personal Day Numbers, I'll once again show you the process using June 26, 1968, my daughter Jamie's birth date. If you recall from Chapter 12, between June 26, 2013, and June 26, 2014, Jamie is in a Personal Year Number 2.

To calculate her Personal Day Number for January 4, 2014, I added the month and day to her Personal Year Number.

Month	Day of Month	Personal Year Number	Add and Reduce	Personal Day Number
1	4	2	1 + 4 + 2	7

As you can see, on January 4, 2014, Jamie would be in a Personal Day Number 7. For this set of numbers, no reduction is necessary.

For an example of one that does use reduction, let's check out her Personal Day Number for New Year's Eve, 2013.

Month	Day of Month	Personal Year Number	Add and Reduce	Personal Day Number
12	31	2	12 reduces to 1 + 2 or 3	9
			31 reduces to 3 + 1 or 4	
			3 + 4 + 2	

So 9 is Jamie's Personal Day Number on New Year's Eve 2013.

Personal Day Number Meanings

Personal Day Numbers, like all the other numbers derived from your date of birth, have to do with timing. When to do—or not do—certain things can be decided with help from the meanings of your Personal Day Numbers.

Personal Day Number 1

Personal Day Number 1 is the time to be independent and not wait for or rely on others. It's the right day to take your life off of the back burner—you know what you want to do, and today is the perfect day to accomplish it.

Be open and direct in all of your dealings today. If you've been sitting on the fence, today's the day to make a decision. Mean what you say and say what you mean (in a nice way, of course). No one can manipulate you today, and somehow that comes across.

Today you are a doer, not a dreamer. Start something new and be persistent—stick with whatever you decide to do. For example, a 1 day is the perfect time to start a diet or join a gym. Forge ahead and keep your eyes and ears wide open.

Personal Day Number 1 is also a good day to make appointments or make a purchase—just be sure you don't let the salesman push you into buying something you don't really want.

On a 1 day, make the first move. You have extra self-confidence, so pick up the phone and contact someone with whom you've been wanting to talk. In personal relationships, listen to your inner voice. Today's the day to turn your clever ideas into romantic realities. It's also a great day to go out on a blind date.

Today, act like the winner you are! You have ambition, so use it. You can and will accomplish a lot at home or at work. Even better, whatever you do today will have your personal stamp on it. You also have the ability to solve problems and think of innovative or simplified ways to accomplish the tasks at hand. Energized and ready to succeed, you have a fresh way of thinking and a new way of acting. At the end of the day, be sure to pat yourself on the back for everything you've accomplished.

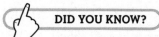 **DID YOU KNOW?**

When your Personal Day Number is the same as your Destiny Number, you're in sync and can do things with ease. You should feel like yourself and in tune with everything you need to accomplish on that particular day.

Personal Day Number 2

On Personal Day Number 2, use your smile and winning ways to "charm the birds right out of the trees." Tact, diplomacy, and politeness get you what you need today. Do you need a favor? This is a good day to ask for it.

Be patient when it comes to making decisions today. Do you have all of the facts you need to make a wise choice? Consider all sides of the question and give others the benefit of the doubt. Even though you may be waiting for something—a check, a phone call, or to hear back after an interview—be patient. Take a deep breath and count to 10 before you lose your cool.

Before you put your foot in your mouth, realize that a 2 day is the time to sit back, listen carefully, and not take things personally. You have two ears and one mouth, so listen twice as much as you speak. Press the Mute button before broadcasting your opinions to others today.

Togetherness and partnership are on your mind on Personal Day Number 2. This is a good day to compromise and not push. You're a wonderful companion today, so make the most of it by, for example, meeting a friend or mate for lunch or dinner. Have plenty of tissues in your purse or briefcase today, because someone might cry on your shoulder! A little sensitive yourself today, you're going to be quite empathetic.

Today, it's important to stay positive and keep negatives out of your thoughts. Don't worry about the ifs, ands, or buts of what could or might happen.

You're also being pulled in two directions today. You might get two offers and want to accept them both. Don't be too concerned; you can accomplish or juggle these two things.

Personal Day Number 3

Personal Day Number 3 is a day to linger over lunch with friends and plan a tête-à-tête dinner with that special someone.

Communication is the key, but easy does it. You're apt to change the subject and be hard to follow as you talk nonstop today. Even if you're in the limelight today, remember that unless someone else is also in Personal Day Number 3, they won't appreciate your chattiness. Take a hint and let others have time to express themselves, too.

Today is like a three-ring circus—your phone may ring constantly, and you're busy from sunup to sundown. Your creative juices are flowing, so you need some kind of a creative outlet. You're filled with vim, vigor, and vitality today. You're feeling not only frisky but flirtatious, so put your personal magnetism to work and attract an array of admirers. You also feel like playing and are in the shopping mood. If you can't hit the malls, you may resort to online shopping for clothes, accessories, or some sort of fun gadget.

Personal Day Number 3 has you feeling either confident or lacking in self-confidence. Remember the song, "Accentuate the positive, eliminate the negative"? If you're tempted to dwell on the downside of an issue, flip it around and think about the positives aspects.

This may be your lucky day to take a calculated risk, so perhaps a lottery ticket is in order.

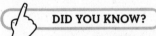 **DID YOU KNOW?**

When your Personal Day Number is the same as your Life Path Number, either opportunities are going to come your way or you learn one of your life's lessons that day.

Personal Day Number 4

Personal Day Number 4 is the day to shop for bargains and avoid paying retail. A word of caution, though: just because it's on sale doesn't mean you really need it or will use it. Be a careful shopper.

This is a day for organization, even if it's your wallet or a desk drawer. It's a good day to pay bills and get your checkbook up-to-date. Luck is what happens when preparation meets opportunity, so get prepared—start building for your future and tighten your financial belt. Concentrate on one goal at a time and don't become scattered. The down-to-Earth plans you make today will pay off in your future.

You have a persevering spirit in Personal Day Number 4. It's an ideal day to clean out your pantry or check the expiration dates on your medicine and perishables.

Everyone in the world—except you, of course—may be running late today. Be patient and don't get yourself in a tizzy over things you can't control. This is a good day to have dental work done, but don't get annoyed if your dentist is running behind schedule. This is also a good day to visit the Department of Motor Vehicles and take your driving test; you'll remember all of the signals and rules of the road and may end up with a perfect score.

Personal Day Number 4 is the day to stick with the tried and true. It's not a good day to try the latest new and exotic restaurant in town. Also, avoid get-rich-quick schemes or a fast-talking salesperson. Be happy with what you have and remember, "If it ain't broke, don't fix it."

Personal Day Number 5

Faster than a speeding bullet, more powerful than a locomotive—is it a bird or a plane? No, it's Personal Day Number 5! Put a snappy "gone fishing" message on your answering machine and get out of Dodge. You've earned it, so take a day off and play hooky.

If you're a loyal employee and do show up at work today, wear clothes that will take you from day to night, because you're sure to get a last-minute invitation. Expect the unexpected. This is not the day for routine tasks, as surprises are sure to derail your plans.

Today's the day you're in perpetual motion. You have so much on your plate today, and 24 hours isn't going to be enough to do what you've got to get finished. *Take the kids to school, go to the dry cleaner, and go grocery shopping. Oops, I forgot something at the market, so it's back to the store. Then it's time to pick up the kids from school and drive off to the orthodontist, followed by a soccer game. Today's too busy to cook dinner, so I need to pick up take-out. Oh, and I'm running low on gasoline, so I need to search for the best gas prices and fill up before heading back home.* Get the picture of what your train of thought is going to be like today? Just do the best you can and try not to get stressed.

Your mind is on fast-forward and is racing as fast as your feet. Plus, your attention span is not at an all-time high, to say the least. If you made a list in your Personal Day Number 4, it comes in handy today. While today isn't the day to make a decision, Personal Day Number 5 is a good day to investigate a new idea you may have. Get the brochures, make a list of pros and cons, and wait.

You have a nose for news and may hear some juicy gossip today. If you even whisper it to one person, it's going to be all over town by nightfall.

Be open to change today. If your plans are changed or you miss your plane flight, it's all for a reason. Enjoy some downtime before you climb into bed so you can relax after a busy day and get a good night's sleep.

> **DID YOU KNOW?**
>
> Unlike many numerologists, I don't use the Master Numbers when it comes to Personal Years, Personal Months, or Personal Days. I always reduce Master Numbers and in fact, I barely glance at Master Numbers most of the time. Why? Behind every Master Number 11 is a 2 and Master Number 22 is a 4; therefore, I personally don't think there's anything super special about Master Numbers.
>
> However, when adults have a Master Number in their Destiny, Soul, or Personality Numbers, I make a mental note and encourage them to live up to their potential.

Personal Day Number 6

Finally, a day for love, home, and family, with some responsibility thrown in as well. Personal Day Number 6 is a perfect day to spend time with someone you love or with someone who needs you. Make yourself and others happy today. This day isn't about you—it's about others. Little things like a hug, a smile, or a kind word mean a lot.

Show an interest in and be protective of loved ones today, letting them know you care. Perhaps you will be called upon to take someone to an appointment or babysit for a niece or nephew. Also, help anyone who needs it—share yourself, your possessions, or whatever someone needs today. Visit a sick friend or someone who needs you. Children and animals tend to be underfoot today, so it's even a good day to take your pet to the groomer or the vet. Florence Nightingale has nothing on you today.

Affection and love are foremost on your mind today. You're reaching out to others and attracting others to you as well. If there's a misunderstanding with those around you, listen to all sides of the story and make compromises. Use a win-win approach all day, and try not to get caught up in any negativity or situations that make you sad.

Whatever you want in life is waiting for you today, whether it's a job, the perfect mate, or the perfect living space. Be generous and focus on quality. A commendable job on your part will be appreciated and rewarded, so accept the praise graciously. It's also a good day for a beauty treatment or self-pampering. On a 6 day, shop for something beautiful, either for your home or to wear.

Personal Day Number 7

Personal Day Number 7 is a day for you; listen to your inner voice today rather than the babbling of others. Avoid the telephone and anything else that will disturb your tranquility today. If you live in the city, escape the hustle and bustle and find a quiet place where you can relax and seek inner peace. If you can't get out of town, take a walk and get some fresh air to clear your head. Today is also a perfect day to pamper yourself with a nap or soak in a hot bath with fragrant bath salts.

The emphasis of Personal Day Number 7 should be inspirational or practical issues. In terms of inspiration, now is the time to research and dig deep for the answers you're seeking; reflect on the past and visualize your future. Also, take the time to read something inspiring or listen to a motivational audio book. On the practical side, this is a good day to work on the computer, enter expenditures in QuickBooks, or meet with your accountant to get things in order. However, make sure you read the fine print before signing any documents.

Today is the day to strive for accuracy and high standards on the job. Be thorough and painstaking, and recheck your work to be sure everything is as perfect as you like it to be. Today is also a great day to spend time on the special skill or hobby you never seem to take the time to enjoy.

You may learn a valuable lesson or read something interesting today. If something has been lost, it may be found today; look in corners, pockets, and under the seat of your car.

If you're feeling unnoticed today, perhaps it's because you're flying under the radar. Take extra care to look neat and well-groomed, and remain poised and reserved today. You may even subconsciously select "keep your distance clothes" that let you blend into a crowd or your surroundings. Be careful choosing who your companions are today. Do you really want to spend time with someone, or would you rather be alone for a change?

This is a good night to stay home and relax. You're going to need your rest before you hit the ground running in your Personal Day Number 8 tomorrow.

 PYTHAGORAS SAYS

How can you use Personal Day Numbers to plan a major event (like a wedding) when both people have different Personal Day Numbers? Look at the Personal Day Numbers for both the bride and groom and try to avoid a Personal Day Number 9 because that's a day of completion and a day for endings, not beginnings.

Personal Day Number 8

Personal Day Number 8 is the time to organize and systematize. Take the initiative, make decisions, and be unlimited in your thinking. All systems are go today, so refuse any form of restriction and be proactive.

Money, power, and success are all on your mind today. You're going to be busy leading and directing others, so be sure to keep your emotions balanced if you get stressed. Time is of the essence, and you've only got 24 hours. Stick to a schedule to stay on task and get everything accomplished today.

This is the day you are destined for success, so pay special attention to how you are "packaged." Be aware of your appearance and the impression you make on others. Today is the day to dress for the job you want, not the job you have. It's also a good day for exercise, so roll up your sleeves and shovel your way through tasks at work and home. Overall, work on a way to improve your self-worth as well as your net worth.

Trust your judgment today. You're the right person at the right time doing the right thing. You won't do anything halfway today because you're hitting on all cylinders.

On an 8 day, anticipate the obvious and avoid any unnecessary activities. However, expect a schedule full of changes; when these changes happen, try to roll with the punches today and temper any frustration. Keep everything in balance today, whether it's your emotions or your checkbook.

If you need to make a major purchase, think of the resale value. Also, look for enduring design and quality workmanship to protect your investment.

Today, focus on your own goal and avoid being overly concerned with the opinion of others. Take stock of yourself and see if you measure up to your own expectations. Remember, you don't compete with anyone but yourself.

Personal Day Number 9

On Personal Day Number 9, you're wearing your heart on your sleeve. Because you're being driven by emotion, today isn't a good day to make purchases lest you have to return them later. Instead of making a hasty decision, sleep on it. Delay a new beginning of any kind until tomorrow.

Be accommodating and willing to help others. You may find yourself sticking up for a friend or underdog today. Although you're helping others today, it's a good time for personal public relations. You have the charisma to project a positive image to the public, so don't hesitate to promote yourself today.

You may fall madly in love with a person, idea, or cause today. Maintain your emotional balance and guard against temperamental outbursts. If you're feeling vulnerable today, try not to take things personally or let your feelings get hurt. It's difficult for you to say no to those less fortunate today; volunteer for a charity or cause that interests you. Give some cash to the homeless person on the street corner, or at the very least, donate some household items or clothing to the Goodwill store or Salvation Army. You're in a very trusting frame of mind, but don't get taken for a ride.

Let the lure of foreign adventure draw you to an ethnic restaurant, and enjoy the interesting patrons as well as the food. It's also a great day to attend a play, musical event, or anything dealing with the arts. Give in to your creative urges and put your imaginative touch on everything you do today.

Personal Day Number 9 is a day of personal expansion. Broaden your horizons and include other people, ideas, and goals. Be tolerant, open-minded, understanding, and accepting of others' faults as well as your own. Encourage others who think differently than you do to give feedback and exchange their views with you. If you keep your ears open and your mouth shut, you might learn something new and be greatly rewarded for the experience.

The Least You Need to Know

- Personal Day Numbers can guide you to the right day to schedule (or avoid) an activity, make large purchases, or get organized.
- Personal Day Numbers are calculated by adding month and day numbers to your Personal Year Number and reducing to a single digit.
- Personal Day Numbers can indicate days of high or low energy, quiet reflection, or energetic interaction.

Tying It All Together

Now that you've learned about numerology's Core Numbers, you can discover how the secondary numbers can provide additional insight into certain times of your life.

Part 4 covers other important numbers that you can use to discover more about yourself. You learn how to calculate your Maturity Number, which indicates the strengths and assets you will enjoy in your golden years. You can also explore the three Malefic Numbers (14, 16, and 19) and the folklore surrounding them. I then teach you to calculate Universal Year Numbers and see how they can pinpoint and even predict important events in history.

In this part, I also help you explore the important, memorable years in your life—your Milestone, Highlight, and Red-Letter Years. You learn how to calculate them, their meanings, and how they help you see how the puzzle of your life fits together.

Finally, I wrap up by taking you through each section of the numerology worksheet, which allows you to collect all of your numbers in one place.

Numerology's Other Numbers

Some numbers you learn in numerology are a bit more general, such as certain traits you'll have late in life and what influence will be felt on a global scale.

In this chapter, I discuss the Maturity Number's place in the pantheon of numerology's numbers, how to calculate it, and what the different values tell you about yourself and your life. Additionally, I give you background on Malefic Numbers and Universal Year Numbers. Finally, I'll wrap up the chapter by discussing what it means when two of your numbers are the same.

In This Chapter

- Learning about your golden years with the Maturity Number

- Malefic Numbers: are they evil?

- Studying what the world is going through with the Universal Year Number

- The significance of two of your numbers being the same

The Maturity Number

Sometimes called the Reality Number or the Ultimate Goal Number by numerologists, the *Maturity Number* describes the true you—the person you have grown and matured to become.

Strangely enough, the Maturity Number is exhibited in childhood through how you play and what your interests are. During your 20s and 30s, your Maturity Number is subtly exhibited while you're typically focused on career, marriage, and family. The Maturity Number's influence is very subtle and it's not usually felt strongly until your 40s or 50s. But while it has some impact in your earlier years, the full effect of the Maturity Number doesn't manifest until you've passed your formative years, which is approximately age 50. This is the time when people start being concerned about their sunset years and want to know what they are going to be like for the remainder of their lives. Also, by this age, you're more discerning and tend not to occupy your life with things that waste your time, money, and energy. To my way of thinking, that's the real meaning of the Maturity Number.

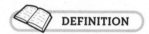

DEFINITION

The **Maturity Number** is meant for your middle-age years and gives hints about how to make the most of your "golden years." It is the reduced sum of your Destiny Number and Life Path Number.

Calculating Your Maturity Number

If you know your Destiny Number and your Life Path Number, you can easily calculate your Maturity Number—you simply add the two values and reduce if necessary. If you don't know one or both of them, review Chapter 3 for your Destiny Number and Chapter 10 for your Life Path Number. The following walks you through the simple steps to finding out your Maturity Number if you don't have your Destiny Number or Life Path Number.

1. Write out your full name and birth date.

2. Write the number values below them.

3. Add the number values together and reduce until you get a single-digit number.

If you recall from Chapters 3 and 10, Jamie has a Destiny Number of 1 and a Life Path Number of 2. If you add those two values together, you get her Maturity Number: 3. If I didn't have that information, though, I could find her Maturity Number by doing the following:

JAMIE LYNN SIMPSON June 26, 1968

11~~495~~ 3755 ~~1947165~~ 6 26 ~~1968~~

2 + 2 (reduced from 20) + 6 + 6 + 8 + 6 = 30

3 + 0 = 3

As you can see, to make the calculation easier (and shorter), I used the trusty "casting out nines" shortcut from Chapter 2. This immediately eliminated the 4, 5, and 9 from her first name; the two 1s, and 4, 5, 7, and 9 from her last name; and the 1, 8, and 9 from her birth year.

PYTHAGORAS SAYS

You may notice that if the Life Path Number is 9, the Destiny Number and the Maturity Number are always the same. Similarly, if the Destiny Number is 9, the Life Path Number and Maturity Number are always the same.

Maturity Number Meanings

The following are the meanings behind each Maturity Number:

Maturity Number 1: If you have a Maturity Number of 1, you're independent, clever, original, determined, direct, and a natural leader. You probably found yourself in leadership roles in your childhood, and later in life is no different. You may need to tone down your sometimes rigid but always strong opinions and thoughts so you have happier relationships in your sunset years.

Maturity Number 2: Always diplomatic, whether in your early years, the prime of your life, or your golden years, you have a talent for getting diverse groups of people working together toward successful outcomes. You have interests and talents that touch others in the humanities (art, music, museums, spiritual activities, and teaching) and anything that's cultured and refined.

Maturity Number 3: Just as was probably the case in your early years, you have a fine ability for a rich and beautiful later life filled with creative activities such as music, art, and literature. You also enjoy humor and possess the ability to express yourself. Be careful not to scatter your forces and waste opportunities in your bountiful later years.

Maturity Number 4: You probably had your early years filled with order, form, and some restriction combined with the practical duties that built for your future. This trend continues in your golden years. There's work to be done, and activities that are systematized and orderly—such as religion, education, publishing, or scientific pursuits—can build for satisfying later years.

Maturity Number 5: Retirement? What's that? Just as the early years of a Maturity Number 5 were busy, your later years are, too. Your golden years are filled with many experiences, including travel and progressive activities, such as freedom of thought, civic involvement, or politics. But be careful not to have too many irons in the fire, which could lead to uncertainty and an inability to get anything accomplished.

Maturity Number 6: Your early years were most likely centered around service to others. The best things in life—such as comfort, financial security, love, and protection—are yours in the latter years. You also have a strong sense of duty and responsibility that makes it easy for you to play by the rules and finish what you start. You're able to accomplish anything you set your mind to with apparent ease.

Maturity Number 7: It's likely that you had specialized talents as a child; now, you should continue to share your knowledge, understanding, and wisdom you've developed through the years with others who seek it. You have opportunities in your golden years for metaphysical and spiritual studies, scientific and educational pursuits, literary interests, and other unique endeavors. When pursuing those interests, you may wish to withdraw, which you probably did when you were a child.

Maturity Number 8: If you've developed organizational skills, courage, good character, and self-discipline through the years, you have the promise of recognition and a position of authority later in life. Anything relating to supervision of real estate, research, philosophical studies, counseling, consulting, or advising others are of interest to you.

Maturity Number 9: In your early years, you were undoubtedly kind and caring, and this kindness carries over later in life. You should be able to live peacefully without jealousy or fears and remain interested in foreign travel and humanitarian affairs. Interest in the humanities (art, music, beauty, and architecture) is a comfort in your later years.

Malefic Numbers

One of my favorite research-based numerology teachers, Earl Miller, introduced me to Malefic Numbers. In his words, "Malefic Numbers represent power we've had in the past that we abused. So now certain things are pushed upon us to learn now what we didn't learn then."

There are three Malefic Numbers: 14, 16, and 19. No special calculation is involved; they are simply values you may come across in your life or when reducing your Core Numbers. You may find them in your calculations before reducing to a single digit. For example, your Soul Number may total 16 before being reduced to a 7, or you may be born on the 14th or 19th of any month.

I personally don't believe Malefic Numbers are bad. But if you believe Malefic Numbers are bad, it's likely they will fulfill your negative expectations.

> **DID YOU KNOW?**
>
> The word *malefic* means "bad" or "evil." Therefore, Malefic Numbers have the connotation of being bad or evil numbers, perhaps undeservedly. But you should remember that dark clouds generally have a silver lining, so what appears negative in the short term could well be beneficial in the long run.

Malefic Number 14

The Malefic Number 14 is related to the physical and sensual aspects of life and relationships. It may represent some form of loss (possessions, a loved one, a job, and so on), sickness, sudden death, unpleasant changes, or physical deformity.

If your Destiny Number is 14 before being reduced to 5, it could represent dashed hopes. You needn't be a pessimist, but a touch of pragmatism could serve you better than unbridled optimism—it's fine to hope for the best, but don't count your chickens until they're hatched.

If your Soul Number is 14 before being reduced to 5, there may be an interruption of emotional affairs. A smooth love life may not be in the cards—just remember that making up can (almost) make the turbulence enjoyable.

If your Personality Number is 14 before being reduced to 5, you may have had a prolific sensual past. Think of the interesting novel you could write! You may want to work to avoid living up to the reputation of being promiscuous if you want your relationships to be more fulfilling.

If the Life Path Number is 14 before being reduced to 5, an important lesson to learn is to "have and to hold and then let go." Your life will be happier if you're less possessive with people and things.

Malefic Number 16

The Malefic Number 16 is related to sensuality and vulnerability. It is a symbol of fallen power, humiliation, discontent, a negative outlook on life, broken promises, gaining love in an inappropriate way, or being a part of unfortunate love affairs.

If your Destiny Number is 16 before being reduced to 7, it may denote the loss of your good name, a compromised professional or social position, or false investments. Often, it means that you once held a high position and then lost your credibility, respect, and power.

If your Soul Number is 16 before being reduced to 7, you may experience a disappointment in love relationships, a broken heart, friends who may not be who you think they are at first meeting, confusion, and general disappointment in children.

If your Personality Number is 16 before being reduced to 7, it can indicate a loss of vitality and health and occasional bouts of depression. It's important for you to see the glass as half full rather than half empty.

If your Life Path Number is 16 before being reduced to 7, you are likely to experience the pain of fallen power. This may manifest as a rise and fall from power, love and loss, prosperity, or financial challenges. You may appear conceited to others but actually be disguising your insecurity. Because you've been let down previously, you often display apathy rather than risk being hurt again.

Malefic Number 19

The Malefic Number 19 is often the most difficult to handle. It can represent extreme suffering when spiritual growth is absent, the break-up of marriages, misuse of power, and serious tests of personal limits and resolve.

If your Destiny Number is 19 before being reduced to 1, it indicates you must relearn lessons throughout your life. Although you run the race or handle life's challenges, you find them especially difficult, as well as both emotionally and physically exhausting. You feel as though you regularly give money, time, and yourself fully but often experience devastating loss or disappointment.

If your Soul Number is 19 before being reduced to 1, it's indicative that all of life's secrets are dragged into the light. You may find that the skeletons in your closet are exposed and that you receive negative public attention. Put your cards on the table early to avoid humiliation and a broken heart.

If your Personality Number is 19 before being reduced to 1, it's likely that others are very slow to trust you. People draw inferences from physical characteristics, such as the impression of "he has shifty eyes." Work on maintaining eye contact and speak directly and distinctly (but not robotically), and you might just gain trust more quickly.

If your Life Path Number is 19 before being reduced to 1, you are going to have to relearn many things throughout your life. These lessons include understanding that you can't get something for nothing, that freedom often comes with a price, and that the universe returns what we send out (karma).

Although Malefic Number 19 seems to be filled with doom and gloom, when it's associated with a Personal Year Number or Pinnacle Number of 19 before being reduced to 1, the following period results in a wiser you. For example, if your marriage or another important relationship ended during this time, you will learn from the experience and approach your next relationship with a richer sense of love.

Universal Year Numbers

Unlike other numbers in numerology, Universal Year Numbers are not "personal" or dependent upon any part of your name or birth date. Universal Year Numbers are something that the world (and everyone in it) is going through at the same time.

The first two digits of any year number (or the first digit between 100 and 999) indicate the rhythm of the century. For example, in the twentieth century (1901 to 1999), the world was under the influence of the 19, which reduces to 1; meanwhile, the twenty-first century is under the influence of the 20, which reduces to 2.

The third number of the four-digit Universal Year indicates the rhythm of the decade. Thus, in 2013, the rhythm of the decade (between 2010 and 2019) is 1; from 2020 through 2029, the rhythm of the decade will be 2; and so forth. Meanwhile, the fourth digit doesn't have any special significance on its own.

The Universal Year Number is determined by adding all four digits of the calendar year and reducing the sum to a single digit. So for the year 2013, the Universal Year Number is 6 (2 + 0 + 1 + 3).

PYTHAGORAS SAYS

Whatever Universal Year Number starts a century also ends the century. For example, 1901 and 2000 have a Universal Year Number of 2, while 2001 and 2100 have a Universal Year Number of 3.

If the sum of the year adds to Master Numbers 11 or 22, it indicates that during the course of that particular Universal Year, great strides and great achievements will be made. It could be significant scientific or technical research, or something politically astounding. However, it's frequently unlikely or impossible for the Master Number to be in effect for the entire year, in which case the year reverts to the reduced number—usually after the occurrence of the significant event.

Universal Year Number 1

Universal Year Number 1 indicates the beginning of a new era or a new nine-year cycle on a worldly level. Initiative and moving forward are the central themes this year. During this time, the Universe needs strong leadership that's courageous and decisive. It's the year for pioneering ideas and charting new courses in human understanding, politics, business, and the arts. A 1 year is also a time for creative activity, progressive planning, and decisive action. The influence of what is begun in a Universal Year Number 1 will be felt for the next eight years.

Universal Year Number 1 Historical Happenings: the assassination of John F. Kennedy (1963); the Watergate break-in (1972) that led to the only presidential resignation in U.S. history; Harrison Ford returned as Indiana Jones at age 65; Tina Fey mocked Sarah Palin on *Saturday Night Live*

PYTHAGORAS SAYS

Of the 11 Universal Year Number 1s in the twentieth century, the first 10 were also Malefic Number 19. To demonstrate that Malefic doesn't always mean bad, both World War I (the so-called "War to End All Wars") and World War II ended in 1918 and 1945 respectively, both Malefic 19 years.

Universal Year Number 2

Whatever began in Universal Year Number 1 is germinating in Universal Year Number 2. This is a year of slow movement—a mild, retiring year in which it's time to collect information or money, sift through things, and put all of the pieces together. During this year, the Universe needs cooperation, tact, and diplomacy. It is a time for peace agreements to be worked out slowly and quietly, so patience is required from all people in all nations.

Universal Year Number 2 Historical Happenings: the League of Nations was founded (1919); CDs replaced records and cassettes (1980); Hillary Clinton elected to the U.S. Senate (2000)

Universal Year Number 3

What began in Universal Year Number 1 and germinated in Universal Year Number 2 begins to show results in Universal Year Number 3. It's a joyful year that offers versatility of interest, with a tendency toward scattering energies in many directions. It's also a time of extravagance, in which money will be spent for pleasure and luxuries. Cultural exchange and sociability are also evident this year.

Universal Year Number 3 Historical Happenings: the Roaring Twenties commenced (1920); the stock market crash that introduced "The Great Depression" (1929); the iPod and XBox were released (2001)

Universal Year Number 4

Universal Year Number 4 is the time in the nine-year cycle when a solid foundation must be laid through hard work and organization. This is the year for order, form, restriction, method, and construction or building for the future. Get ready to buckle down, roll up your sleeves, and get to work on internal organization. A strict sense of values is also especially critical this year.

Universal Year Number 4 Historical Happenings: the creation of the PG-13 movie rating (1984); the introduction of the Macintosh computer (1984); the accounting firm Arthur Andersen dissolved due to a fraud scandal (2002); the last mission in the Space Shuttle Program with *Atlantis* (2011)

Universal Year Number 5

Universal Year Number 5 brings activity, recreation, change, and new life in old trends. The world is busy this year, and travel is universal. A 5 year is also a time of rejuvenation and a time to discard useless and burdensome endeavors that hold one back—people are in the mood for change. Opportunities come through speculation, rather than safe and secure investments.

Universal Year Number 5 Historical Happenings: the introduction of Legos (1955); the rapid worldwide spread of SARS or Severe Acute Respiratory Syndrome (2003); Obama's re-election campaign, with a theme of "Change" (2012)

 PYTHAGORAS SAYS

To determine a Universal Year Number for any century, simply add the first two digits of any year. For example, from 2000 to 2099, people are under the influence of a Universal Year Number 2.

Universal Year Number 6

The freedom of Universal Year Number 5 is replaced by an emphasis on security and reliability. This is a year of adjustments and seeking balance. This year, the world also shows interest in education and health programs, food and diet, emotions, the law of attraction in relationships, ecology, and civic improvements. Business is also good, particularly in industries and commodities that concern the improvement of health.

Universal Year Number 6 Historical Happenings: the issuance of the first credit card (1950); the landing of the Mars Explorer Rover on Mars (2004); the low-carb diet the South Beach Diet became popular (2004); tsunami killed thousands of people in Indonesia (2004)

Universal Year Number 7

Universal Year Number 7 is a time for analysis and introspection, with a goal of refining and perfecting the results of past efforts. It's not a time for expansion or change, as the Universe is rejecting force, limitation, and restriction. Change occurs and alliances are made only through mutual attraction. Obscurity also abounds this year, leading to confusion, fear, and insecurity, particularly on the part of those who are practical-minded. The scientific research developing in Universal Year Number 7 will be realized in Universal Year Number 1.

Universal Year Number 7 Historical Happenings: the first color television set was released (1951); Mark Zuckerberg debuted Facebook (2005); Sudoku became popular (2005)

Universal Year Number 8

Universal Year Number 8 could free the accumulated irritations and confusions experienced during the past seven-year period, as the Universe is seeking justice and a fair deal for all. An endeavor undertaken in the past seven years is harvested this year. It's a time to move forward and branch out for material success and gain—prosperity, expansion, and success are achieved by thinking big. This is a powerful year dealing with money, power, success, and health that gives recognition to those who take authority and efficiently organize to reap financial success.

Universal Year Number 8 Historical Happenings: Margaret Thatcher winning a (very rare) third term as Prime Minister of Britain (1987); the Wii, Tickle Me Elmo, and Dora the Explorer sold millions (2006)

Universal Year Number 9

The Universal Year Number 9 indicates the end—one cycle ends and a new one is ready to begin. It's a time for big business, fulfillment, and completion, with the arts being especially significant. All limitations and self-imposed restrictions must be discarded—no loose ends should be carried over into the subsequent Universal Year Number 1. This year also calls for universal love and sponsors generosity and understanding. Nations and groups must put aside petty concerns and differences and work toward harmony.

Universal Year Number 9 Historical Happenings: the Allied D-Day invasion of Normandy (1944); the Cuban Missile crisis (1962); the publishing of the Pentagon Papers (1971); the first Starbucks opened in Seattle, Washington (1971); Charles Manson and his followers were convicted for the killing of Sharon Tate (1971); MP3s were developed (1998)

Master Universal Year Number 11

A year has an 11 master vibration when futuristic ideals come to the forefront. It is an idealistic year in which people want to know more about the deep inner truths of the self and how they relate to the Universe. It's also a time of surprising or shocking events, and a time to trust intuition and to innovate and invent. The world is ready to explore and to take up new idealistic causes.

Master Universal Year Number 11 Historical Happenings: the founding of U.S. Steel (1901); the indictment, trial, and conviction of Illinois Governor Ron Blagojevich for his attempt to sell the U.S. Senate seat formerly held by President Barack Obama (2009); *Avatar* won Best Film at the Academy Awards (2009); singer Michael Jackson died (2009)

Master Universal Year Number 22

Master Universal Year Number 22 is a time to bring practical idealism into play and develop practical solutions for the burdens of the time which creates unusual types of businesses. It requires construction, organization, and cooperation using the highest of social principles. If international governments cooperate, there are opportunities for solutions to worldwide problems during this period.

Master Universal Year Number 22 Historical Happenings: the creation of the U.S. Air Force out of what was previously the U.S. Army Air Corps as the consequence of the Key West Agreement (1948); the Russian launch of the first man-made orbiting satellite, *Sputnik I* (1957); the creation of the Miranda Warning as a result of the *Miranda* vs. *Arizona* case (1966); Trivial Pursuit games and Cabbage Patch Kids dolls were wildly popular (1984); *Jurassic Park* opened in theaters (1993)

When Two of Your Numbers Are the Same

Metaphysicians believe that coinciding numbers have a special significance and provide you with additional information about yourself. The following are some of the overlaps you might encounter with your numbers and what they mean.

- **Destiny Number and Life Path Number:** When your Destiny Number and Life Path Number are the same, it means you're perfect the way you are. You have no lessons to learn in this lifetime, because you were born knowing all you need to know.

- **Soul Number and Personality Number:** What you see is what you get! In other words, because who you are on the inside (Soul Number) and who you appear to be on the outside (Personality Number) are the same, you're a very genuine person. You don't have any pretenses.

- **Destiny Number and Personal Year Number:** Because your Destiny Number indicates your talents and goals and your Personal Year Number tells you what your activities and experiences will be like for the year, you should feel in sync this year. The activities and things you pursue during this overlap will exemplify you and who you really are—in short, you'll make a name for yourself. Not only will you gain self-understanding, but people will also recognize and notice you for your accomplishments.

- **Personal Year Number and Life Path Number:** The outcome of this combination depends upon how you handle it and the attitude you adopt. Your Life Path Number indicates your opportunities as well as your lessons in life, while your Personal Year indicates the experiences during a particular year. Therefore, you may have opportunities that help you reach your goal with this overlap, or you could be learning some of your life's lessons during the matching Personal Year Number.

- **Soul Number and Personal Year Number:** This overlap can indicate a very interesting year for love or romance. Your Soul Number is the inner you, while your Personal Year Number tells your experiences and activities during a particular year. When they're the same, it means you could have opportunities to fulfill your hopes, wishes, and desires during that year. On the other hand, you might have some issues concerning love and romance, whether it's finding true love or your mate disappointing you (typically in a Personal Year Number 7 or 9).

The Least You Need to Know

- Maturity Numbers don't come to the forefront until middle age. They are calculated by adding your Destiny Number to your Life Path Number and reducing to a single digit.
- Malefic Numbers are the constants 14, 16, and 19.
- Universal Year Numbers apply to the world as a whole and aren't specific to an individual.
- An overlap in your Destiny and Life Path Numbers, Soul and Personality Numbers, Personal Year and Life Path Numbers, or Soul and Personal Year Numbers can have a special significance and provide more information about yourself.

Important Year Numbers

As you've seen, everything in numerology is based on Pythagoras' belief that nature and time are cyclical. Not coincidentally, in this chapter, you'll explore a few cycles of significant importance: Milestone Years, Overtone Numbers, Highlight Year Numbers, and Red-Letter Years.

If you're like most of my clients, you'll be intrigued by how your different important-year numbers correspond to events that made your life memorable. Whether happy or bittersweet, your calculations will once again prove that "numbers do not lie."

In This Chapter

- Looking at the significance of Milestone Years

- Studying the activities between Milestone Years with Overtone Numbers

- How you're progressing through life: Highlight Year Numbers

- How Red-Letter Years pinpoint the special moments in your life

What Are Milestone Years and Overtone Numbers?

Milestone Years are the pinpointed years in your life that are significant for some reason. Perhaps you started or graduated from school, met your first love, or moved to a new home or city. Maybe you started a new job, got a promotion, started your own company, took a sabbatical, or even retired. Overtone Numbers give the entire panorama of events that are apt to occur in the time span between Milestone Years.

PYTHAGORAS SAYS

A Milestone Year is like a mile marker on the highway of your life. Sometimes there's no exit and you just continue along the path of your life without any significant occurrences. On other occasions, something important happens and you can change direction, take another road, or just take a rest before continuing your journey.

Calculating Your Milestone Years and Overtone Numbers

Now it's time to calculate your Milestone Years and Overtone Numbers. You can use the following chart to fill in your information.

1. Write your four-digit birth year on the top-left line of the chart.

2. Reduce to a single digit, and write the single-digit number beneath your four-digit birth year. The single-digit number is an Overtone Number.

3. Add the two values together. This gives you your first Milestone Year.

4. Repeat this process until you have enough equations equal to the number of letters in your first, middle, and last names.

5. Write the letters of your full name vertically on the right side of the chart. Within a year after your first, middle, and last names end is when your problems are said to be over!

```
_____ Birth Year
+_____ Reduced Birth Year ___ Letters of Your Name
+____
+____                        ___
+____                        ___
+____                        ___
+____                        ___
+____                        ___
+____                        ___
+____                        ___
+____                        ___
+____                        ___
+____                        ___
+____                        ___
+____                        ___
+____                        ___
+____                        ___
+____                        ___
+____                        ___
+____                        ___
+____                        ___
+____                        ___
```

Use this chart to fill in your Milestone Year and Overtone Number calculation information.

Let's look at an example for a person born in 1951 with the given name of Jerry Lee Johnson. To calculate his Milestone Years and Overtone Numbers, start with 1951, the four-digit year Jerry was born. Add the digits of the year and reduce to a single digit.

$$1 + 9 + 5 + 1 = 16$$

$$1 + 6 = 7$$

Next, add the 7 to the four-digit year he was born.

1951 + 7 = 1958

Jerry's first Milestone Years are 1951 and 1958, and the Overtone Number between 1951 and 1958 is 7. To find Jerry's next Milestone Year, add and reduce the digits in 1958.

1 + 9 + 5 + 8 = 23

2 + 3 = 5

Next, add the 5 to the previous Milestone Year of 1958.

1958 + 5 = 1963

Jerry's next Milestone Year is 1963, and the Overtone Number between 1958 and 1963 is 5.

The following chart shows the rest of Jerry Lee Johnson's Milestone Years and Overtone Numbers.

$$
\begin{array}{r}
1951 \\
+\quad 7 \\
\hline
1958 \\
+\quad 5 \\
\hline
1963 \\
+\quad 1 \\
\hline
1964 \\
+\quad 2 \\
\hline
1966 \\
+\quad 4 \\
\hline
1970 \\
+\quad 8 \\
\hline
1978 \\
+\quad 7 \\
\hline
1985 \\
+\quad 5 \\
\hline
1990 \\
+\quad 1 \\
\hline
1991 \\
+\quad 2 \\
\hline
1993 \\
+\quad 4 \\
\hline
1997 \\
+\quad 8 \\
\hline
2005 \\
+\quad 7 \\
\hline
2012 \\
+\quad 5 \\
\hline
2017 \\
+\quad 1 \\
\hline
2018
\end{array}
$$

As you can see, Jerry's Milestone Years are 1951, 1958, 1963, 1964, 1966, 1970, 1978, 1985, 1990, 1991, 1993, 1997, 2005, 2012, 2017, and 2018; his Overtone Numbers are 7, 5, 1, 2, 4, 8, 7, 5, 1, 2, 4, 8, 7, 5, and 1.

It's then time to go back and write in every letter of Jerry's given name in each cluster.

$$
\begin{array}{r}
1951 \\
+\quad 7 \;\; J \\
\hline
1958 \\
+\quad 5 \;\; E \\
\hline
1963 \\
+\quad 1 \;\; R \\
\hline
1964 \\
+\quad 2 \;\; R \\
\hline
1966 \\
+\quad 4 \;\; Y \\
\hline
1970 \\
+\quad 8 \;\; L \\
\hline
1978 \\
+\quad 7 \;\; E \\
\hline
1985 \\
+\quad 5 \;\; E \\
\hline
1990 \\
+\quad 1 \;\; J \\
\hline
1991 \\
+\quad 2 \;\; O \\
\hline
1993 \\
+\quad 4 \;\; H \\
\hline
1997 \\
+\quad 8 \;\; N \\
\hline
2005 \\
+\quad 7 \;\; S \\
\hline
2012 \\
+\quad 5 \;\; O \\
\hline
2017 \\
+\quad 1 \;\; N \\
\hline
2018
\end{array}
$$

According to the system, in the year 2018, Jerry Lee Johnson's problems will be over and he can enjoy the remainder of his life problem free. Lucky Jerry!

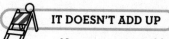

Not everyone's troubles end at or before their demise. Just because your problems are due to end when you're 90 is no guarantee you'll live to see that end. To avoid leaving difficulties for your loved ones, try to wrap up your affairs ahead of time so you don't leave them as your legacy.

Overtone Number Meanings

The numbers between your Milestone Years have special significance. The following describes each Overtone Number.

Overtone Number 1: During this period, you should find the answers to any questions you might have about your life or other people. This is a time to use your intuition and be your own best friend. As silly as it sounds, if the answers you're seeking don't come to you readily, wash your car, scrub floors, or accomplish a task that requires water, and the answers will follow. This is also the time to stand on your own two feet—if you want a job done right, do it yourself. You'll be comfortable being direct, but remember to be polite as well.

Overtone Number 2: Cooperation is essential to your success during this period. Partnership is good, but try to choose a partner who isn't too headstrong. You may also feel pulled in two different directions or may have a choice between two alternatives. Don't allow your surroundings to influence your decisions too much—be diplomatic for the best outcome. This may be a waiting time, so exercise patience.

Overtone Number 3: This is a time to express yourself and showcase your talents. During this period, it's essential for you to be optimistic and look at the bright side, even though you have many plates spinning simultaneously. Concentrate on finishing one project before undertaking the next. Because you're so busy, you must be sure to take extra care of your health. This is a time of expansion, so unless you want to add inches to your waistline, watch what you eat and stick to an exercise routine.

Overtone Number 4: This is a time for hard work and leading a disciplined life. Work to make your practical ideas a reality—your perseverance will pay off. Also, be steadfast and loyal during this period; otherwise, your infidelity will be found out. Spending time in nature can restore your soul and help you to relax. This is a period of time for home and family, so pay special heed to any honey-do items or relationships that need extra attention.

Overtone Number 5: This is a time of restlessness, curiosity, and high energy. During this period, you seek answers to any questions you may have. A butterfly out of the cocoon flying in many different directions, you desire freedom in all forms, including travel. There may also be moves, changes, and lots of activity around you. Understand that change is inevitable, and expect the unexpected. Be adaptable and ready to fit into different types of situations at any time.

Overtone Number 6: Love, home, family, and responsibility dominate during this period. This is the time to put your own needs aside and help others. Don't insist on getting your way—be flexible. You may have family responsibilities or extra duties at work. Even if you don't get paid overtime, pitch in to assist in whatever needs to be accomplished.

Overtone Number 7: This is a time when you need to analyze your life along with everyone and everything in it. Take the time to be by yourself long enough to figure out where you've been, where you are, and where you're going. Read between the lines and look below the surface to discover what is *not* being said. It's also the time to inspire others around you who may be at a crossroad in life and could benefit from some encouragement from you. You may go from one extreme to the other—avoid being fanatical or too much of an introvert. Because of your strong opinions during this period, you may be a bit difficult to live with.

Overtone Number 8: This is a period to be balanced in all of your dealings and affairs. Organize your entire existence and attend to your financial well-being. Also, think big—be open-minded and avoid narrow points of view. Even though you're busy, take some time for romance during this period. You have a warm heart and are generous to others in need.

Overtone Number 9: This is a universal time period during which you need to think on a grand scale and see the big picture. As a humanitarian with universal appeal, you have the power now to inspire others. Therefore, this is a good time to disperse your knowledge and teach what you know—share yourself with the world. This also may be a time of endings and ridding yourself of that which you no longer need.

What Are Highlight Year Numbers?

Some numerologists refer to the Highlight Year Number as "race consciousness"—not in an ethnic sense, but rather as your awareness of your progress or race through your life. As you progress toward your goals, you'll find increased awareness about your advances in your career and personal life.

Calculating Highlight Year Numbers

It's easy to find your Highlight Years. All you need is your current age and the age you'll be on your next birthday.

1. Add your current age to the age you'll be on your next birthday.

2. Reduce to a single digit.

For example, let's say you're 40 now and will be 41 after your next birthday. Add your current age, 40, to the age at your next birthday, 41: $40 + 41 = 81$. Then reduce 81 to a single digit: $8 + 1 = 9$. Between your 40th and 41st birthdays, you'll be in a Highlight Year Number of 9.

PYTHAGORAS SAYS

I don't deal with Master Numbers for Highlight Years. The sum before reducing two consecutive numbers is always an odd number—therefore, 22 and 44 will never occur. When it comes to the other Master Numbers, 11 only happens for a 5-year-old (5 + 6 = 11), and 33 only happens for a 16-year-old (16 + 17 = 33).

Highlight Year Number Meanings

But what does your Highlight Year Number entail? The following provides a description for each.

Highlight Year Number 1: A 1 year indicates an ending followed by a new beginning and often involves a leap of faith. This may be the year when you give up something you've been pursuing and start something new that you've been wanting to try. You may take up a new hobby, learn a new language, or pursue a new job or career path.

Highlight Year Number 2: This is a tricky vibration, so it's up to you whether you experience inspiration or limitation. Highlight Year Number 2 can indicate a change of residence, a trip of some sort, or a change of business or occupation. Perhaps you work for a large chain and were asked to relocate to a new area and become the regional manager. You can say "yes" and get a higher salary, or you can decide to stay put and be satisfied with your current pay. Alternatively, you may be contacted by a headhunter for an entirely different position out of town, and after being offered the new position and weighing all of the pros and cons, decide to remain where you are.

Highlight Year Number 3: A 3 year indicates a new beginning, often in a social or artistic field. You also have an opportunity to make a choice of some kind this year. Perhaps you decide to join a bridge group, join a hiking or running group, attend an aquatic exercise class at the Y, learn to line dance or Zumba, or decide to sign up for a sketching class at your local Recreation Center. Highlight Year Number 3 also indicates reaping what you have sown. Accept the good that comes into your life, because more is on the way.

Highlight Year Number 4: This indicates a possible change in your business or domestic routine. It's a time to change your habits or the manner in which you are handling things. However, it's not a time of action; the change is more apt to come from some outside influence rather than your own choice. Perhaps you were asked to change shifts at work, or, if you're a teacher, maybe your school developed a new schedule and your vacation dates are changed.

Highlight Year Number 5: This period indicates change of an artistic or social nature. It can also be a time for remodeling in ways as simple as rearranging furniture. Highlight Year Number 5 is a good time for sales or taking short trips. It could mean you start thinking about a trip you've always wanted to take by researching group tours to various locations, or maybe you join a charter bus trip to a nearby casino to play the slots.

Highlight Year Number 6: This usually indicates change in the home, whether it's something as simple as planting new flowers in the garden or repainting a room. On the relationship side, Highlight Year Number 6 could mean the arrival of a new baby or a marriage in the family that welcomes new family members into your home. The period could also mean the time for a couple to bury the hatchet, work out their differences, and appreciate each other more.

> **DID YOU KNOW?**
>
> When clients come to me in Highlight Year Number 6 and mention that they're unhappy and considering ending a relationship, I'm not surprised. Only after they mention their unhappiness will I mention that Highlight Year Number 6 can indicate either a marriage or a divorce. Highlight Year Number 6 can also mean the unhappy couple can resolve their disagreements through counseling.

Highlight Year Number 7: A 7 year can indicate several things: a marriage for a female, a period of introspection, metaphysical study (you may even be reading this book in Highlight Year Number 7), a time to research and study, and a time to watch finances and health. You may decide you're tired of being overweight and finally do something about it this year, possibly by researching various eating plans and diets. This also may be the year you decide to take a computer course and further your skills.

Highlight Year Number 8: This indicates that certain business or executive matters are probably going to be closed with satisfactory financial arrangements. For example, perhaps a slip-and-fall accident case is settled and you receive compensation, the estate you're due an inheritance from is settled and you receive a check or various items from Grandma, or an audit with the IRS turns out in your favor and you don't have to pay additional taxes. Expect pleasant surprises in Highlight Year Number 8.

Highlight Year Number 9: A 9 year indicates the close of a situation followed by a new beginning in the near future. This may mean finishing high school and starting college; graduating from college and starting a new job; or moving out of your parent's home and getting your own apartment, condo, or house. Highlight Year Number 9 can also mean something as mundane as ending your current cell-phone contract and getting a better plan with another provider.

Red-Letter Years

Sometimes called *Forecasting,* Red-Letter Years are an interesting exploration of a person's life cycle. Red-Letter Years are actually the specific ages in your life that are memorable or when something significant occurs. Perhaps the Red-Letter Year is when you graduated from college, moved into an apartment with a roommate, got a terrific job in your chosen career, bought your first car, made a major move, got married, bought a home, or had your first child.

Calculating Your Red-Letter Years

The following shows you how to calculate Red-Letter Years. I provided a chart to help you fill in your name and information. While following the steps, feel free to use a calculator. Some people also like to use three different-color pens—one color for the first name, another color for the middle name, and another color for the last name—because it is easier to distinguish the calculations for each name.

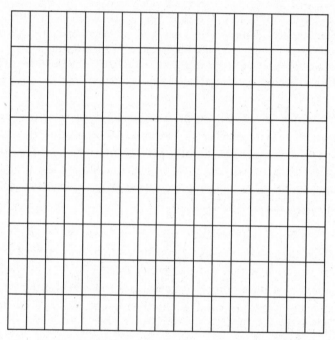

Use this chart to fill in your full name and Red-Letter Years.

1. On the top row of the chart, print your full birth-certificate name, one letter to a square. Remember to leave space between your first, middle, and last names—each part of your name will be dealt with separately.

2. For your first name, put the numeric value of the first letter under it.

3. Add the numeric value of the second letter to the numeric value of the first letter, and write the total below the second letter. Continue to add the numeric value of the current letter to the value under the preceding letter and write that total under the letter.

4. Once you have a value for the last letter, circle back and begin again with the first letter, placing the total on a row below the previous row. Keep adding and starting over until you reach a value close to 100.

5. Repeat the addition process for the middle and last names separately.

6. After you do your calculations for each name, check for the repetition of specific years (ages). Those are your Red-Letter Years.

 PYTHAGORAS SAYS

Because Red-Letter Years are actually ages, you shouldn't reduce the numbers to a single digit, as you've become accustomed to doing.

To give you an example of the process, let me show you part of the calculation process of the Red-Letter Years I did for a client named Dennis Robert Cohen.

I started by writing down his first name, Dennis, making sure to leave space between the letters. Unlike previous calculations, where the numeric values are placed under their respective letters, I instead only put the numeric value of the *first letter of the first name* under the letter. For Dennis, I wrote the numeric value of D (which is a 4) under the D.

D   E   N   N   I   S
4

Next, I added the numeric value of the second letter, E (5), to the numeric value of the previous letter, D (4). I wrote that total, 9 (4 + 5 = 9), below the E.

D   E   N   N   I   S
4   9

I then added the numeric value of the third letter, N (5), to the previous total (9). I wrote the total, 14 (5 + 9 = 14), under the N. Notice that I didn't reduce the number (which is actually an age) to a single digit.

D   E   N   N   I   S
4   9   14

Next, I added the numeric value of the next letter, N (5), to the total under the previous letter (14). N (5) + previous total (14) = 19, so I wrote 19 under the N.

D	E	N	N	I	S
4	9	14	19		

I then added the numeric value of the next letter, I (9), to the total under the previous letter (19). I wrote the total, 28 (9 + 19 = 28), under the I.

D	E	N	N	I	S
4	9	14	19	28	

Continuing along, I added the numeric value of the next letter, S (1), to the total under the previous letter (28). S (1) + previous total (28) = 29, so I wrote 29 under the S.

D	E	N	N	I	S
4	9	14	19	28	29

What now? I circled back and began again with the first letter of the first name, only this time I started another row below the previous row. I added the sum under the S (29) to the numeric value of the first letter of the first name, D (4). I then wrote the total, 33 (29 + 4 = 33), under the D.

D	E	N	N	I	S
4	9	14	19	28	29
33					

Next, I added the numeric value of the second letter, E (5), to the previous total (33). I wrote the total, 38 (33 + 5 = 38), below the E.

D	E	N	N	I	S
4	9	14	19	28	29
33	38				

I then continued on until I reached 100, give or take, for the first name. I followed by doing the same calculations for the middle and last names separately. The following chart shows the final results for Dennis Robert Cohen.

D	E	N	N	I	S		R	O	B	E	R	T		C	O	H	E	N
4	9	14	19	28	29		9	15	17	22	31	33		3	9	17	22	27
33	38	43	48	57	58		42	48	50	55	64	66		30	36	44	49	54
62	67	72	77	86	87		75	81	83	88	97			57	63	71	76	81
91	96													84	90	98		

Interpreting Red-Letter Years

The enlightening part of this exercise is seeing a pattern of repeating numbers in the first, middle, and last names. You can either underline or circle the numbers you see repeated in each of your names. Those are your Red-Letter Years—the ages at which something special will occur or which are memorable to you in some way. You can also look for age "runs" of sequential years in a row; some can be as few as two sequential years and some "runs" may be three, four, or more years sequentially.

Looking at Dennis's chart, 9 seems important, occurring under all three names. Number (age) 22 is repeated twice, so it's also considered a Red-Letter Year. Number 57 is repeated two times, denoting another Red-Letter Year, followed by age 58, so both of those ages are important. Numbers 57 and 58 and 71 and 72 are two-year runs. Numbers 29, 30, and 31; 42, 43, and 44; 48, 49, and 50; 62, 63, and 64; 75, 76, and 77; and 96, 97, and 98 are all sequential three-year runs.

The Least You Need to Know

- The important year numbers are years and ages of significance in your life.
- Milestone Years mark the beginning of a cluster of one or more years in your life through which a consistent theme runs (signified by Overtone Numbers).

- Highlight Year Numbers are calculated by adding your current age to your age after your next birthday and reducing the sum to a single digit.

- Red-Letter Years are a more involved calculation, where the letters of your entire birth-certificate name are cycled to look for repetitions and sequences of ages.

Introducing the Worksheet

Numbering imposes order, or at least the impression of order. Numerology focuses on numbers and how they describe the order and organization of your life. Now that you know how to calculate the many numbers that are important to your life, you need to have a place to collect all the data. That's where the worksheet comes in.

In this chapter, I give you a tour of the worksheet and tell you how to fill in the different worksheet sections with the appropriate data. You can then go to Appendix C of this book, which contains a full version of the worksheet, to write in all of your information.

In This Chapter

- The Recap Section
- The Pinnacles and Challenges Chart
- The Hidden Cross
- The Type and Traits Chart and the Karma, Intensification, and Subconscious Response Number Chart
- Progressed letters and the Hidden Essence and Essence Numbers

The Recap Section

The Recap Section is where you record your full name as listed on your birth certificate and your date of birth. From there, you use that information to find your Destiny Number (see Chapter 3), Soul Number (see Chapter 4), Personality Number (see Chapter 5), Point of Security Number (see Chapter 7), Life Path Number (see Chapter 10), and Maturity Number (see Chapter 16).

																				Soul Number	
Vowels																					
Name																			Point of Security Number	
																			Destiny Number	
Consonants																			Personality Number	
																			Maturity Number	
Birth Date																				
																			Life Path Number	

Here's how to fill out the Recap Section. The blank rows can be used to help you with your calculations, if you haven't already done them:

1. Print your full name in the "Name" row.

2. Count the number of letters in your name, not including suffixes, and place that value in the box to the left of "Point of Security Number." Enter the reduced result in the box to the right of "Point of Security Number."

3. Below the "Name" row, enter the numeric values for the letters in your name. Place the total for those in the box to the left of "Destiny Number," and enter the reduced result in the box to the right.

4. Enter the numeric values for each vowel in your name (remember, Y isn't considered a vowel) in the "Vowels" row. Place the total for those in the box to the left of "Soul Number," and enter the reduced result in the box to the right.

5. Enter the numeric values for each consonant in your name in the "Consonants" row. Place the total for those in the box to the left of "Personality Number," and enter the reduced result in the box to the right.

6. Enter the numbers of your birth date in the "Birth Date" row. Place the total for those in the box to the left of "Life Path Number," and enter the reduced result in the box to the right.

7. Add the single-digits of your Destiny Number and Life Path Number together, reduce to a single-digit if necessary, and enter the reduced result to the right of "Maturity Number."

The following is a filled-out Recap Section using my daughter Jamie's name and date of birth.

	1	2	3	4	5	6	7	8	9	10	11	12	13	14	15	16	17	18	19	Total	Label	Value
			15					+							15					30	Soul Number	3
Vowels		1		9	5								9				6					
Name	J	A	M	I	E		L	Y	N	N		S	I	M	P	S	O	N		16	Point of Security Number	7
	1	1	4	9	5		3	7	5	5		1	9	4	7	1	6	5				
			20			+		20			+			33						73	Destiny Number	1
Consonants	1		4				3	7	5	5		1		4	7	1		5				
			5			+		20			+			18						43	Personality Number	7
Birth Date	0	6		2	6		1	9	6	8												
			6		+		8		+		24									38	Life Path Number	2
																					Maturity Number	3

The Pinnacles and Challenges Chart

Below the Recap Section is a row of four charts. The leftmost chart is the Pinnacles and Challenges Chart (see Chapter 11). It lists your four Pinnacle and Challenge age ranges and the numbers associated with each Pinnacle and Challenge. In this version of the chart, I've included quick reminders of how to calculate each of the Pinnacle and Challenge Numbers; these boxes are blank in Appendix C's full worksheet.

	Pinnacle Number	Challenge Number	Start Age	Thru	End Age
1st	Month + Day	Difference between Month and Day	0	—	36 – Life Path Number
2nd	Day + Year	Difference between Day and Year	36 – Life Path Number	—	2nd Start Age + 9
3rd	1st + 2nd	Difference between 1st and 2nd	2nd End Age	—	3rd Start Age + 9
4th	Month + Year	Difference between Month and Year	3rd End Age	—	No entry needed here

Here's how to fill out the Pinnacles and Challenges Chart:

1. In the column labeled "Pinnacle Number," enter each of your Pinnacle Numbers.

2. In the column labeled "Challenge Number," enter each of your Challenge Numbers.

3. In the column labeled "Start Age," enter each of the starting ages for your Pinnacles and Challenges. You should only have starting ages for the last three; your first one is at birth, or 0.

4. In the column labeled "End Age," enter each of the ending ages for your Pinnacles and Challenges. You should only have ending ages for the first three; the fourth is your age at your death, which you don't know.

Once again, I'm going to use Jamie's data as the example of how the Pinnacles and Challenges Chart looks filled out.

	Pinnacle Number	Challenge Number	Start Age	Thru	End Age
1st	5	2	0	—	34
2nd	5	2	34	—	43
3rd	1	0	43	—	52
4th	3	0	52	—	?

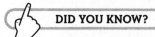

DID YOU KNOW?

The transition from one set of Pinnacles and Challenges to the next takes up to two years—one year before the change and one year after the change.

The Hidden Cross

The chart on the far right of the row of four is the Hidden Cross (see Chapter 10). This is where you place the numbers of your birth date.

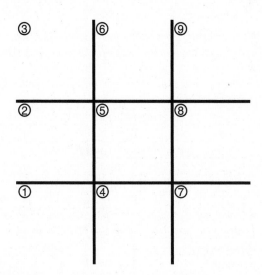

Here's how you fill out the Hidden Cross:

1. Enter the values of your birth date that correspond to the number of the square.

2. If you have any zeroes, place them in any square you'd like to fill out more.

The following shows the Hidden Cross filled out for my daughter Jamie.

	666	9
2		8
1		

PYTHAGORAS SAYS

If you're going in order, you can use the numbers for your date of birth that you filled in for the Recap Section to fill in the Hidden Cross.

The Type and Traits Chart and the Karma, Intensification, and Subconscious Response Number Chart

The two charts in the middle of the row use the results derived from the letters in your name: the Type and Traits, Karma Number, Intensification Number, and Subconscious Response Number (see Chapter 7).

Karma Number								
1	2	3	4	5	6	7	8	9
Intensification Number								
1	2	3	4	5	6	7	8	9
Subconscious Response Number								
1	2	3	4	5	6	7	8	9

Type		Traits				
Physical		4s				5s
Mental		1s				8s
Emotional		2s		3s		6s
Intuitive		7s				9s
Total						

Here's how to fill out the chart for Karma Numbers, Intensification Numbers, and Subconscious Response Numbers and the Type and Traits Chart:

1. Under "Karma Number," circle any numeric values that are missing from your name.

2. Under "Intensification Number," circle any numeric values of letters that you have more than average of in your name.

3. Under "Subconscious Response Number," circle the numeric value you get when you subtract the sum of your Karma Numbers from 9.

4. For the Type and Traits Chart, enter the frequency of each number's occurrence in your name in the box to the left of that number. Add the numbers on each row and place the sum in the box to the right of its respective type, then write the sum of all the numbers together in the "Total" box.

The following show the tables with Jamie's information filled in.

Karma Number								
1	(2)	3	4	5	6	7	(8)	9
Intensification Number								
(1)	2	3	(4)	(5)	6	(7)	8	9
Subconscious Response Number								
1	2	3	4	5	6	(7)	8	9

Type		Traits					
Physical	6	2	4s			4	5s
Mental	4	4	1s			0	8s
Emotional	2	0	2s	1	3s	1	6s
Intuitive	4	2	7s			2	9s
Total	16/7						

The Life Chart

At the bottom of the numerology worksheet is a large chart on which you progress the letters of your name and calculate your Hidden Essence and Essence Numbers (see Chapter 8). This is called the *Life Chart*. The following image represents the first block of the Life Chart. Because there's inadequate space to present a usable chart with squares for every year of a typical life span, the Life Chart is broken into three virtually identical blocks, each covering 32 years—0 to 32, 33 to 65, and 66 to 98. For this chapter, I'm just going to show you the first block—ages 0 through 32—as the length of the blocks is the same. The full Life Chart is in Appendix C.

Year																																	
Age	0	1	2	3	4	5	6	7	8	9	10	11	12	13	14	15	16	17	18	19	20	21	22	23	24	25	26	27	28	29	30	31	32
First Name																																	
Middle Name																																	
Middle Name 2																																	
Last Name																																	
Hidden Essence Number																																	
Essence Number																																	
Personal Year Number																																	
Universal Year Number																																	
Pinnacles																																	
Challenges																																	
Highlight Year Number																																	

Here's how you fill in your Life Chart:

1. In the first row, labeled "Year," enter the year you were born above each age entry, starting with your birth year for age 0.

2. In the "First Name" row, progress the letters of your first name, starting at age 1.

3. If you have a middle name, progress its letters in the "Middle Name" row, starting at age 1. If you have additional middle names, progress the letters in the "Middle Name 2" row, and add rows as needed.

4. In the "Last Name" row, progress the letters of your last name, starting at age 1.

5. Beginning with the year you turned 1, add the values for the progressed letters in each column of your year and enter each sum in the "Hidden Essence" row for that year.

6. Reduce each Hidden Essence Number to a single digit, if necessary, and enter the result in the "Essence Number" row for that year.

7. Starting with age 0, calculate and enter your Personal Year Numbers in the "Personal Year Number" row. Your Personal Year Number at birth is the same as your Life Path Number.

8. Starting with age 0, calculate and enter the Universal Year Number for each year in the "Universal Year Number" row.

9. Enter your Pinnacle Number for each year in the "Pinnacles" row. You can refer back to your Pinnacles and Challenges from Chapter 11.

10. Enter your Challenge Number for each year in the "Challenges" row. You can refer back to your Pinnacles and Challenges from Chapter 11.

11. Calculate and enter your Highlight Year Number for each year in the "Highlight Year Number" row.

PYTHAGORAS SAYS

You don't have to compute every Personal Year Number or Universal Year Number. Because time is cyclic, simply calculate the first year in the series and add 1 each year and, if necessary, reduce to a single digit.

The following shows my daughter Jamie's completed Life Chart.

Year	68	69	70	71	72	73	74	75	76	77	78	79	80	81	82	83	84	85	86	87	88	89	90	91	92	93	94	95	96	97	98	99	00
Age	0	1	2	3	4	5	6	7	8	9	10	11	12	13	14	15	16	17	18	19	20	21	22	23	24	25	26	27	28	29	30	31	32
First Name		J	A	M	M	M	M	I	I	I	I	I	I	I	I	I	E	E	E	E	E	J	A	M	M	M	M	I	I	I	I	I	I
Middle Name		L	L	L	Y	Y	Y	Y	Y	Y	Y	N	N	N	N	N	N	N	N	N	N	N	L	L	L	Y	Y	Y	Y	Y	Y	Y	N
Middle Name 2																																	
Last Name		S	I	I	I	I	I	I	I	I	I	M	M	M	M	P	P	P	P	P	P	P	S	O	O	O	O	O	O	N	N	N	N
Hidden Essence Number		5	13	16	20	20	20	25	25	25	25	18	18	18	18	21	17	17	17	17	17	11	5	13	17	17	17	22	22	21	21	19	19
Essence Number		5	4	7	2	2	2	7	7	7	7	9	9	9	9	3	8	8	8	8	8	2	5	4	8	8	8	4	4	3	3	1	1
Personal Year Number	2	3	4	5	6	7	8	9	1	2	3	4	5	6	7	8	9	1	2	3	4	5	6	7	8	9	1	2	3	4	5	6	7
Universal Year Number	6	7	8	9	1	2	3	4	5	6	7	8	9	1	2	3	4	5	6	7	8	9	1	2	3	4	5	6	7	8	9	1	2
Pinnacles	5	5	5	5	5	5	5	5	5	5	5	5	5	5	5	5	5	5	5	5	5	5	5	5	5	5	5	5	5	5	5	5	5
Challenges	2	2	2	2	2	2	2	2	2	2	2	2	2	2	2	2	2	2	2	2	2	2	2	2	2	2	2	2	2	2	2	2	2
Highlight Year Number	1	3	5	7	9	2	4	6	8	1	3	5	7	9	2	4	6	8	1	3	5	7	9	2	4	6	8	1	3	5	7	9	2

The Least You Need to Know

- The Recap Section is where you record your full name and date of birth and includes your Core Numbers.
- The Pinnacles and Challenges Chart lists your Pinnacle and Challenge Numbers, along with the start and end dates for each.
- The Hidden Cross is where you write in the numbers of your birth date.
- The Type and Traits Chart and the chart for Karma Number, Intensification Number, and Subconscious Response Number relate to the letters in your name.
- The Life Chart is where you fill in the progression of the letters in your name and your Hidden Essence and Essence Numbers.
- A full version of the worksheet can be found in Appendix C.

Fun Things to Do and Know

Now that you know more about numerology and the different calculations behind it, you can put it into effect in your own life with naming and numbering.

Part 5 shows you how to use numerology to choose important names and numbers in your life—including your business name, vanity license plate, phone number, address, email address, and user IDs—and how carefully selected ones can mean the difference between success or struggle. I even take you through the pros and cons of changing your own name.

In this part, I also discuss how you can influence your future child's talents, strengths, and even personality by using numerology to choose a birth name. You can even choose the best day for a scheduled delivery using numerology.

Choosing the Names and Numbers in Your Life

While many of the numbers in this book are calculated based on predetermined names and numbers, you do have some control over what numerology values appear in your life. Whether it's a password or even your business, you can find a way to make the names and numbers have a certain effect on your life.

In this chapter, you learn how to choose names and numbers for a license plate, phone number, email and password, business, and home address. I also discuss the impact of one of the biggest choices you could make—changing your name.

In This Chapter

- Picking a vanity license plate
- Selecting a phone number
- Finding a PO Box number
- Numbers for the World Wide Web: email addresses, passwords, and website names
- Choosing a business name
- Finding the correct address for your home, apartment, or office
- Changing your name: should you do it?

Vanity License Plates

Vanity license plates are not only fun, they're also highly individualized. Whizzing past, I've seen VROOM on a high-speed Ferrari, LUV2DNC on a ballet teacher's car, FLIRT on a cute blonde teenager's car, and FinchX4 on the family SUV of the Finch family of four. Each is an accurate description of the owner both on the surface and in terms of the numeric values you get when calculating for each name.

Want to cause a stir and get more phone calls? Use your area code and phone number on your plate (if all of the numbers can fit). Want to advertise your business? Use a shortened version of your business name on your plates, perhaps by deleting the vowels. Whatever you decide, make sure the numbers work for you.

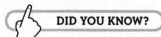

DID YOU KNOW?

I must admit, when I wrote my first book, *Shisha Mirror Embroidery: A Contemporary Approach,* I succumbed to using SHISHA on my license plate. Everywhere I went, people asked me what it meant. My personalized plate proved to be an excellent way to advertise my book!

To find the right vanity license plate, pick some letters, numbers, or a combo of the two that you're considering and calculate the values. You can then check out the basic meanings and see what works best for you; if you need a reminder of what the values mean, check out Chapter 2.

Post Office Boxes

Renting a PO Box at the U.S. Post Office will likely limit your selection of box numbers. However, if you visit a UPS Store or Mail Boxes Etc., you can possibly select a box number from available ones. When choosing a PO Box, I suggest finding one that's the same as your favorite number, your Destiny Number, or the day of the month you were born.

You may also decide to choose one based on its intended use. For example, if the PO Box is for business, you may want to select one with a numeric value of 8 (indicates money, success, and power) or 9 (indicates completion).

The choice is totally up to you. However, if you're not sure what PO Box you want, let the clerk select a random box number for you and then calculate to see the number you were given.

Phone Numbers

What do you want your phone number to say about you? You can use the following as a guideline to pick the number that's right for you:

- If you want to be more independent and have the courage of your convictions, choose a phone number that adds and reduces to 1.

- If you want to have harmonious partnerships and be more diplomatic and tactful, select a phone number that adds and reduces to 2.

- If you want to be more expressive with your feelings or emotions, pick a phone number that adds and reduces to 3.

- If you want to be more focused on details, choose a phone number that adds and reduces to 4.

- If you want to have more friends and be on the go more, select a phone number that adds and reduces to 5.

- If you want to attract a romantic partner and have more dates, you probably want to choose a number that adds and reduces to 6.

- If you want to be left alone and have more solitude, select a phone number that adds and reduces to 7.

- If you want to attract more money, choose a phone number that adds and reduces to 8.

- If you have a business that deals with art, music, or something international, choose a phone number that adds and reduces to 9.

Most phone companies will give you a bank of numbers to choose from when you place your order. The only trick is that you have to choose the number you want while you're on the line with the phone company, so you may want to have a calculator handy to speed the process. If you're lucky and can multitask, you can make small talk with the representative while you calculate away. You may even want to give the rep a mini numerology lesson so he or she knows what you're looking for and can possibly help you calculate the numbers.

Internet Addresses and Passwords

Email addresses and passwords can be anything you choose. If you feel drawn to a certain number or name, then use it. If you calculate the numbers from your choice, nine times out of ten it will be a number that resonates with either one of your Core Numbers or your Personal Year Number. First, choose the name or names you like, then calculate the numbers later.

Because your email address is what's most personal to you, don't calculate the extension of the service provider (for example, @gmail or @yahoo.com). You share that part of your address with millions of other users; however, the first part of your address is unique to you.

If your email address or password includes a number, simply add it into your calculation at its face value.

IT DOESN'T ADD UP

Don't drive yourself crazy selecting special numbers for everything. Numbers don't make things happen, but they do give off various vibrations inherent in each number meaning. In the end, our beliefs are what make things happen. For example, if you believe a certain password for your online banking account is going to help you not only earn more money but also save more money, then that's what you'll experience. When deciding whether to choose a special number for something, keep in mind my favorite quote: "Thoughts are things and what we think about we bring about."

Business Names

When selecting a name for your business, the first thing you need to consider is the type of business you're starting. Is your business going to sell beauty products, sports equipment, household appliances, provide babysitting, or offer limousine service? Start by brainstorming and write down all possible names you can think of; you can even ask your friends and relatives for possible suggestions. Then convert each of the names into a single-digit number and select the one you like best. Notice I said the one *you* like best, because if this is your business, the name as well as the number have to resonate with you.

There aren't any particular numbers that are "best" for a business—any and all numbers are good numbers. There are also no bad numbers, but some numbers are better than others for certain types of businesses. Does this mean that your business will suffer if you select the wrong number? No! But for the ease of your customers and your business in general, you might focus first on finding the name before worrying about the number associated with it—after all, you don't want to have an oddly spelled business name just because it reduces to the number you picked out.

When I assist clients choosing a business name, I always ask for their input. Frankly, my vote is for a clever name that attracts attention before a number that you like. You can always incorporate under a name and corresponding number that you like, but call the business by a catchy name. For example, when I had a business that designed and packaged mirror embroidery needlework kits, my husband thought of the name Kitsophrenia. Without even doing the numbers, I immediately said, "That's it!" As it turned out, Kitsophrenia adds and reduces to a 1, which definitely related to the business; it was inventive and ahead of its time.

Whether you decide to focus on the numeric value before or after choosing a business name, make sure to check out the following sections to understand the meanings behind each Business Name Number.

Business Name Number 1

This is an ideal number for a business that deals with anything that's unusual, unique, or not run-of-the-mill. If you customize the product or it's made to order, 1 is the right number for your business.

> **DID YOU KNOW?**
>
> Have you heard of the chain Color Me Mine, where you can sit and paint ceramics? A novel idea, that business name adds and reduces to 1. Similarly, one of the first cosmetic superstores in virtually every mall in every large city in America is Sephora, which adds and reduces to 1.

Business Name Number 2

A Business Name Number of 2 is good for partnerships or anything that's sold in pairs, such as tires, socks, shoes, or gloves. A 2 is also ideal for any business that gives one-on-one instruction, such as a behind-the-wheel driving school. This is also an excellent number for anything creative, such as writing services or graphic design. Successful sales businesses that add up to 2 often include textiles, jewelry, toys, beverages, and art.

Business Name Number 3

A Business Name Number of 3 is great for anything dealing with creativity or words. Three would be a terrific numeric value for a business dealing with résumé writing and editing, an art-supply store, or an art gallery. A 3 would also be a good number for a business that sells cosmetics or age-defying products or deals with plastic surgery in the form of Botox, Juvaderm, or facelifts.

Business Name Number 4

The number of details, 4 also represents order and form. What better name for a firm dealing with payroll, bookkeeping, and tax preparation than one that adds and reduces to this number? Additionally, an architectural, drafting, or contracting company that deals with plans and details is a prime candidate for Business Name Number 4.

Business Name Number 5

Do you want more walk-in traffic? Is there a lot of coming and going with your product or service? Business Number 5 is for you! Anything that deals with travel or motion benefits from a 5 name. Therefore, it's the perfect choice for car dealerships, gasoline stations, yacht sales, answering services, chauffeur services, hotels, motels, and fast-food or take-out restaurants.

Business Name Number 6

Businesses dealing with makeup, beauty supplies, hair styling, massages, facials, manicures and pedicures, jewelry, bridal gowns, or any service appealing to women would be wise to pick a 6 business name. A 6 is also the ideal name value for a business giving advice or counseling, such as a physician, insurance broker, or politician.

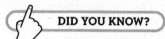 **DID YOU KNOW?**

Although taken from its founder's name, one of the best-known businesses in beauty supply is Vidal Sassoon, which adds and reduces to 6. This is very fitting, as 6 relates best to beauty and other lifestyle businesses.

Business Name Number 7

A religious or metaphysical organization; spa; bookstore; or business specializing in analysis, research, technology, or scientific pursuits would do well with a Business Name Number 7. These businesses often revolve around an individual owner/operator rather than a company with a large staff. Entrepreneurs and inventors also often have a Business Name Number 7.

Business Name Number 8

My personal number preference for the success of any business is number 8, which indicates money, power, and success. Business Name Number 8 is also an ideal number for anything dealing with management, organization, health, exercise, and emotions. Companies that add and reduce to this number could be a vitamin or health-food store or deal with personal training and sports equipment.

Business Name Number 9

Number 9 is great for anything dealing with art, music, beauty, or big business on an international scale. Have you heard of Arthur Murray Dance Studio? The dance-instruction company is franchised around the world and adds to a 9. Business Name Number 9 is also an ideal number for anything dealing with attorneys, doctors, hospitals, humanitarian efforts, or long-distance travel.

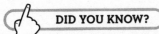

Houses, Apartments, or Offices

Just like people, addresses have a personality of their own. They are an indication of the energy of the place. I've lived in a number of different homes, and the numbers are always spot-on! House Numbers are calculated just like a Life Path Number or a Destiny Number—you simply add the numbers in the address together and reduce to a single digit.

I have found that using only the house number and not including the street name is the most accurate way to interpret your individual numbers. After all, everyone on your street shares the street name, but only you have your unique address.

But what about addresses that include a letter? Let's say you live at 203 Main Street, Apartment 2B. The 201 (2 + 0 + 1 = 3) part of your address applies to the entire building, making it a 3; however, 2B is unique to you, so your apartment has the energy of 4 (2 + 2 = 4).

What should you do if you really love a particular place but don't like the House Number? You can do what my mother did and petition the city and then the county and see if you can have the number changed. If that doesn't work, should you move or not buy the place? That's up to you. Maybe the place just isn't right for you. Or perhaps you've attracted a karmic lesson and need to live in a particular place. My suggestion: even if it doesn't have the numeric value you want, put your own touches on the place and give it the character you want it to have. And if it's a place you already live in, stay put and renovate.

The following sections detail the meaning behind each House Number. Despite the name, these numeric values can also apply to apartments and offices.

House Number 1

A place with an address that reduces to 1 is a marvelous place for creative pursuits and independence. There's something quite unique or special about it, as well as the people who live or work there—the residents either already have or develop strength of character and a strong determination in this place.

House Number 1 brings many interesting experiences—to the people inside the place or their careers, or to the people who come to it. This isn't a place for shrinking violets who vacillate and can't make up their minds; it requires the residents or workers to be decisive leaders who have integrity.

There are often new beginnings while living or working in a place with a House Number of 1. Inventors and self-reliant people who think out of the box are happy living in a House Number 1 because it encourages the inhabitants to follow their own instincts and think for themselves. This address can be difficult if teamwork is essential to a business's success. Those who work in a House Number 1 tend to do their own thing rather than work as a unified group. However, House Number 1s can be lonely if the resident doesn't like to be alone some of the time.

House Number 2

A place with an address that reduces to 2 has a quiet, cooperative vibe to it. This area insists on cooperation and patience from the inhabitants. Because of this, intuitive, sensitive souls are often drawn to places with a House Number of 2.

House Number 2 brings companionship and closeness to the people who reside or work there. For example, it's a great place for couples who share household duties and are helpful to each other. If you're strong-willed, argumentative, impatient, and want to spend most of your time alone, this environment isn't the best choice for you.

People who live or work in House Number 2 tend to be quite detailed and are most likely collectors or have a lot of "stuff" and mementos. It's hard for them to part with the sentimental objects, which may overtake the living or working space, because they're sensitive souls who simply can't bear to part with any of their treasures.

Because 2 is also the number of creativity and beauty, House Number 2 is ideal for designers, artists, and even antique dealers.

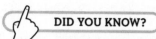 **DID YOU KNOW?**

Before I was even born, my parents bought a lot and built a home. My mother—who had no knowledge or interest in metaphysics or numerology—told me that when they built the house, the actual address according to the county was 2901. However, she had gone to the city and then the county to get the address changed to 2900, because she liked the two zeros and the 11. It's interesting because my Destiny Number and my Life Path Number are 11/2, so apparently I grew up in the perfect home.

House Number 3

If you want to express your feelings with words or are very creative, this numeric value is a happy choice for you. House Number 3s are fun, light-hearted, full of laughter and joyfulness, have lots of goings and comings, and are great for giving parties and entertaining friends. Visitors who speak various languages are probably going to be some of your favorite guests.

If you raise your children in House Number 3, they are apt to put a creative spin on everything they undertake and use a lot of words—either writing or speaking eloquently. You might as well buy some extra air mattresses, because House Number 3 is going to be the place for sleepovers and social events.

The inhabitants in House Number 3 tend to spend a lot of money either updating, remodeling, or decorating the place. Therefore, those living or working in House Number 3 are cautioned to not scatter their energy or burn the candle at both ends.

If you like lots of peace and quiet and tend to be a penny pincher who follows a budget, House Number 3 may be a challenge for you. That doesn't mean you wouldn't be happy living there; it just means you would have to go with the flow and become more flexible.

House Number 3 is ideal for communicating. This is a busy address with many phone calls, emails, meetings, and socializing. Because the energy can sometimes feel chaotic, it's important to schedule some quiet time to recharge.

House Number 4

If you're a detail-oriented person who enjoys following a budget and believe home or office ownership is an investment that should pay dividends, a place that reduces to a numeric value of 4 is a good choice. Chances are, House Number 4 has a solid foundation and is well built, with straight walls and a properly hung door. People who live or work in places with a value of 4 tend to be practical, loyal, have good common sense, and want to get value for the money they spend. They tend to be hard workers and like to putter, fixing things themselves to minimize expensive service calls from plumbers, electricians, and so on.

If you're a homebody who needs harmony in all relationships, you'll enjoy House Number 4. However, if you like to be on the go constantly and can't sit still, or if you "rob Peter to pay Paul," this probably isn't the place for you.

House Number 4 can indicate a place where career and commitments often take precedence over family or social lives. If you have a home office in a House Number 4, be sure to put a door on your office and adhere to fixed business hours to ensure a balance between work and family.

House Number 5

If you like being in the middle of the action and having constant activity, a House Number 5 is a good bet. Maybe you like to remodel and update your surroundings, hear the sound of ringing telephones, or want to be able to lock up the house and pack your bags for quick getaways. If so, House Number 5 has your name on it. And because House Number 5s tend to have a list of several former owners, this place is great if you want investment property to use as a rental.

If you want to work from home (perhaps you're in sales or publishing), this is the ideal spot. Best of all, you'll never be lazy in House Number 5. Instead, you'll be full of enthusiasm, with a zest for life. A place with a numeric value of 5 is also nice if you're a nonconformist who likes the unusual.

If you are the retiring type who likes order and quiet solitude, you should probably pass on purchasing or renting a House Number 5. What if you already live or work in House Number 5 and don't want to move but want some peace and quiet? Like a five-pointed star, House Number 5 may have an unusual layout that can be converted to suit your needs.

Because a number 5 often represents change, be sure to take your time in making decisions at this address. It's best to do your research rather than regret making a snap decision.

House Number 6

House Number 6 isn't a house, it's a home. If you're into love, home, family, and tradition, you'll be happy here. These places usually have a lovely garden and, when you're inside, you bring the outdoors inside with large windows and a nice view.

When driving up the street, do you see colorful flowers, a nicely manicured lawn, and a flag flying out front of a certain house? If you were to walk up to the front door, you could probably smell the aroma of fresh apple pie baking in the oven and see home-schooled children in neatly pressed clothes. Check the address—it's probably a House Number with a value of 6.

House Number 6 may not be elegant, but it's always in good taste. For example, it's important to have a pleasant-sounding doorbell or ringer on a 6 home. Forget the Chinese gong that can be heard a block away or a loud, irritating buzzer—this place needs a melodic sound similar to a harp or chirping birds to announce a guest's arrival.

When painting House Number 6, take the time to carefully choose the colors. This comes from personal experience, as I visited one of my House Number 6 clients and commented on the beautiful color of her dining room. She said, "That color is called 19 gallons," because it had taken her 19 gallons of paint to get the perfect color she wanted: a rich terracotta hue with a hint of peach.

If your family talks loudly, tends to bicker, and doesn't care about the quality of furniture, you may not want to buy a 6 place. However, if you welcome guests seeking your good advice and enjoy helping others, this is the home for you. A word of caution for the inhabitants of House Number 6, though—don't be nosy and pay too much attention to the neighbors. What happens at the neighbor's house should stay at the neighbor's house and is none of your beeswax.

This is also an ideal address for visual artists such as painters, photographers, and graphic designers. Because the number 6 represents harmony, residents and co-workers in a House Number 6 will enjoy strong and productive relationships.

House Number 7

Do you thrive on peace, quiet, and solitude? Do you need your space to write, read, compose, or pursue technical, scientific, or metaphysical studies? Do you like lots of privacy in order to rest and have time to recharge your batteries? If so, House Number 7 is an ideal choice for you.

The inhabitants of House Number 7 seek solitude, like nature and healthy food, and require lots of fresh air. House Number 7s should be decorated with calm and serene colors and may have a mini-forest of trees, a swimming pool, or some water element (such as a waterfall) in it. You may also find an organic vegetable garden, too, tucked away in the backyard.

House Number 7 is a terrific place for musicians, writers, accountants, attorneys, mystics, pastors, rabbis, scientists, computer specialists, or private people who need to spend much of their time contemplating and thinking. This isn't the place for someone who enjoys being in a beehive of activity.

Note that if your prospective place is a 16/7, you'd better have a thorough inspection before signing your name on the dotted line. Invariably, there is something hidden in a 16/7 house— either a leaking pipe, mold, or something that isn't in plain sight. Oh yes, and check for dry rot in the wood, termites, and a faulty shower pan.

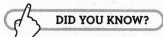 **DID YOU KNOW?**

Possibly the most famous House Number 7 address in the world is 1600 Pennsylvania Avenue—the White House.

House Number 8

People who are organized and impressed by money, power, and success are attracted to House Number 8. You're likely to find an oversized garage for multiple vehicles, an office with file cabinets and adding machines (the inhabitants like money and want to know their bank balance in off-shore accounts), or well-organized closets and drawers with everything in its place. It's important to stay balanced, both financially and emotionally, in House Number 8.

House Number 8 is as impressive to look at, as are the people who reside or work there. If you're attracted to this numeric value, you're likely to be respected in the community and recognized in your career; however, you need to be careful to avoid being boastful. Also, this is a place that will attract big money, but you shouldn't expect to save lots of money while you live or work there. Inhabitants of an 8 place know the intrinsic value of location, location, location, and even if House Number 8 is a fixer-upper when purchased, it's going to be the nicest house on the block when finished.

Repairs and expenses tend to be higher in House Number 8, because the inhabitants like quality and want things to be done correctly. If you live or work in an 8 place, you may gravitate toward higher-end contractors and experienced technicians who are hired upon recommendations from friends and co-workers.

House Number 9

See the Hacienda-style home with the curved arches and cobalt flower pots filled with red geraniums and the leather Mexican chairs on the front porch? Or do you see an office that resembles a Japanese tea house, with Shoji screens covering the windows, lots of bamboo plants, and a koi pond out front? Check the address, because it's almost sure to be a place with a House Number of 9.

The inhabitants of a 9 place are usually tolerant and understanding of the customs of diverse groups of people; this isn't a place for bigots and narrow-minded people. There's an artistic, universal vibration about the environment and the people who live or work there. House Number 9 is a good place for completing projects and meeting deadlines.

You'd like a place with a House Number of 9 if you enjoy international cuisine and themes and are apt to have artwork filling your walls. This place is also a perfect fit if you're a frequent traveler who has Airport Express picking up your luggage more than the usual person.

To Change Your Name, That Is the Question

I believe you were given the name at birth that your soul chose. Therefore, I don't think you should change your name if you want a different experience in your life. But why? In the words of author Jon Kabat-Zinn, "Wherever you go, there you are." What does that mean? It means that while you can move, change careers, change your looks, and even change your name, you'll always be the same *you*, with the same personality and the same problems.

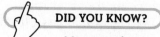 **DID YOU KNOW?**

Most metaphysicians believe that it takes about five years for a new name's effects to be fully felt.

But suppose you have another reason for wanting to change your name. For example, perhaps your grandmother named you Murgatroid and you hate it (I understand why). Whatever the reason is, you need to remember that your given name from birth is the real you and you will take its energies with you, no matter where you go and what you do.

However, if you *really* want to change your name, here's how to do it using numerology:

1. Make a list of all of the possible names you're considering.

2. Convert each name to a Destiny Number, a Soul Number, and a Personality Number.

3. Compare the values of the Core Numbers for your potential name changes with the values from your original birth-certificate name and see how they correspond to your Life Path Number.

    •   If your original numbers are mostly even numbers, try to select a new name that calculates to even numbers. Conversely, if your original numbers are odd numbers, try to select a new name that contains odd numbers.

    •   Also, quite often, the name or names you've selected are similar numbers to your original Destiny, Soul, and Personality Numbers. If that's the case, and you truly want to change your name, go for it. But if the numbers are completely different and have no resemblance to your original name numbers, go back to the drawing board and rethink your selections.

 PYTHAGORAS SAYS

Try to avoid changing your name to something that adds up to one of your Challenge Numbers, unless you've already conquered those challenges.

If you're unsure you want to change your name but you want to change your experiences in life, here's what I recommend: change your thinking. It may not be as easy as it sounds, but what you think about, you bring about. A change in perspective can go a long way and doesn't require a name change.

The Least You Need to Know

•   Employ numerology to help you select vanity license plates, PO Boxes, telephone numbers, and internet (including email) addresses and passwords to reinforce the message you're trying to send.

•   You can use numerology to choose a business name that resonates with your target customer.

- Addresses for a home, office, or apartment are almost like a person's name, in that a harmonious number conveys the place's personality.

- Choosing to change your name is not something to be taken lightly. Make sure you understand the numerical consequences that can go with it.

What About the Baby?

Choosing a name for your baby is very special. Not only do you get to decide what your child will be known as the rest of his or her life, you also get to pick something with numerological values that you feel are important.

And if you're going to have your baby via C-Section or induction, there's a possible numerological upside—you often get to schedule the delivery date. When you have dates from which to choose, you can often pick the one that best conveys to your child the path you hope for him or her.

In this chapter, you learn how you can use numerology to pick your child's name and possible due date.

In This Chapter

- Picking your baby's name
- Nicknames and unique names for your baby
- Baby Destiny Numbers
- Is it possible to plan your baby's birth date?

What Should You Name Your Baby?

That's the $64,000 question. One thing is certain—if anyone other than the mother names the baby, the baby probably won't like his or her name.

Over time, I've had clients come to me for help naming their baby. To see if the name or names they're thinking about work, I ask for the following information:

- The mother and father's full names and birth dates, so I can calculate their Core Numbers (Soul, Destiny, Personality, and Life Path)

- The names and birth dates of any siblings of the baby, so I can also calculate their Core Numbers

- A list of possible names for the baby, for which I calculate the Destiny, Soul, and Personality Numbers for each

When I do these calculations, an incredible thing happens that never ceases to amaze me. Nine times out of 10, the names the parents have chosen either contain the same numbers as the mother's and father's—or at the very least, the potential names blend well with the parent's numbers.

The following is a chart you can copy and use to collect the numbers that will surround your baby. You can then use the numbers as guidance in selecting the baby's name.

Vowels																		
Name																		
Consonants																		
Birth Date																		

Even though you may get a good idea of the name you want your baby to have now, don't make the final decision until he or she arrives—that way, you'll also have the birth date, which will allow you to select a name that resonates with the baby's Life Path Number.

> **DID YOU KNOW?**
>
> When I had my children, ultrasounds weren't commonly used, so there was usually a great element of surprise about the gender of babies. Each time I was pregnant, I was convinced I was going to deliver a boy; I had even chosen the name Chad Wellington Simpson III. You can imagine my surprise when every baby was a girl! I didn't know enough numerology then to calculate the numbers, but as fate would have it, each of my girls loves the name I chose for her and has the perfect numbers. Did their souls choose their names, or was I picking up telepathic messages from each daughter on what to name her? Whatever the case, it worked out.

Nicknames

Choose nicknames for your baby carefully, as they can be difficult to shed later in life. For example, the second child of my daughter and her husband is named Carpenter. However, he was given the nickname Carpi Doodles around the age of 3. While it was adorable then, the name isn't so great at the age of 15. Doodles has been dropped (except by family members), but Carpi seems to have stuck.

Also, your child may prefer a different name later in life. If you name your child Michael, he might want to be called Michael and not Mike or Mikey. Or if you have a son named James, he may prefer Jim or Jimmy. Alexandra might opt for Alex or even Ali.

In the end, calling someone by a nickname isn't going to change who they really are—that's determined by their given name at birth. So when choosing the birth name, don't worry about what the intended or eventual nickname is or becomes.

Unique Names

What about the trend toward unusual baby names? Do you want your child to have a unique moniker? While unique names certainly excel at grabbing attention (bad or good), it's worth doing the numbers on a name before finalizing the birth certificate. After all, you're setting the stage for your child's future and his or her true characteristics.

Nowhere is the unique-name trend more apparent than with celebrities. For example, Kanye West and Kim Kardashian named their baby North West (no middle name). North West has a Destiny Number of 7 (analytical and conservative), a Soul Number of 2 (harmony and cooperation), and Personality Number of 5 (energetic). Although they plan to call her Nori why didn't they just name her that?), the numbers of the actual name on her birth certificate will drive her life. North will undoubtedly be a quiet, introspective, and shy child who enjoys spending time by herself. She'll also enjoy nature and being in or near water.

And when Gwyneth Paltrow and Chris Martin named their daughter Apple Blythe Alison Martin, they reported that they thought the name conjured an image of something sweet, wholesome, and biblical. The name has a Destiny Number of 6 (nurturing and civic-minded), a Soul Number of 6 (generous and loving), and a Personality Number of 9 (approachable and warm), which does, in fact, denote a very sweet, kind person. (I just hope she isn't teased later in life and called Apple Martin[i] or Appletini.)

Whatever you decide for your child, remember that even the most simple names can have the characteristics of a trend-setter or innovator based on their numerological interpretation.

How Your Baby's Name Can Affect Your Family

Most metaphysicians believe that the soul (baby) chooses its name and birth date according to what the baby has come to Earth to accomplish. Similarly, they also believe that parents are given the baby they were meant to have according to what karmic lessons the parents are supposed to learn.

Suppose you're a Destiny Number 7 parent and have a Destiny Number 5 baby. While you may enjoy peace and quiet, with a love of reading and nature, your perpetual-motion Destiny Number 5 baby wants to be on the go continually. What happens? You guessed it—you learn to adapt.

What if you're a strong-willed Destiny Number 1 parent who has an equally strong-willed Destiny Number 1 baby? You've met your match in life!

If you're a globetrotting, humanitarian Destiny Number 9 parent, what do you do if you have a home-loving Destiny Number 6 baby? Your baby will probably adapt and make his or her home out of a suitcase.

Or imagine you're a budget-minded, frugal Destiny Number 4 parent who has a generous Destiny Number 9 baby, who wants to share everything and give away things to its friends. What do you do? You may need to develop a prosperity consciousness and learn that as you give, you receive.

All these scenarios illustrate that there is give and take in life, and no matter what your numbers, you have adjustments to make and lessons to learn in life. Nowhere is that more apparent than with your baby. The following are some potential traits you may see in your baby based on his or her Destiny Number.

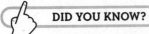

DID YOU KNOW?

Trouble agreeing upon a baby name is a challenge as old as the ages. In 1897, Ole Halverson of Eastskill, New York, sued a minister who christened his baby with the name provided by the mother, rather than the father's preferred moniker of Oscar. Ole claimed that he suffered loss of authority in his household and serious disappointment, for which he requested damages.

Destiny Number 1 Baby

The Destiny Number 1 baby is an independent youngster from the moment of his first breath. When he whimpers, you had better hop to and attend to this assertive wee one. His distinctive cry lets you know if he is hungry, cold, or warm; wants to be cuddled; or needs a fresh diaper. This baby makes his wants and needs known. However, just because your baby's independent doesn't mean he can't get his feelings hurt.

There's nothing subtle about a Destiny Number 1 baby. He creates his own schedule (never mind what you want) and smiles, coos, rolls over, sits up, walks, gives up his bottle, and climbs out of his crib long before you expect it. And in the realm of food, a Destiny Number 1 baby knows what he likes and dislikes without any doubt—his dislikes may be spit out so many times that you give up and give in to feeding him his favorites. When it comes to family, the family pet is at his beck and call, as are any siblings and his parents and grandparents.

As Destiny Number 1 baby grows up, he is apt to favor unusual and colorful toys, things that make sounds (the louder the better), and anything that's a challenge to operate. For example, he enjoys putting keys in locks and undoing buckles and bows. A Destiny Number 1 baby also needs plenty of privacy and alone time because he enjoys his own company and is able to entertain himself.

When he's old enough to toddle off to preschool, expect a wave good-bye without a backward glance. When he comes home after his first day, he will tell you all about how he was first in line for snacks, first to be noticed by the teacher for his impeccable manners, and first to be chosen to play Duck, Duck, Goose by his newest best friends. And speaking of friends, the Destiny Number 1 child enjoys spur-of-the-moment play dates with someone who's just as independent and unique as he is.

Destiny Number 2 Baby

The Destiny Number 2 baby is tuned into the Almighty Telephone and Telegraph Company— the Universe. She is highly intuitive and instinctively knows who loves her most (you, of course). A Destiny Number 2 baby can flash those innocent doe eyes at you so you'll happily spend endless hours cuddling her in her favorite place—the rocking chair. And as you hum lullabies to her, she may do her best to hum along because she likes being part of a duet.

A Destiny Number 2 baby is sweet and adaptable. She can sense your moods and will do her best to be even sweeter if she senses that you're stressed. She also enjoys being close to you, so you may want to invest in a baby sling or front carrier so she can nuzzle next to you. The Destiny Number 2 baby may also be satisfied holding onto a stuffed animal or having a sibling or the family pet in close range.

This precious soul is soothed by quiet music like Baby Mozart and musical mobiles. She enjoys sharing and having two of everything—one for each hand—so you might as well give her two books or two toys at a time to play with. And be sure to have drawers and shelves for her collections—everything from seashells to colorful pieces of paper and pretty leaves. By the way, when your child gets old enough to talk, don't even think of cleaning her room and tossing things out without asking first!

Your Destiny Number 2 baby works hard to please and will be the teacher's pet from the first step over the classroom threshold. When she comes home from the first day of school, she will proudly tell you about how she is everyone's best friend at school. She will be a lifelong student with multiple interests, so she may have a difficult time deciding which avenue to pursue.

Destiny Number 3 Baby

From the moment of birth, a Destiny Number 3 baby is irresistible. He's the one in the nursery getting all of the attention, because you can hear him down the hall. See those bright eyes and happy face with personality? That's a Destiny Number 3 baby in action.

This child is a creative soul who needs color and activity in the nursery—a sound machine playing rain or ocean wave sounds, bright walls, and mobiles hanging above the crib. He also coos and begins to mimic your words and sounds at an early age.

A Destiny Number 3 baby comes in two varieties: he either goes to anyone to be held, or he winces when strangers try to hold him. This youngster is a free spirit and doesn't like to be bound by convention. Don't expect him to enjoy a strict schedule, and good luck to you if you expect him to follow it.

He's going to enjoy preschool because he likes being around other children. The Destiny Number 3 child can either be shy or the class clown and may not like being told to sit in the exact spot on the rug every day. Don't worry, though; he'll always be lovable and keep you in stitches with knock-knock jokes.

As the Destiny Number 3 baby grows up, he'll want to be the first on the block to have the latest and greatest toy advertised on television. Therefore, you should teach him the value of the dollar early on.

Destiny Number 4 Baby

You won't need an alarm clock when your Destiny Number 4 baby arrives on the scene—she comes with one already built in. Want to get an extra half hour's sleep past your normal time in the morning? Forget it! Your Destiny Number 4 baby lets you know when it's time to be fed at 6:00 A.M., not 6:15 or 6:30.

A Destiny Number 4 baby likes to be dry, fed, and at just the right temperature in the nursery. Enjoying all the creature comforts, she flourishes when she has the same routine and the same foods day in and day out. The nursery also needs to be simple, calming, and, above all, neat; otherwise, your Destiny Number 4 baby will sense if things are out of place or the lighting isn't just so. So don't even consider leaving a pile of laundry to fold in the middle of the room or the mini-blinds pulled up to different levels.

Your Destiny Number 4 baby has incredible manual dexterity and may reach up to help hold her bottle, mesmerized by her own hands. The Destiny Number 4 baby loves to fiddle with parts and put round pegs in round holes. She also enjoys puttering in the garden with you and being near nature. As your baby grows, she'll enjoy playing with puzzles, blocks, Legos, and Tinker toys.

At school, the Destiny Number 4 child listens intently, follows the rules, and remembers to do her homework without being reminded. Because she aims for perfection, a Destiny Number 4 child will get upset if scolded.

Destiny Number 5 Baby

The Destiny Number 5 baby probably kept you alert before his birth with sudden kicks and an elbow jab in your ribs. When this curious little creature makes his grand entrance into the world, his eyes are wide open, intently checking out the surroundings.

 DID YOU KNOW?

The Destiny Number 5 child is a multitasker from the get-go. Early on he can suck his thumb, stroke his satin blanket, and rock back and forth in your lap simultaneously. Later on he can watch television, do his homework, and surf the internet all at once. Restless and inquisitive, he needs constant stimulation.

Don't expect the Destiny Number 5 baby to sleep isolated in a quiet nursery. Your active baby has two speeds—go and stop—and he will fight going to sleep. However, when he finally succumbs, he likes to crash in the midst of the action so as to not miss out on any fun.

It's doubtful that your Destiny Number 5 baby likes being swaddled, because he wants to move his arms and legs like the whirling dervish he is. And if you put him in a playpen, be sure it's stocked with lots of visual and hands-on amusements, such as toys that move and have buttons with flashing lights and noise—the noisier the better.

Your Destiny Number 5 baby is a born traveler, so strap him into the car seat and zoom off; he's content on a boat, plane, or anything that moves. He's also happy playing peek-a-boo until he gets bored, at which time you can put him in a bouncy chair or automatic swing. Curiosity is this tyke's middle name, so be sure to child-proof the house.

When he's ready for school, choose a preschool that isn't overly structured and allows him to get up and move about. Warn the teacher that he needs lots of mental and physical stimulation because he gets bored easily and loves to ask the question "Why?"

Destiny Number 6 Baby

This little bundle of joy can charm you with a sweet smile and winning ways. All the Destiny Number 6 baby wants is for the people around her to be content and happy. As for her own needs, she desires to be loved, cherished, and adored. She also wants comfort with a capital C—no scratchy onesies, no wet or dirty diapers, no loud noises, not too hot and not too cold, and no garish colors in the nursery, please.

It doesn't take much to keep this precious Destiny Number 6 baby happy. She may smile and play goo-goo gah-gah with her dancing eyes. Also, she loves to be held, have her head stroked, and have a soft, satin blanket to hold onto.

If there are siblings in the family and family pets, so much the better—everyone loves a Destiny Number 6 baby. People gravitate to a Destiny Number 6 baby, and undoubtedly you'll receive offers to babysit her at no charge. It's also hard to resist not gently pinching the cheeks or poking the chubby thighs on a Destiny Number 6 baby.

When she toddles off to preschool, she initially might have a bit of separation anxiety because home and family mean so much to her. But in no time at all, she'll be her teacher's little helper and favorite child. She'll also be popular at school and love painting, doing arts and crafts, and playing rhythm instruments during music lessons.

The Destiny Number 6 baby is adaptable and will be happy wherever she is in the future, provided that her surroundings are peaceful and she's cherished and adored. And when you're old and gray, the good news is that she'll always come home and care for you.

PYTHAGORAS SAYS

The higher-vibration Destiny Master Number 33 can hold powerful creative and artistic energy. It can also indicate a lack of control and sometimes a tragic life. Celebrities with a Master Destiny Number 33 include Helen Keller, Babe Ruth, Mother Theresa, Michael Jackson, Amy Winehouse, and Whitney Houston.

Destiny Number 7 Baby

From the moment of birth in the delivery room, a Destiny Number 7 baby is content looking around and taking it all in. He has an inquisitive look about him, and his piercing eyes look straight through you and seem to read your mind.

His nursery should be decorated with serene colors and be as peaceful and dignified as he is. He enjoys soft voices and listening to soothing music. The sound of heavy metal or loud drums makes him jump as if he has been struck by a bolt of lightning. The Destiny Number 7 baby is discerning and will instantly know the difference if you switch formulas. Even though he enjoys splashing in the warm water at bath time, he doesn't appreciate wet diapers.

Chances are your Destiny Number 7 baby has a discerning palate. When food is introduced, he'll most likely favor fresh food to frozen and be fussy about textures. And during his first birthday party, it's doubtful that he'll sink his hands into the frosting, because he doesn't like to get messy.

A Destiny Number 7 baby enjoys looking at picture books and has a knack for thumbing through pages of big-people books, too. He may like being outdoors, watching the leaves move to and fro and listening to the rustling of the branches. He may also like the water, so the sooner he has swimming lessons, the better. For companionship, a Destiny Number 7 baby or child needs a cat or dog as his special friend.

When your Destiny Number 7 child starts school, his favorite spot will be sitting on the bean-bags in front of the bookshelves in the corner of the classroom. Let's hope his teacher is a good researcher because Destiny Number 7's favorite question is "Why?" As he ages, his caring and inquisitive nature will continue. That's a good thing, because when you're old and gray, your Destiny Number 7 will be by your side, sensing your every need, and not allowing you to take any medication until he's researched the pros, cons, and side effects.

Destiny Number 8 Baby

It's no surprise when you adhere to your Destiny Number 8 baby's schedule; there's something so irresistible about her that you simply follow her lead. She believes in eight hours of sleep, eight hours of play, and eight hours of eating. And oh, does she like to eat! Does she have a hollow leg? No, she's just a Destiny Number 8 baby!

The Destiny Number 8 baby is a born leader and needs a staff to cater to her needs. She also lets you know in no uncertain terms if she wants to be fed differently or if she wants to be held or to be left alone.

The nursery of this little delegator needs to have lots of drawers and shelves, because she will have a system for organizing toys and her favorite things—she wants a place for everything and everything in its place. Be sure to give your Destiny Number 8 a piggy bank, because she was born knowing the value of a penny saved.

You'll be able to easily spot your Destiny Number 8 child on the playground when she starts school—she's the one in the middle of a throng of peers organizing the games and giving directions. You'll always be able to count on your Destiny Number 8 offspring; for example, be assured that she'll handle everything if you downsize and move to an assisted-living facility.

Destiny Number 9 Baby

Your Destiny Number 9 baby may capture the hearts of everyone in the delivery room with his sweet demeanor and interest in what's going on around him. He's an adaptable and happy little tyke who's adored by everyone.

The Destiny Number 9 baby is in love with love and is happiest when you hold him. He loves colorful artwork on his nursery walls and calms down when listening to music. When it comes to music, vary the type, as he enjoys it all.

A Destiny Number 9 baby is like no other number when it comes to his tastes in food. He has a refined sense of taste and will like things you never dreamed possible. Snails with garlic butter? Sure, he'll try them at least once. As he grows up, he'll enjoy ethnic foods as he globetrots around the world.

When he goes to preschool, he'll be very tolerant of other children. Nonjudgmental, he understands what makes people tick and will have unusual friends. A Destiny Number 9 will also be popular among his peers because he's willing to share and cares deeply about the feelings of others. A rule follower and teacher's little helper throughout his school years, your Destiny Number 9 child will always make you proud.

Planning Your Baby's Birth Date

The number-one thing to remember when given a choice of possible dates for inducing a baby or having a C-Section is safety. What does the doctor recommend? What do you feel is the right day to deliver the baby? Medical science should always prevail.

However, you can calculate the Birthday Number of your baby (see Chapter 9) based on the selected or anticipated date of birth to see what characteristics it may hold.

- Are you hoping for an independent child who will always be the leader of the pack? Keep your fingers crossed for a baby born on the 1st, 10th, 19th, or 28th of the month.

- Do you dream of a peaceful child who gets along well with everyone he meets? If your baby is born on the 6th, 15th, or 24th, he'll bring harmony to everyone he touches.

- Would you enjoy having your home be the meeting place where all of your child's friends congregate? Then hope your baby arrives on the 3rd, 12th, 21st, or 30th.

- Would you like your child to have high hopes and big dreams? A baby born on the 9th, 18th, or 27th will love to take long trips with you.

- Do you like to be on the go and expect your baby to adapt to your busy lifestyle? A baby born on the 5th, 14th, or 23rd will be ready for action, and plenty of it.

- Do you have a tandem bicycle and want your baby to ride along? A baby born on the 2nd, 11th, 20th, or 29th loves twosomes.

- Do you want your child to be an entrepreneur and earn her own spending money? A baby born on the 8th, 17th, or 26th will be the first on the block with a lemonade stand.

- Do you daydream about having an inquisitive child who putters in the garden with you? Then hope your baby arrives on the 7th, 16th, or 25th.

Guess what? The baby will arrive when it's supposed to arrive. Sometimes you can make all the plans in the world for a special date and have the plans fly out the window when the baby decides to arrive a week or two early. There are just some things in life that you aren't able or supposed to control, and the birth of a baby is at the top of the list. Trust the Universe to have the baby arrive safely when it wants to grace your presence.

The Least You Need to Know

- You can choose your baby's name to give the talents and personality traits and corresponding numbers you desire for the child.
- Nicknames don't count in numerology. The true individual is the name as it is on the birth certificate.
- When choosing a unique name, remember that the name and its corresponding energies will be with your child for the rest of his or her life.
- You can occasionally pick a particular date for delivery; however, your best-laid plans might be overridden by the baby deciding to set his or her own schedule.

Glossary

Abjad numerals   Predating Arabic numerals, this refers to the assignment of numeric values to the 28 letters of the Arabic alphabet. Arabic numerologists use the assigned values to foretell the future and explain the past.

Arabic numerals   The familiar 10 digits (0 through 9) used virtually worldwide today are called the Arabic Numerals.

Challenges   These foretell potential stumbling blocks in reaching your Pinnacles or goals for a certain time period. Unlike most numbers in numerology that range from 1 to 9, Challenge Numbers range from 0 to 8.

Core Number   The four core, or important, numbers in numerology—your Destiny, Soul, Personality, and Life Path Numbers.

Destiny Number   A Core Number that describes your character, talents, and goals, and reveals what you need to do to reach your ultimate success in life. It's derived by adding the numeric values of the letters in the given name you received at birth and then reducing to a single digit.

Essence Number   What you get when you reduce the Hidden Essence Number to a single digit. Your Essence Number provides additional information concerning what to expect in a given year and guidance on how to deal with it. *See also* Hidden Essence Number.

Hidden Cross   A grid similar (but not identical) to the Lo Shu Square, it's used to determine your strength levels on the physical, mental, and emotional planes. You use your date of birth to fill out each square of the Hidden Cross grid.

Hidden Essence Number   A number based on the numeric values of the letters in your given name. To find the Hidden Essence Number, add the numeric values of the progressed letters in your name for any given year. *See also* Essence Number.

Highlight Year Number   Sometimes referred to as "race consciousness" by other numerologists, this number gives you awareness as you race through life. It is the reduced sum of your current age and the age you'll be after your next birthday.

Life Path Number   One of the Core Numbers in numerology, it gives you clues to your opportunities in life and what you may need to learn in order to accomplish your goals. It is obtained from the digits of your birth date.

Lo Shu Square   Also known as the "Magic Square," it's a grid with squares that correspond to the numbers 1 through 9, and the sum of each row, each column, and both diagonals total 15. The bottom row references the practical, the middle row is emotional, and the top row is mental. *See also* Hidden Cross.

Maturity Number   This number is meant for your middle-age years and gives hints about how to make the most of your "golden years." It is the reduced sum of your Destiny Number and Life Path Number.

Personal Day Number   This number tells you what you can expect on a given day and suggests appropriate actions and activities. This is the reduced sum of a day and month of interest to you and your Personal Year Number.

Personal Month Number   This number indicates the overall tone of the coming month and helps track how your feelings, attitudes, and circumstances change. It is the reduced sum of the number value of a certain month and your Personal Year Number.

Personal Year Number   A number that's used in the calculation of many other numerology values, this tells you where you are and where you're going for the year. This number comes from the reduced sum of the day of the month on which you were born, the month in which you were born, and the year in which you last celebrated your birthday.

Personality Number   This Core Number represents the outer you, or the traits perceived by others. It is obtained by adding and reducing the numeric value of the consonants in your birth name.

Pinnacles   Four long-term cycles along your life path. Each Pinnacle represents a lesson on which you are working during that cycle. The first cycle lasts from birth until an age between 27 and 35 (the ending age is the difference between your Life Path Number and 36), the second and third Pinnacle periods are both nine years in duration, and the fourth Pinnacle is with you for the remainder of your life.

Pythagoras   Ancient Greek mathematician and philosopher who believed that "all is number," meaning everything in the world is connected to numbers. His mystical teachings about the numerical nature of everything form the core of modern numerology.

Pythagorean numerology   This modern system of numerology is based on the teachings of Pythagoras and is founded on the principle that all letters have a corresponding number 1 through 9. This system interprets names and birth dates, providing insight into personality; talents; heart's desire; and the past, present, and the future.

Soul Number   Sometimes called the Heart Number, this Core Number represents the inner you, including your values, hopes, wishes, dreams, and innermost desires as well as your thoughts, feelings, and attitudes toward life and love. It is the reduced sum of the numeric values of the vowels in your birth name.

Triad Numbers   These reveal more detailed information for each of the four-month periods within your Personal Year. They are calculated using the age at your last birthday, your Life Path Number, and the four-digit year of your birth.

Type and Traits Chart   This conveys information about the physical, mental, emotional, and intuitive aspects. It is based on the numeric values of the letters in your given name.

Universal Year Number   Known as the "rhythm of the universe," this describes the current year in general terms—not personal terms. It is the reduced sum of the digits in the current year.

Resources

In this appendix, I provide some information on some of my favorite books and websites to help you learn even more about numerology and related disciplines.

Books

Adrienne, Carol. *The Numerology Kit*. New York: Penguin, 1988.

———. *Your Child's Destiny: A Numerology Guide for Parents*. New York: Penguin, 1994.

Balliett, Dow. *How to Attain Success Through the Strength of Vibration*. Whitefish, MT: Kessinger Publishing, LLC, 2010.

Brill, Michael. *Numerology for Healing: Your Personal Numbers as the Key to a Healthier Life*. Rochester, VT: Destiny Books, 2009.

———. *Numerology for Decoding Behavior: Your Personal Numbers at Work, with Family, and in Relationships*. Rochester, VT: Destiny Books, 2011.

Bunker, Dusty, and Victoria Knowles. *Birthday Numerology*. Rockport, MA: Para Research, 1997.

Camp, Robert. *Destiny Cards: Your Birth Card and What It Reveals About You & Your Past, Present & Future*. Naperville, IL: Sourcebooks, Inc., 2004.

Campbell, Florence. *Your Days Are Numbered*. Marina del Rey, CA: DeVorss & Co., 1982.

Crawford, Saffi, and Geraldine Sullivan. *The Power of Birthdays, Stars, & Numbers: The Complete Personology Reference Guide*. New York: Ballantine, 1998.

Decoz, Hans. *Numerology: The Key to Your Inner Self.* New York: Penguin Putnam, 2002.
DiPietro, Sylvia. *Live Your Life by the Numbers.* New York: Penguin, 1991.

Fairchild, Dennis, and Peter Weber. *The Portable Book of Birthdays.* Philadelphia: Running Press, 2003.

Goodwin, Matthew. *Numerology, The Complete Guide, Vol. II.* Franklin Lakes, NJ: New Page Books, 2005.

Heline, Corrine. *Sacred Science of Numbers.* Marina del Rey, CA: DeVorss & Co., 1991.

Hitchcock, Helyn. *Helping Yourself with Numerology.* New York: Prentice Hall Press, 1988.

Jordan, Juno. *Numerology: The Romance in Your Name.* Marina del Rey, CA: DeVorss & Co., 1984.

———. *Your Right Action Number.* Marina del Rey, CA: DeVorss & Co., 1983.

Lagerquist, Kay, PhD, and Lisa Lenard. *The Complete Idiot's Guide to Numerology, Second Edition.* New York: Amaranth Illuminare, Alpha Books, 2004.

Line, Julia. *Discover Numerology.* New York: Sterling Publishing, 1993.

Millman, Dan. *The Life You Were Born to Live: A Guide to Find Your Life Purpose.* Tiburon, CA: HJ Kramer, 1993.

Moore, Julian. *Numerology: Numbers Past and Present With the Lo Shu Square (Speed Learning) (Volume 5).* (Kindle Edition). Charleston, SC: CreateSpace Independent Publishing Platform, 2013.

Newmont, Nick. *Numerology: From Sex to Stocks, It's All in the Numbers.* San Diego, CA: Jodere Group, 2003.

Phillips, David. *The Complete Book of Numerology: Discovering the Inner Self.* Carlsbad, CA: Hay House, Inc., 2005.

Randall, Edith, and Florence Campbell, MA. *Sacred Symbols of the Ancients: The Mystical Significance of Our Fifty-Two "Playing" Cards and Their Amazing Connection with Our Individual Birthdays.* Marina del Rey, CA: DeVorss & Co., 1989.

Schimmel, Annemarie. *The Mystery of Numbers.* New York: Oxford University Press, 1994.

Simpson, Jean. *Hot Numbers: Discover What Makes Your Lover, Boss, Friends, Family and You Really Tick.* New York: Gramercy Books, 1998.

Strayhorn, Lloyd. *Numbers and You: A Numerology Guide for Everyday Living.* New York: The Ballantine Publishing Group, 1997.

Websites

NumberQuest Numerology (numberquest.com): On this site, you can find links to paid numerology readings.

Numerologist.com (numerologist.com): This site has great general information about numerology, as well as a blog and personalized reports for purchase.

Numerology.com (numerology.com): This is a comprehensive source of background information on numerology, including detailed material about various interpretations and numerology calculators.

Your Life in Numbers (yourlifeinnumbers.com): Developed by numerologist Michel Kassett, a former numerology client of Dr. Helena Davis, this site offers a more spiritual viewpoint on readings.

The Numerology Worksheet

The worksheet presented here consolidates all the numbers and calculations I've covered in this book. If you need a refresher on how to fill out each section of the worksheet, check out Chapter 18.

If you want to "do the numbers" for friends or family members, feel free to make copies of these pages. However, if you only plan to do this process one time, you can just transfer the numbers you calculated as you went through the book to these pages, in order to have everything in one easy-to-reference location.

Soul Number		Point of Security Number		Destiny Number	Personality Number	Maturity Number		Life Path Number
Vowels	Name			Consonants		Birth Date		

Type	Traits		
Physical	4s		5s
Mental	1s		8s
Emotional	2s	3s	6s
Intuitive	7s		9s
Total			

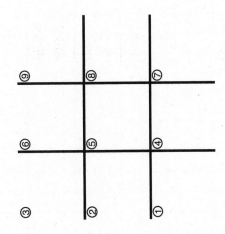

	Pinnacle Number	Challenge Number	Start Age	Thru	End Age
1st				—	
2nd				—	
3rd				—	
4th				—	?

Karma Number

1	2	3	4	5	6	7	8	9

Intensification Number

1	2	3	4	5	6	7	8	9

Subconscious Response Number

1	2	3	4	5	6	7	8	9

Year																																	
Age	0	1	2	3	4	5	6	7	8	9	10	11	12	13	14	15	16	17	18	19	20	21	22	23	24	25	26	27	28	29	30	31	32
First Name																																	
Middle Name																																	
Middle Name 2																																	
Last Name																																	
Hidden Essence Number																																	
Essence Number																																	
Personal Year Number																																	
Universal Year Number																																	
Pinnacles																																	
Challenges																																	
Highlight Year Number																																	

Year	33	34	35	36	37	38	39	40	41	42	43	44	45	46	47	48	49	50	51	52	53	54	55	56	57	58	59	60	61	62	63	64	65
Age																																	
First Name																																	
Middle Name																																	
Middle Name 2																																	
Last Name																																	
Hidden Essence Number																																	
Essence Number																																	
Personal Year Number																																	
Universal Year Number																																	
Pinnacles																																	
Challenges																																	
Highlight Year Number																																	

Year	66	67	68	69	70	71	72	73	74	75	76	77	78	79	80	81	82	83	84	85	86	87	88	89	90	91	92	93	94	95	96	97	98
Age																																	
First Name																																	
Middle Name																																	
Middle Name 2																																	
Last Name																																	
Hidden Essence Number																																	
Essence Number																																	
Personal Year Number																																	
Universal Year Number																																	
Pinnacles																																	
Challenges																																	
Highlight Year Number																																	

Index

D

E

F

N

Q-R

S

T

U

Personal Numerology Reading
With
Jean Simpson

For many people, doing their own numbers is a fun activity, giving them insight into themselves, friends, and family members. But a personalized reading with a renowned numerologist provides a tailored and comprehensive look at what the numbers have to say.

A personal numerology reading can provide unique insight into your hidden talents, life's path, relationships, lessons in life, personal year, and more! Consultations are customized to provide the information you want to know. You will have adequate time to have your questions answered. Possible topics include compatibility, baby names and birth dates, company names, addresses, wedding dates, name changes, and so much more!

To schedule a personal numerology reading by telephone, the following information is needed.

_____   _____

Birth Name   **Birth Date**
(exactly as it appears on your birth certificate)

Additional names, if you're purchasing the 60-minute reading:

_____   _____

Birth Name   **Birth Date**
(exactly as it appears on the birth certificate)

_____   _____

Birth Name   **Birth Date**
(exactly as it appears on the birth certificate)

_____   _____

Birth Name   **Birth Date**
(exactly as it appears on the birth certificate)

Your information:

_____   (   )_____
Full Name   **Day Telephone**

_____   (   )_____
Email   **Evening Telephone**

Your order should be emailed to jeansimpsonnumerology@gmail.com. Upon receipt of your order, you will receive an invoice by email. You may pay the invoice via cashier's check, money order, or Paypal only. Payments should be mailed to:

Jean Simpson
2060-D East Avenida de los Arboles #205
Thousand Oaks, CA 91362

Once we have received your payment, you will be contacted to determine the best time for your personal reading. Readings may be scheduled seven days a week from 6:00 A.M. to 7:00 P.M. PST.

Still have questions? Feel free to email jeansimpsonnumerology@gmail.com or call (805) 449-1429 for more information about personal readings, fees, appointment availability, classes, and lectures.

30-minute personal phone reading: $100

60-minute personal phone reading: $190

Prices subject to change without notice.